Contents

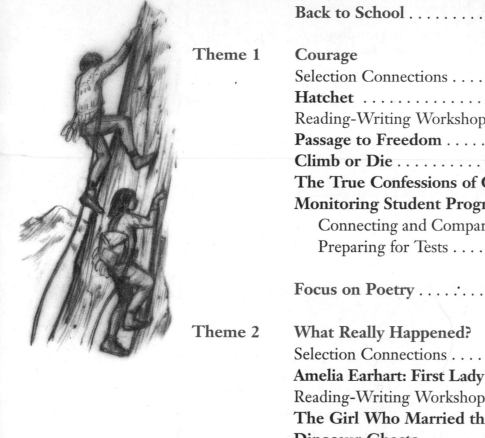

Weeks-Townsend Memorial Library
Union College
Barbourville, KY 40906

Contents

Strategy Workshop

As you listen to the story "A Mummy Mystery," by Andrew Clements, you will stop from time to time to do some activities on these practice pages. These activities will help you think about different strategies that can help you read better. After completing each activity, you will discuss what you've written with your classmates and talk about how to use these strategies.

Remember, strategies can help you become a better reader. Good readers

- use strategies whenever they read

- use different strategies before, during, and after reading

- think about how strategies will help them

Copyright © Houghton Mifflin Company. All rights reserved.

Name _____

Strategy 1: Predict/Infer

Use this strategy before and during reading to help make predictions about what happens next or what you're going to learn.

Here's how to use the Predict/Infer Strategy:
1. Think about the title, the illustrations, and what you have read so far.
2. Tell what you think will happen next—or what you will learn.
3. Thinking about what you already know on the topic may help.
4. Try to figure out things the author does not say directly.

Listen as your teacher begins "A Mummy Mystery." When your teacher stops, complete the activity to show that you understand how to predict what the story might be about and what the mystery might be.

Think about the story and respond to the question below.

What do you think the story is about, and what might the mystery be?

_____

_____

_____

_____

_____

As you continue listening to the story, think about whether your prediction was right. You might want to change your prediction or write a new one below.

_____

_____

_____

_____

_____

Copyright © Houghton Mifflin Company. All rights reserved.

Name _____

Strategy 2: Phonics/Decoding

Use this strategy during reading when you come across a word you don't know.

Here's how to use the Phonics/Decoding Strategy:

1. Look carefully at the word.
2. Look for word parts you know and think about the sounds for the letters.
3. Blend the sounds to read the words.
4. Ask yourself: is this a word I know? Does it make sense in what I am reading?
5. If not, ask yourself what else can I try? Should I look in a dictionary?

Listen as your teacher continues the story. When your teacher stops, use the Phonics/Decoding Strategy.

Now write down the steps you used to decode the word *Dynasty*.

_____

_____

_____

_____

_____

_____

_____

_____

_____

Remember to use this strategy whenever you are reading and come across a word that you don't know.

Copyright © Houghton Mifflin Company. All rights reserved.

Name _____

Strategy 3: Monitor/Clarify

Use this strategy during reading whenever you're confused about what you are reading.

Here's how to use the Monitor/Clarify Strategy:

- Ask yourself if what you're reading makes sense—or if you are learning what you need to learn.
- If you don't understand something, reread, use the illustrations, or read ahead to see if that helps.

Listen as your teacher continues the story. When your teacher stops, complete the activity to show that you understand what's happening in the story.

Think about the mummy and respond below.

1. Describe what happened with the mummy's hand.

_____

_____

_____

_____

2. Can you tell from listening to the story how everyone reacts to the mummy's hand moving? Why or why not?

_____

_____

_____

_____

3. How can you find out what made the mummy's hand move?

_____

_____

_____

_____

Copyright © Houghton Mifflin Company. All rights reserved.

Name _____

Strategy 4: Question

Use this strategy during and after reading to ask questions about important ideas in the story.

Here's how to use the Question Strategy:

- Ask yourself questions about important ideas in the story.
- Ask yourself if you can answer these questions.
- If you can't answer the questions, reread and look for answers in the text. Thinking about what you already know and what you've read in the story may help you.

Listen as your teacher continues the story. Then complete the activity to show that you understand how to ask yourself questions about important ideas in the story.

Think about the story and respond below.

Write a question you might ask yourself at this point in the story.

_____

_____

_____

_____

_____

_____

If you can't answer your question now, think about it while you listen to the rest of the story.

Copyright © Houghton Mifflin Company. All rights reserved.

Name _____

Strategy 5: Evaluate

Use this strategy during and after reading to help you form an opinion about what you read.

Here's how to use the Evaluate Strategy:

- Tell whether or not you think this story is entertaining and why.
- Is the writing clear and easy to understand?
- This is a mystery story. Did the author make the characters believable and interesting?

Listen as your teacher continues the story. When your teacher stops, complete the activity to show that you are thinking of how you feel about what you are reading and why you feel that way.

Think about the story and respond below.

1. Tell whether or not you think this story is entertaining and why.

_____

_____

_____

_____

2. Is the writing clear and easy to understand?

_____

_____

_____

3. This is a mystery story. Did the author make the characters interesting and believable?

_____

_____

_____

_____

Copyright © Houghton Mifflin Company. All rights reserved.

Name _____

Strategy 6: Summarize

Use this strategy after reading to summarize what you read.

Here's how to use the Summarize Strategy:

- Think about the characters.
- Think about where the story takes place.
- Think about the problem in the story and how the characters solve it.
- Think about what happens in the beginning, middle, and end of the story.

Think about the story you just listened to. Complete the activity to show that you understand how to identify important story parts that will help you summarize the story.

Think about the story and respond to the questions below:

1. Who is the main character?

_____

_____

_____

2. Where does the story take place?

_____

_____

_____

_____

3. What is the problem and how is it resolved?

_____

_____

_____

_____

Now use this information to summarize the story for a partner.

Copyright © Houghton Mifflin Company. All rights reserved.

Name _____

Courage

The characters in this theme show courage in dangerous or challenging situations. After reading each selection, complete the chart below to show what you learned about the characters.

	Hatchet	**Passage to Freedom**
What challenge does the main character face?	Brian has to survive in the wilderness and build a fire with only a hatchet as a tool. **(2.5 points)**	Mr. Sugihara has to decide whether to obey his superiors or help save the lives of hundreds of refugees. **(2.5)**
Where does the challenge take place?	in the wilderness, in modern times **(2.5)**	in Lithuania, during World War II **(2.5)**
In what ways does the main character show courage?	Brian learns to cope with being alone in the wilderness. He learns to build a fire from sparks. **(2.5)**	Mr. Sugihara disobeys his superiors and puts his own job at risk to help the refugees. **(2.5)**
What do you think the character learns from his or her experience?	Brian learns that he can make a fire from wood scrapings and a spark, and that he can handle difficult situations by himself. **(2.5)**	Mr. Sugihara learns that sometimes one must follow one's conscience instead of obeying orders. **(2.5)**

Copyright © Houghton Mifflin Company. All rights reserved.

Assessment Tip: Total **10** Points per selection

Name _____

Courage continued

	Climb or Die	**The True Confessions of Charlotte Doyle**
What challenge does the main character face?	Danielle and Jake must climb a steep, icy mountain without the right climbing tools. **(2.5)**	Charlotte must climb to the top of the royal yard to prove she is fit to be a sailor. **(2.5)**
Where does the challenge take place?	on a snowy mountain in modern times **(2.5)**	on a sailing ship in the 1800s **(2.5)**
In what ways does the main character show courage?	Danielle and Jake bravely complete the climb, using only the tools they have. **(2.5)**	Charlotte completes the climb even though she is terrified. **(2.5)**
What do you think the character learns from his or her experience?	Danielle and Jake learn that they are resourceful and stronger than they thought. **(2.5)**	Charlotte learns that she can climb to the top of the royal yard without falling or getting sick. **(2.5)**

What have you learned about courage in this theme?

Sample answer: Sometimes people surprise themselves with strength they didn't

know they had. **(2)**

Assessment Tip: Total **10** Points per selection and **2** points for the final question

Copyright © Houghton Mifflin Company. All rights reserved.

Name _____

Words in the Wild

Answer each of the following questions by writing a vocabulary word.

Copyright © Houghton Mifflin Company. All rights reserved.

1. Which word tells what you should seek in a rainstorm so you won't get wet? shelter **(1 point)** _____

2. Which word describes what a snake is doing when it moves across the ground? slithering **(1)** _____

3. Which word names a tool used to chop wood? hatchet **(1)** _____

4. Which word describes small pieces of wood needed to build a fire? kindling **(1)** _____

5. Which word means "very frightened"? terrified **(1)** _____

6. Which word names the sharp spines a porcupine uses to defend itself? quills **(1)** _____

7. Which word means "the process of staying alive"? survival **(1)** _____

8. Which word describes a feeling a person has when he or she keeps trying to do something but cannot do it? frustration **(1)** _____

Write two questions of your own that use vocabulary words from the list above.

9. Accept reasonable answers. **(1)** _____

10. Accept reasonable answers. **(1)** _____

Vocabulary

hatchet
quills
shelter
survival
terrified
frustration
slithering
kindling

Theme 1: **Courage**   11
Assessment Tip: Total **10** Points

Name _____

Details Chart

Page(s)	Brian feels _____.	Details that show how Brian feels
30	terrified	• his nostrils widened and he opened his eyes wider • he thought of every monster he had ever seen • his heart hammered in his throat **(3 points)**
32–33	in pain; hurt **(1)**	• the eight quills in his leg seem like dozens • his pain spreads • catches his breath when he pulls the quills out
33–34	sorry for himself **(1)**	• He thinks, "I can't take this" and "I can't do this." • He cries until he is cried out.
34–35	frustrated	• can't understand what his father and Terry are telling him in his dream • thinks "so what" and "I know" when he thinks about the fire in his dream **(2)**
36–37	motivated; excited; happy **(1)**	• realizes the hatchet can make sparks • recognizes the message about fire from his dreams • begins to make sparks to start a fire
38–41	determined	• doesn't give up when his first attempts fail to start a fire • takes two hours to gather tree bark • finally succeeds in lighting the fire **(3)**
43	satisfied	• smiles and calls the fire a good friend **(1)**

Assessment Tip: Total **12** Points

Copyright © Houghton Mifflin Company. All rights reserved.

Name _____

What Really Happened?

These sentences tell about Brian and the things that happen to him in the story. Write T if the sentence is true. Write F if the sentence is false. If the sentence is false, correct it to make it true.

1. __F__ Brian wakes up when he hears a bear growling outside his shelter.

   Brian wakes up when he hears the wind growling outside his shelter. **(1 point)**

2. __F__ Brian's leg gets injured when he kicks out in the darkness and hits the hatchet.

   Brian's leg gets injured when he kicks out in the darkness and hits a porcupine. **(1)**

3. __T__ After crying for a long time, Brian realizes that feeling sorry for yourself changes nothing.

   (1) _____

4. __F__ Seeing his father and his friend Terry in a dream makes Brian feel happy.

   Seeing his father and his friend Terry in a dream makes Brian feel frustrated. **(1)**

5. __F__ In Brian's dream, his friend Terry shows him a path out of the forest.

   In Brian's dream, his friend Terry shows him a fire in a barbecue pit. **(1)**

6. __T__ Brian thinks that throwing his hatchet to protect himself from wild animals is a bad idea.

   (1) _____

7. __T__ By hitting the hatchet against a hard black rock, Brian is able to make sparks.

   (1) _____

Copyright © Houghton Mifflin Company. All rights reserved.

Assessment Tip: Total **7 Points**

Name _____

Seeing the Solution

Read the story. Then complete the activity on page 15.

The Water Tree

Paul and I had been hiking for six hours. We came upon a dry creekbed that ran through the desert. Paul frowned, and I sighed. "I hope this isn't the creek we've been trying to reach," I said.

"See, Tom, I told you we should have brought more water," said Paul. Between the two of us, we had only about a third of a bottle left. Our clothes were wet with sweat and our throats were dry, but we dared not drink any more water yet. Even if we headed back right away, it was at least a six-hour hike back to our campground.

Paul and I just stared at the dry creekbed. "Check the map," I said to Paul. "Is there any other water within a mile of here?" I thought that even if there was another creek nearby, it might be dry too.

"There's nothing but lava rocks and an occasional cactus for another three miles," he reported grimly as he pulled out his map. Then his eyes lit up. "Wait a second, Tom," he said in a much happier voice. "A cactus!" He grinned and slapped me on the back.

"A cactus what?" I said. I wondered how he could be so excited about desert plants at a time like this.

"Don't you remember what we learned at camp last summer?" Paul asked. Then my own face curled into a smile. At camp they had shown us how to get water from a cactus.

"Do you have a knife?" I asked. "I have a handkerchief we can use to strain the water from the cactus flesh." Within minutes we were squeezing water out of a prickly pear cactus into our water bottles, through a funnel fashioned from a sun visor. We didn't get much water per squeeze, but there were more than enough cacti around. We'd make it back to camp with water to spare.

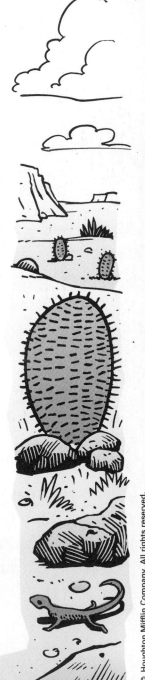

Copyright © Houghton Mifflin Company. All rights reserved.

Name _____

Seeing the Solution continued

Answer these questions about the story on page 14.

1. How do Paul and Tom feel when they reach the dry creekbed? Why?
   They feel discouraged because the creek is dry and they are
   almost out of water. **(2 points)**

2. What details in the first paragraph help you figure out how the
   boys feel?
   Paul frowns. Tom sighs. **(2)**

3. What kind of danger are the boys in? What details help you
   understand the danger?
   They could run out of water. They are in the hot desert with only a
   third of a bottle of water left, and must hike at least six hours back
   to their campground. **(2)**

4. How does Paul feel when he remembers that they can get water from
   a cactus? How do you know his feelings change?
   He is suddenly happy. His eyes light up and he says "A cactus!" in
   a happy voice. He then grins and slaps his friend on the back. **(2)**

5. How do the boys make use of what they have to get water?
   They use a handkerchief to strain the water from the cactus pulp.
   They use a visor to funnel the water into their water bottles. **(2)**

6. Do you think that the task of filling the water bottles will be a fast
   one or a slow one? Why?
   It will probably be slow because they don't get very much water
   per squeeze. **(2)**

Copyright © Houghton Mifflin Company. All rights reserved.

Name _____

Suffixes Aflame

**Circle the words with the suffixes *-ful*, *-less*, and *-ly* in the flames.
Use the circled words to complete the story.**

OXVPOWERLESSABLE
BRIEFLYHMBRQZTEND
CAREFULLYTOAND
FINALLYOADBEAUTIFUL
SERMEANINGLESSJUS
SKILLFULBLIYLFRCH
INCREDIBLYXGAN
HANDFULOZZMEK

Brian's strange dream at first seemed _meaningless **(1 point)**_____, until he

realized that he needed a fire. In one _handful **(1)**_____ after another,

he gathered tiny bits of _beautiful **(1)**_____ white birch bark. He made

a nest out of the _incredibly **(1)**_____ fine bits of bark, but it stayed alight

only _briefly **(1)**_____. He seemed _powerless **(1)**_____

to keep the flame going. _Finally **(1)**_____, he discovered how to fan

the flames with his breath. In time, he would become _skillful **(1)**_____

at building a fire.

Which word has *two* suffixes?

_carefully **(2)**_____

Assessment Tip: Total **10** Points

Copyright © Houghton Mifflin Company. All rights reserved.

Name _____

Short Vowels

A short vowel sound is usually spelled *a*, *e*, *i*, *o*, or *u* and is followed by a consonant sound.

/ă/ cr**a**ft   /ĕ/ d**e**pth   /ĭ/ f**i**lm   /ŏ/ b**o**mb   /ŭ/ pl**u**nge

Write each Spelling Word under its short vowel sound.
Order of answers for each category may vary.

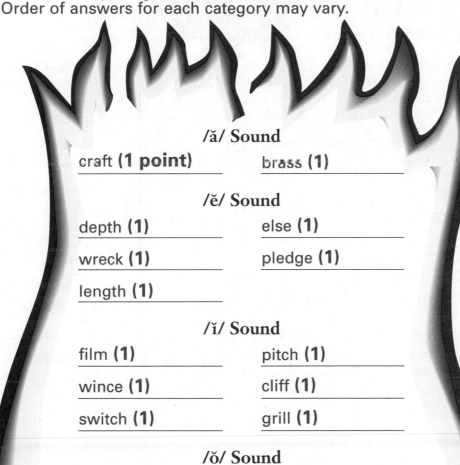

/ă/ Sound

craft **(1 point)**   brass **(1)**

/ĕ/ Sound

depth **(1)**   else **(1)**

wreck **(1)**   pledge **(1)**

length **(1)**

/ĭ/ Sound

film **(1)**   pitch **(1)**

wince **(1)**   cliff **(1)**

switch **(1)**   grill **(1)**

/ŏ/ Sound

bomb **(1)**   prompt **(1)**

/ŭ/ Sound

plunge **(1)**   stung **(1)**

sunk **(1)**   bulk **(1)**

scrub **(1)**

Spelling Words

1. depth
2. craft
3. plunge
4. wreck
5. sunk
6. film
7. wince
8. bomb
9. switch
10. length
11. prompt
12. pitch
13. else
14. cliff
15. pledge
16. scrub
17. brass
18. grill
19. stung
20. bulk

Copyright © Houghton Mifflin Company. All rights reserved.

Theme 1: **Courage**   17
Assessment Tip: Total **20** Points

Name _____

Spelling Spree

Change the Word Write a Spelling Word by adding one letter to each word below.

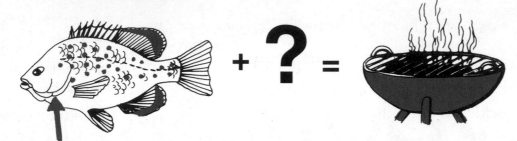

Spelling Words

1. depth
2. craft
3. plunge
4. wreck
5. sunk
6. film
7. wince
8. bomb
9. switch
10. length
11. prompt
12. pitch
13. else
14. cliff
15. pledge
16. scrub
17. brass
18. grill
19. stung
20. bulk

1. ledge   pledge **(1 point)**
2. bass   brass **(1)**
3. sun   sunk **(1)**
4. itch   pitch **(1)**
5. raft   craft **(1)**

6. wine   wince **(1)**
7. lunge   plunge **(1)**
8. gill   grill **(1)**
9. bob   bomb **(1)**
10. sung   stung **(1)**

Word Detective Write a Spelling Word to fit each clue.

11. great size or volume   bulk **(1)**
12. the measure of being long   length **(1)**
13. something used in a camera   film **(1)**
14. an overhanging rock face   cliff **(1)**
15. other or different   else **(1)**
16. what's left after a crash   wreck **(1)**
17. the quality of being deep   depth **(1)**
18. a device used to turn on the power   switch **(1)**
19. to clean very well   scrub **(1)**
20. right on time   prompt **(1)**

Assessment Tip: Total 20 Points

Copyright © Houghton Mifflin Company. All rights reserved.

Proofreading and Writing

Proofreading Circle the five misspelled Spelling Words in this journal entry. Then write each word correctly.

Copyright © Houghton Mifflin Company. All rights reserved.

> I spent all day today starting a fire. Building a fire is a real craft! I began by trying to light pieces of a torn twenty-dollar bill. Then I decided to swich to strips of birch bark. I gathered some pieces of the right lenth and width and made them into a ball. I lit the ball with the sparks made by striking my hatchet against the rock wall. It was hard work, but I don't know what els I could have used to start the fire. I still winse when I think about another night without one. My next goal is to figure out how to make a gril that I can cook on.

Spelling Words

1. depth
2. craft
3. plunge
4. wreck
5. sunk
6. film
7. wince
8. bomb
9. switch
10. length
11. prompt
12. pitch
13. else
14. cliff
15. pledge
16. scrub
17. brass
18. grill
19. stung
20. bulk

1. switch **(1 point)**
2. length **(1)**
3. else **(1)**
4. wince **(1)**
5. grill **(1)**

✏️ **Write an Opinion** What do you think about the way the writer of this journal entry went about building a fire? Was there anything about his or her behavior that you admired? Is there anything you would have done differently?

On a separate piece of paper, write a paragraph in which you give your opinion of the writer's way of doing things. Use Spelling Words from the list. Responses will vary. **(5)**

Name _____

A Search for Meaning

Your friend doesn't know the meaning of some words in a story she's reading. Use context clues to help her figure out the underlined words, and then fill in the chart. Sample answers shown.

From a safe distance, Marcy <u>squatted</u> low and watched the burning storage barn. The flames were <u>consuming</u> one section after another, as though the building were an enormous meal. The fire left almost nothing behind, so she thought all the building materials must be <u>flammable</u>. She was <u>gratified</u> to hear sirens in the distance. Her 911 call had been heard.

Word	Clues from Context	Meaning
squatted	A person doing this is in a position low to the ground. **(1 point)**	crouched down low in a sitting position **(1)**
consuming	This action is compared to an enormous meal. **(1)**	eating up; destroying totally **(1)**
flammable	Almost nothing of the building is left. **(1)**	capable of burning easily and rapidly **(1)**
gratified	She had placed a 911 call, and help was on the way. **(1)**	pleased; satisfied **(1)**

Assessment Tip: Total **8** Points

Copyright © Houghton Mifflin Company. All rights reserved.

Name _____

What Is a Spiny Pig?

Kinds of Sentences A **declarative** sentence makes a statement. It ends
with a **period**. An **interrogative** sentence asks a question. It ends with
a **question mark**. An **imperative** sentence gives an order or makes a
request. It ends with a **period**. An **exclamatory** sentence shows
excitement or strong feeling. It ends with an **exclamation point**.

**Add the correct end punctuation to each sentence. Then label
each sentence *declarative*, *interrogative*, *imperative*, or *exclamatory*.**

1. Porcupines are rodents. **(1)** <u>declarative **(1)**</u>

2. They have long, sharp quills. **(1)** <u>declarative **(1)**</u>

3. Treat all animals with respect. **(1)** <u>imperative **(1)**</u>

4. Have you ever seen a porcupine? **(1)** <u>interrogative **(1)**</u>

5. How big the tail is! **(1)** <u>exclamatory **(1)**</u>

6. Do porcupines have fine or coarse fur? **(1)** <u>interrogative **(1)**</u>

7. Please let me see your porcupine quill. **(1)** <u>imperative **(1)**</u>

8. What a sharp tip it has! **(1)** <u>exclamatory **(1)**</u>

9. Did you know the word *porcupine* means "spiny pig" in Latin? **(1)**
<u>interrogative **(1)**</u>

10. *Porcupine* comes from Latin *porcus* (meaning "pig") and *spina*
(meaning "spine"). **(1)** <u>declarative **(1)**</u>

Copyright © Houghton Mifflin Company. All rights reserved.

Campfires Need . . .

Subjects and Predicates The **subject** of a sentence tells whom or what the sentence is about. The **complete subject** includes all the words in the subject. The **simple subject** is the main word or words of the complete subject.

The **predicate** tells what the subject does, is, has, or feels. The **complete predicate** includes all the words in the predicate. The **simple predicate** is the main word or words of the complete predicate.

Draw a line between the complete subject and the complete predicate in each sentence below. Then write the simple subject and the simple predicate on the lines.

1. Brianna | needed kindling for a fire. **(1 point)**

   Simple subject: Brianna **(1)**

   Simple predicate: needed **(1)**

2. A fire | needs oxygen. **(1)**

   Simple subject: fire **(1)**

   Simple predicate: needs **(1)**

3. A roaring fire | will keep them warm. **(1)**

   Simple subject: fire **(1)**

   Simple predicate: will keep **(1)**

4. The first spark | has faded quickly. **(1)**

   Simple subject: spark **(1)**

   Simple predicate: has faded **(1)**

5. I | am learning about building safe campfires. **(1)**

   Simple subject: I **(1)**

   Simple predicate: am learning **(1)**

Copyright © Houghton Mifflin Company. All rights reserved.

Assessment Tip: Total **15** Points

Name _____

This and That

Combining Sentences A good writer avoids writing too many short, choppy sentences. Combine short sentences by creating **compound subjects** or **compound predicates**.

Moose live in these woods.
Caribou live in these woods too. } **Compound Subject**
Moose and caribou live in these woods.

I ate quickly.
I gulped my juice. } **Compound Predicate**
I ate quickly and gulped my juice.

Combine subjects or predicates in each group of sentences below.

Example: I sighed. Then I sat down.
I sighed and sat down.

1. Rebecca was prepared for an emergency.
   The other hikers were prepared for an emergency.

   Rebecca and the other hikers were prepared for an emergency. **(1 point)**

2. The scout built the fire.
   The scout stoked the fire.

   The scout built and stoked the fire. **(1)**

3. Hatchets should be used with caution.
   Axes should be used with caution.
   Other sharp tools should be used with caution.

   Hatchets, axes, and other sharp tools should be used with caution. **(1)**

4. The birch trees swayed in the wind.
   The birch trees creaked in the wind.

   The birch trees swayed and creaked in the wind. **(1)**

5. Conrad will gather wood.
   Sam will gather wood.

   Conrad and Sam will gather wood. **(1)**

Copyright © Houghton Mifflin Company. All rights reserved.

Name _____

Writing Instructions

In *Hatchet*, Brian is stranded alone in the Canadian wilderness. The only tool he has is a hatchet. How could Brian explain to someone else how he used the hatchet to start a fire? **Instructions** tell readers how to do or make something. Good written instructions clearly explain the materials needed and the order in which the steps are to be followed.

Use this page to plan and organize your own written instructions. First, choose a process you would like to explain. Then list the materials that are needed. Finally, write each step in the process, giving details that readers will need to know.

How to _____

Materials (2 points)	
Steps	**Details**
Step 1	(2)
Step 2	(2)
Step 3	(2)
Step 4	(2)
Step 5	(2)

Using the information you recorded, write your instructions on a separate sheet of paper. You can either number each step or use sequence words such as *first, next,* and *finally*. Include diagrams or pictures to help readers picture this process. (10)

Assessment Tip: Total **22** Points

Copyright © Houghton Mifflin Company. All rights reserved.

Name _____

Using Sequence Words and Phrases

Following steps correctly is a matter of life or death for Brian in *Hatchet*. A careful writer gives clear instructions so that a reader can complete the steps in a process. Sequence words and phrases in instructions help readers understand a process and keep track of the order of steps.

The following page is from a first-aid manual. The instructions tell readers how to treat puncture wounds like those Brian suffered from the porcupine quills in his leg. In the blanks provided, add sequence words and phrases from the list to make the connection between steps clearer. Remember to capitalize sequence words as needed.

Sequence Words and Phrases

first	after	by the time
during	prior to	finally
before	then	as soon as possible

First **(2 points)** _____, you will need to wash your hands with soap and water. After **(2)** _____ you have washed your hands, remove the object with a pair of tweezers.

Then **(2)** _____ control any bleeding with direct pressure and elevation. Wash the puncture wound thoroughly with soap and water.

Finally **(2)** _____, cover the wound with a sterile dressing.

Check with a doctor to find out whether a tetanus shot is needed. If you see any signs of infection, such as pus, pain, redness around the wound, or a fever, call the doctor back as soon as possible **(2)** _____.

Copyright © Houghton Mifflin Company. All rights reserved.

Name _____

Revising Your Personal Narrative

Reread your narrative. Put a checkmark in the box for each sentence that describes your paper. Use this page to help you revise.

Loud and Clear!

☐ The beginning catches the reader's interest.

☐ All events are focused on a single experience. They are also told in order.

☐ Many details and exact words bring the story to life.

☐ My writing sounds like me. You can tell how I feel.

☐ Sentences flow smoothly, and there are few mistakes.

Sounding Stronger

☐ The beginning could be more interesting.

☐ A few events are out of order, and a few are unrelated.

☐ More details and exact words are needed.

☐ My voice could be stronger. It doesn't always sound like me.

☐ The sentences don't always flow smoothly. There are some mistakes.

Turn Up the Volume

☐ The beginning is missing or weak.

☐ The story is not focused. The order is unclear.

☐ There are no details or exact words.

☐ I can't hear my voice at all.

☐ Most sentences are choppy. Mistakes make it hard to read.

Copyright © Houghton Mifflin Company. All rights reserved.

Name _____

Improving Your Writing

Varying Sentences Rewrite the paragraphs in the spaces provided. Each paragraph should include at least one example of each type of sentence: declarative, interrogative, imperative, and exclamatory. **(4 points each)**

Backstage Pass NO SENTENCE VARIATION I shook hands with Whole New Crew! I was at their concert! I went backstage! I met Jeff! I met Pinky! I met Wanda! I met Therese! At first, I was so excited I could hardly breathe! And guess what — they ignored me! After a while it got boring! So we went home!	**Backstage Pass** SENTENCE VARIATION _____ _____ _____ _____ _____
Jalapeño Biscuits NO SENTENCE VARIATION Do I know how to make biscuits? Sort of. Did I put in the flour, butter, and baking powder? I did. Did I add jalapeño peppers? Accidentally. What did it taste like? It was sort of good. Then why did I end up running to get a drink of water? Because it was so HOT.	**Jalapeño Biscuits** SENTENCE VARIATION _____ _____ _____ _____ _____
Early Start NO SENTENCE VARIATION The coach said to meet at 6 A.M. for Saturday's game. Anyone late would not play, the coach said. On Friday, I set my alarm for 5. I went to the field. Everyone was there — except the coach. We finally found her. Her car had broken down. She said, "I guess I don't get to play."	**Early Start** SENTENCE VARIATION _____ _____ _____ _____ _____

Copyright © Houghton Mifflin Company. All rights reserved.

Name _____

Spelling Words

Most of the Spelling Words on this list are often misspelled because they are **homophones,** words that sound alike but have different meanings and spellings. Look for familiar spelling patterns to help you remember how to spell the words on this page. Think carefully about the parts that you find hard to spell in each word.

Write the missing letters and apostrophes in the Spelling Words below.

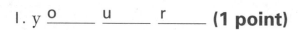

1. y <u>o</u> <u>u</u> <u>r</u> **(1 point)**

2. you <u>'</u> <u>r</u> <u>e</u> **(1)**

3. th <u>e</u> <u>i</u> r **(1)**

4. th <u>e</u> r <u>e</u> **(1)**

5. th <u>e</u> <u>y</u> <u>'</u> re **(1)**

6. it <u>s</u> **(1)**

7. it <u>'</u> <u>s</u> **(1)**

8. w <u>o</u> <u>u</u> <u>l</u> dn't **(1)**

9. we <u>'</u> <u>r</u> <u>e</u> **(1)**

10. t <u>o</u> **(1)**

11. t <u>o</u> <u>o</u> **(1)**

12. tha <u>t</u> <u>'</u> <u>s</u> **(1)**

13. k <u>n</u> ew **(1)**

14. <u>k</u> <u>n</u> ow **(1)**

Spelling Words

1. your
2. you're
3. their
4. there
5. they're
6. its
7. it's
8. wouldn't
9. we're
10. to
11. too
12. that's
13. knew
14. know

Study List **On a separate piece of paper, write each Spelling Word. Check your spelling against the words on the list.**
Order of words may vary. **(2)**

Assessment Tip: Total **16** Points

Copyright © Houghton Mifflin Company. All rights reserved.

Name _____

Spelling Spree

Homophone Blanks The blanks in each of the following sentences can be filled with homophones from the Spelling Word list. Write the words in the correct order.

Spelling Words

1. your
2. you're
3. their
4. there
5. they're
6. its
7. it's
8. wouldn't
9. we're
10. to
11. too
12. that's
13. knew
14. know

1–3. I think that _____ sitting over _____ on _____ blanket.

4–5. If you don't hurry, _____ going to miss _____ bus.

6–7. The pizza's still _____ hot _____ eat.

8–9. Since _____ so hot today, the school is letting _____ students go home early.

1–3. they're, there, their **(3)** _____

4–5. you're, your **(2)** _____

6–7. too, to **(2)** _____

8–9. it's, its **(2)** _____

Word Addition Write a Spelling Word by adding the beginning of the first word to the end of the second word.

10. than + Pat's

11. we'll + score

12. knack + flew

13. work + shouldn't

14. knight + grow

10. that's **(1)** _____

11. we're **(1)** _____

12. knew **(1)** _____

13. wouldn't **(1)** _____

14. know **(1)** _____

Copyright © Houghton Mifflin Company. All rights reserved.

Name _____

Proofreading and Writing

Proofreading Circle the five misspelled Spelling Words in this poster. Then write each word correctly.

Spelling Words

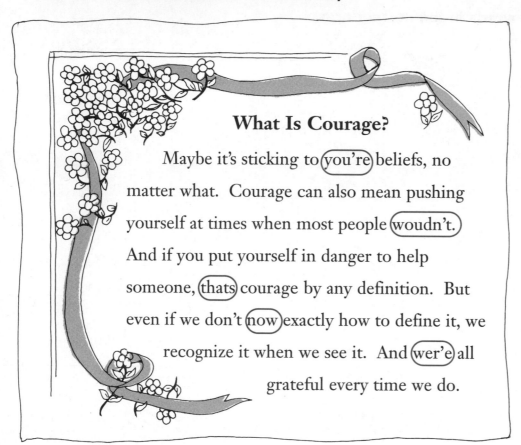

What Is Courage?

Maybe it's sticking to (you're) beliefs, no matter what. Courage can also mean pushing yourself at times when most people (woudn't.) And if you put yourself in danger to help someone, (thats) courage by any definition. But even if we don't (now) exactly how to define it, we recognize it when we see it. And (wer'e) all grateful every time we do.

Spelling Words

1. your
2. you're
3. their
4. there
5. they're
6. its
7. it's
8. wouldn't
9. we're
10. to
11. too
12. that's
13. knew
14. know

1. <u>your</u> **(2 points)**   4. <u>know</u> **(2)**

2. <u>wouldn't</u> **(2)**   5. <u>we're</u> **(2)**

3. <u>that's</u> **(2)**

Writing Headlines Suppose that a newspaper were going to write articles covering the events that take place in each of the selections in this theme. What would some good headlines be?

On a separate piece of paper, write a headline for each selection in the theme. Use Spelling Words from the list. Responses will vary. **(5)**

Assessment Tip: Total **15** Points

Copyright © Houghton Mifflin Company. All rights reserved.

Name _____

The Official Word

Read the word in each box below from *Passage to Freedom*.
Then write a word from the list that is related in meaning.
Use a dictionary if necessary.

Copyright © Houghton Mifflin Company. All rights reserved.

> **Vocabulary**
>
> bosses
> documents
> envoy
> organization
> choice
> approval
> victims

superiors	**government**	**visas**
bosses **(2 points)**	organization **(2)**	documents **(2)**

refugees	**diplomat**	**decision**
victims **(2)**	envoy **(2)**	choice **(2)**

permission
approval **(2)**

Choose *three* words from the list above. Write a short paragraph
about what Hiroki Sugihara's father did in *Passage to Freedom*.

Accept reasonable answers. **(4)**

_____

_____

_____

_____

_____

Theme 1: **Courage**   31
Assessment Tip: Total **24** Points

Name _____

Judgments Chart

	Facts from the Selection	Own Values and Experiences	Judgment
What kind of person is Mr. Sugihara?	He sees a sad, needy child in a store who doesn't have enough money to buy what he wants, and he gives the child some money. **(2 points)**	I think people should do what they can to help those in need. **(2)**	Mr. Sugihara has done a good thing and has shown himself to be a compassionate person. **(2)**
Is Mr. Sugihara's decision right or wrong?	First Mr. Sugihara says he will only write a few visas. After talking with the refugees, although his goverment refuses permission, he says he will issue visas to everyone. When his wife offers to help, he writes the visas alone for safety's sake. **(2)**	I think a person should do what he or she knows to be right, but not involve others in the process. **(2)**	Mr. Sugihara's values are excellent. He decides to give the refugees visas and not to listen to his government. **(2)**
What kind of a person is Hiroki's mother?	Hiroki's mother says they must think about the people outside before themselves. She massages her husband's arm; she encourages him when he is too tired to write. **(2)**	I think that to be unselfish, you have to think of others in big and small ways. **(2)**	Hiroki's mother is a good person because she puts the well-being of others ahead of her own. **(2)**

Assessment Tip: Total **18** Points

Copyright © Houghton Mifflin Company. All rights reserved.

Name _____

Award for a Hero

Complete the fact sheet below about Chiune Sugihara. Then on a separate sheet of paper design an award that honors Mr. Sugihara.

FACT SHEET

Who Chiune Sugihara was:	the Japanese consul to Lithuania **(1 point)**
Where he was from:	Japan **(1)**
Where he was working at the beginning of World War II:	in a small town in Lithuania **(1)**
What his job was:	to represent the Japanese government in Lithuania **(1)**
Why people needed his help:	to give the refugees visas—written permission to travel east through another country **(1)**
What conflict he faced:	The Japanese government refused to allow Sugihara to issue visas to the refugees, but Sugihara knew the refugees would probably die if they didn't escape to the east. **(1)**
What decision he made:	to write visas for as many refugees as he could, and to go against the wishes of his government **(1)**
Why he is remembered:	He saved thousands of lives by writing the visas and had the courage to do the right thing. **(1)**

Copyright © Houghton Mifflin Company. All rights reserved.

Name _____

Judge for Yourself

Read the passage. Then answer the questions on page 35.

A South African Hero

In 1918, Nelson Mandela was born into a royal African family in South Africa. He was raised to be a chief, but instead chose to become a lawyer. He hoped to help blacks win equal rights in South Africa. At the time, the country was ruled by a white minority that discriminated against blacks. This policy was later called *apartheid*.

In the 1940s, Mandela earned his law degree. He helped set up the first black law firm in South Africa. He also joined the African National Congress (ANC), a group that worked to end apartheid. Mandela soon became a top official in the ANC and a leader of nonviolent protests.

The government cracked down on the ANC, however, and responded to peaceful protests with violence. In 1960, Mandela decided to abandon nonviolence and support armed struggle against apartheid. "The government left us no other choice," he said. Arrested several times for his work, he was tried for treason in 1963. At his trial, Mandela declared, "I have cherished the ideal of a democratic and free society. . . . It is an ideal which I hope to live for and to achieve. But if needs be, it is an ideal for which I am prepared to die."

Mandela was sentenced to life in prison and spent the next twenty-seven years behind bars. The struggle for equal rights in South Africa continued, however, and people around the world called for an end to apartheid. The government offered to free Mandela in exchange for his cooperation, but he refused. Finally, in 1990, the government released him from prison. He later won the Nobel Peace Prize and became South Africa's first black president. As president, Mandela called for peace and harmony in South Africa and tried to ensure equal rights for all South Africans.

Copyright © Houghton Mifflin Company. All rights reserved.

Name _____

Judge for Yourself continued

Answer these questions about the passage on page 34.

1. What was important to Nelson Mandela as a young man?
   He valued equal rights for blacks in South Africa. **(2 points)**

   _____

2. What facts from the passage reveal his values as a young man?
   He chose to become a lawyer to help blacks win equal rights. He
   became a top official in the ANC and worked to end apartheid. **(2)**

3. Circle three words you would use to describe Nelson Mandela. Sample answers
   (selfless)   (compassionate)   uninspired   shown.
   powerless   alienated   (determined)

4. Write each word you circled below. Then tell why you made that
   judgment about Mandela's character. Use facts from the passage to
   support your judgment.

Word	Reasons for Judgment
selfless **(1)**	He was willing to go to prison and even to die for equal rights. **(2)**
compassionate **(1)**	He believed that every person should have equal rights and that apartheid should end. **(2)**
determined **(1)**	Even after 27 years in jail, he held to his beliefs. **(2)**

5. How have your own experiences and beliefs helped you make a
   judgment about Nelson Mandela's character and actions?
   Sample answer: I have seen other people sacrifice for their beliefs.

   This shows that a person is selfless and determined. **(2)**

Copyright © Houghton Mifflin Company. All rights reserved.

Theme 1: **Courage**   35
Assessment Tip: Total **15** Points

Name _____

Sugihara Syllables

**Write each underlined word on the line below. Add slashes
between the syllables of each word. Then write another sentence
using the word correctly.**

1. My father was a Japanese <u>diplomat</u> working in Lithuania.
   dip/lo/mat **(1 point)** Example: I would like to become a diplomat for
   the United States and live abroad. **(2)**

   _____

2. <u>Hundreds</u> of refugees gathered outside our house.
   hun/dreds **(1)** Example: I have hundreds of sports cards in my
   collection. **(2)**

   _____

3. They needed <u>visas</u> to leave the country.
   vi/sas **(1)** Example: Visas allow people to move from one country
   to another. **(2)**

   _____

4. My father <u>replied</u> that he would help each one of the refugees.
   re/plied **(1)** Example: When my brother asked a favor, I replied
   yes. **(2)**

   _____

5. My life changed <u>forever</u> because of my father's action.
   for/ev/er **(1)** Example: Endangered species are gone forever. **(2)**

   _____

Assessment Tip: Total **15 Points**

Copyright © Houghton Mifflin Company. All rights reserved.

Name _____

Long Vowels

A long vowel sound may be spelled vowel-consonant-*e* or with two vowels written together.

/ā/ g**aze**, tr**ait**   /ē/ th**eme**, pr**each**, sl**ee**ve   /ī/ str**ive**

/ō/ qu**ote**, r**oa**m   /yōō/ m**ute**

Write each Spelling Word under its long vowel sound.
Order of answers for each category may vary.

Spelling Words

1. theme
2. quote
3. gaze
4. pace
5. preach
6. strive
7. trait
8. mute
9. sleeve
10. roam
11. strain
12. fade
13. league
14. soak
15. grease
16. throne
17. fume
18. file
19. toast
20. brake

/ā/ Sound

gaze **(1 point)**

pace **(1)**

trait **(1)**

strain **(1)**

fade **(1)**

brake **(1)**

/ī/ Sound

strive **(1)**

file **(1)**

/ē/ Sound

theme **(1)**

preach **(1)**

sleeve **(1)**

league **(1)**

grease **(1)**

/ō/ Sound

quote **(1)**

roam **(1)**

soak **(1)**

throne **(1)**

toast **(1)**

/yōō/ Sound

mute **(1)**

fume **(1)**

Copyright © Houghton Mifflin Company. All rights reserved.

Name _____

Spelling Spree

The Third Word Write the Spelling Word that belongs with each group of words.

1. pocket, collar, sleeve **(1 point)**
2. association, group, league **(1)**
3. vapor, gas, fume **(1)**
4. feature, quality, trait **(1)**
5. crown, castle, throne **(1)**
6. advise, counsel, preach **(1)**
7. passage, excerpt, quote **(1)**

Spelling Words

1. theme
2. quote
3. gaze
4. pace
5. preach
6. strive
7. trait
8. mute
9. sleeve
10. roam
11. strain
12. fade
13. league
14. soak
15. grease
16. throne
17. fume
18. file
19. toast
20. brake

Code Breaker Some Spelling Words have been written in code. Use the code below to figure out each word. Then write the words correctly.

```
CODE:    J X B M S L T O W K E G C N I Z H
LETTER:  A B D E F G H I K L M O R S T U V
```

8. LCMJNM grease **(1)**
9. ITMEM theme **(1)**
10. SOKM file **(1)**
11. SJBM fade **(1)**
12. XCJWM brake **(1)**
13. IGJNI toast **(1)**
14. NGJW soak **(1)**
15. CGJE roam **(1)**

Assessment Tip: Total 15 Points

Copyright © Houghton Mifflin Company. All rights reserved.

Name _____

Proofreading and Writing

Proofreading Circle the five misspelled Spelling Words in this screenplay. Then write each word correctly.

Mr. Sugihara enters his home. He walks to a chair and collapses into it. He sits (muet) for a few seconds, and then he speaks.

MR. SUGIHARA: I've been filling out visas all day at an incredible (pase.) I don't know how much longer I can take the (strane) . . . *(His voice begins to fade as his head droops to his chest.)*

MRS. SUGIHARA: *(She looks at her husband.)* I know, but you must think of the people. You can't just leave them to roam the countryside. They need a place to go.

MR. SUGIHARA: *(He slowly lifts his head and meets his wife's (gaiz.)* You're right, of course. I should (striv) to help as many as I can. If I don't, what will happen to them?

1. mute **(1 point)**
2. pace **(1)**
3. strain **(1)**
4. gaze **(1)**
5. strive **(1)**

Write a Persuasive Letter You have a chance to send Mr. Sugihara a letter on behalf of the refugees. You know he is unsure of what action to take. What will you write to convince him to help them?

On a separate piece of paper, write a persuasive letter to Mr. Sugihara. Include several reasons why he should help the refugees. Use Spelling Words from the list.
Responses will vary. **(5)**

Spelling Words

1. theme
2. quote
3. gaze
4. pace
5. preach
6. strive
7. trait
8. mute
9. sleeve
10. roam
11. strain
12. fade
13. league
14. soak
15. grease
16. throne
17. fume
18. file
19. toast
20. brake

Copyright © Houghton Mifflin Company. All rights reserved.

Name _____

Word-Order Sets

For each set of words, decide which two would be the guide words if all three words were on a dictionary page. On each "page," write the guide words in the correct order on the first line, and the other word on the line below.

office	ceiling	gown	refugees	emergency
offer	celery	government	refuse	embody
offside	celebration	gourmet	refrigerator	embraced

offer **(1 point)** / offside **(1)**

office **(1)**

ceiling **(1)** / celery **(1)**

celebration **(1)**

refrigerator **(1)** / refuse **(1)**

refugees **(1)**

gourmet **(1)** / gown **(1)**

government **(1)**

embody **(1)** / emergency **(1)**

embraced **(1)**

Assessment Tip: Total **15** Points

Copyright © Houghton Mifflin Company. All rights reserved.

Name _____

Safety and Freedom

Conjunctions A **conjunction** is a word that connects words or sentences. The words *and*, *but*, and *or* are conjunctions.

In each sentence below, add a conjunction. Then on the line, write *words* or *sentences* to show what the conjunction joins.

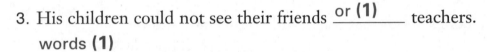

> **Example:** The escape was risky ____and____ frightening.
> words _____

1. The diplomat had courage, __and (1)__ he had compassion.
   sentences **(1)** _____

2. He knew it was risky, __but (1)__ he helped the people.
   sentences **(1)** _____

3. His children could not see their friends __or (1)__ teachers.
   words **(1)** _____

4. His wife __and (1)__ family members agreed to help.
   words **(1)** _____

5. The women, men, __and (1)__ children escaped to a safer place.
   words **(1)** _____

Copyright © Houghton Mifflin Company. All rights reserved.

Name _____

Should We Run, or Should We Hide?

Compound Sentences A **compound sentence** is two simple sentences joined by a comma and a conjunction (*and*, *but*, or *or*).

Add a comma followed by *and*, *but*, or *or* to combine the simple sentences below into compound sentences. Conjunctions used will vary.

> **Example:** Our escape was dangerous. We made it safely.
>
> *Our escape was dangerous, but we made it safely.*

1. World War II brought many hardships. People showed great courage.

   World War II brought many hardships, but people showed great

   courage. **(2 points)**

2. Have you read any books about that war? Did you see any movies about it?

   Have you read any books about that war, or did you see any

   movies about it? **(2)**

3. Bombs fell in many places. They did not fall in America.

   Bombs fell in many places, but they did not fall in America. **(2)**

   _____

4. My great-grandfather was in the Navy. He showed me his uniform.

   My great-grandfather was in the Navy, and he showed me

   his uniform.**(2)**

5. Our town built a war memorial in the park. My class went to see it.

   Our town built a war memorial in the park, and my class went to

   see it. **(2)**

Assessment Tip: Total **10** Points

Copyright © Houghton Mifflin Company. All rights reserved.

Name _____

I Can Speak Italian, but I Can't Speak Japanese

Combining Sentences: Compound Sentences Sometimes combining short, choppy sentences into longer sentences makes your writing more interesting. Use a comma and *and*, *but*, or *or* to combine sentences.

Lee has written a letter to Aunt Lucy. Revise the letter by combining simple sentences to make compound sentences. Insert your marks on, above, and below the line, as shown in the example. The last sentence will not change. (1 point each)

                                    , or
Tomorrow I'd like to go to the zoo. I'd like to visit Mel.

Dear Aunt Lucy,

          , but
    I think I'd like to be a diplomat someday. I don't know

where I'd like to live. Italy would be an interesting place to

  , or   , but
live. I might live in Japan. You taught me to speak Italian.

I don't know anyone who can teach me Japanese. Maybe I

        , and
could study it in school. I could study Japanese history too.

        , and
My teacher visited Japan. He showed us beautiful pictures.

The next time I visit, may I see your photos of Italy?

               Love,
               Lee

Copyright © Houghton Mifflin Company. All rights reserved.

Assessment Tip: Total **5** Points

Name _____

Writing a Memo

Chiune Sugihara was a diplomat in Lithuania in 1940. He probably wrote different forms of business communication, such as letters, reports, and memos. A **memo** is a brief, informal message that is sent from one person to others in the same company, group, or organization.

Imagine that you are Mr. Sugihara. Plan and organize a memo to your superiors in the Japanese government about the plight of the Jewish refugees from Poland. Follow these steps: (10 points)

1. Name the person or persons to whom you are writing the memo.
2. Tell who is writing the memo.
3. Write the date.
4. Identify the subject of the memo.
5. Write the body of the memo. Begin by stating your reason for writing. Use clear, direct language and a business-like tone. Be brief but include all the important information. If you want a response, end by asking a question or by requesting that a specific action be taken.

To: _____

From: _____

Date: _____

Subject: _____

_____

_____

_____

_____

Copy your memo on a separate sheet of paper and exchange it with a classmate. Then, using the format above, write a response memo from the officials in the Japanese government to Chiune Sugihara in which you deny him permission to grant visas to the Polish refugees.

44   Theme 1: **Courage**
Assessment Tip: Total **10** Points

Copyright © Houghton Mifflin Company. All rights reserved.

Copyright © Houghton Mifflin Company. All rights reserved.

Name _____

Capitalizing and Punctuating Sentences

To communicate effectively, a writer must write sentences correctly. When you write, remember to begin all sentences with a capital letter and to capitalize the names of people and places. Also, remember to end sentences with a period, a question mark, or an exclamation mark.

Proofread the following memo. Look for errors in capitalizing and punctuating sentences. Use these proofreading marks to add the necessary capital letters and end punctuation. (1 point each)

⊙	Add a period.	! ∧	Add an exclamation mark.
═	Make a capital letter.	? ∧	Add a question mark.

To: Mrs. Masue Okimoto, Office Manager

From: Mr. Kenji Hamano

Date: August 25, 1940

Subject: Request for Office Supplies

<u>my</u> assistant <u>boris</u> Lavhas informed me that we need to restock some

office supplies⊙<u>will</u> you kindly send the items listed below?

1. two hundred visas and permission forms

2. one dozen fountain pens

3. two dozen bottles of ink

<u>please</u> ship these supplies to my office in <u>lithuania</u> immediately!

<u>thank</u> you for your prompt action in this matter⊙

Name _____

Complete the Climb

Complete each sentence about mountain climbing with the correct word from the list.

Vocabulary

carabiners
pitons
foothold
desperate
improvising
belay
ice ax
overcome
functioned
fatigue

1. Metal spikes with a hole at the end through which you pass a rope are called <u>pitons</u> **(1)** _____.

2. Metal rings you use to attach rope to pitons are called <u>carabiners</u> **(1)** _____.

3. To cut into the ice and support your upper body while climbing, you might use an <u>ice ax</u> **(1)** _____.

4. In order to remain steady on your feet, it is important to find a secure <u>foothold</u> **(1)** _____.

5. If you and another climber are helping each other climb up the mountain while attached to the same rope, you are on <u>belay</u> **(1)** _____.

6. Do not push yourself too hard, or you may experience extreme <u>fatigue</u> **(1)** _____.

7. If you get lost and feel nearly hopeless that help will arrive, you feel <u>desperate</u> **(1)** _____.

8. If you don't have the proper equipment, you might look for other tools you have and try <u>improvising</u> **(1)** _____.

9. If you climb cautiously and with safety in mind, you will never have to face an obstacle you won't be able to <u>overcome</u> **(1)** _____.

10. Safe climbers have always <u>functioned</u> **(1)** _____ as role models for others.

Assessment Tip: Total **10** Points

Copyright © Houghton Mifflin Company. All rights reserved.

Name _____

Event Chart

1. **Page 75** At first Danielle hits the rock with Dad's hammer. Then she turns the hammer around and uses its claw like an ice ax. **(1)**

2. **Page 77** The hammers work. Next, Jake and Danielle start to climb up the icy trench. **(1)**

3. **Page 78** Danielle gets to the top of the trench first. Then she turns to help Jake reach the top. **(1)**

4. **Pages 80–81** Jake and Danielle are happy to be at the top. Then they realize they can't see a weather station anywhere. **(1)**

5. **Page 82** Crying, Jake and Danielle hug each other. Then Danielle pushes Jake away. Suddenly, Jake realizes that she is trying to show him something. **(1)**

6. **Page 84** Through the clouds, they see the weather station on a ridge above them. **(1)**

7. **Pages 84–85** Danielle is getting weaker. When they finally knock on the weather station door, no one answers it. **(1)**

8. **Page 86** Jake improvises by banging on the door with the hammer. As a result, a man finally opens the door. **(1)**

Copyright © Houghton Mifflin Company. All rights reserved.

Theme 1: **Courage**   47

Assessment Tip: Total **8** Points

Name _____

Interview with the Ice Climbers

Complete the interview below by writing the answers Danielle and Jake would give to tell about their experience.

Q: Jake, why did you and your sister climb Mount Remington in the first place?

A: Danielle and I had to get help for our parents after our car crashed in a blizzard. I had seen a weather station on Mt. Remington on TV, so we decided to go there for help. **(1 point)**

Q: Danielle, how did you and your brother manage to climb without proper equipment?

A: We improvised. We used hammers as ice axes, screwdrivers as pitons, and a nylon leash as a carabiner. **(1)**

Q: What happened when you reached the top of the trench?

A: We were happy at first because we thought we were at the top. Then we suddenly got scared when we realized we couldn't see the weather station anywhere. **(1)**

Q: Jake, how did you and your sister feel at that moment?

A: I felt guilty for having been wrong about the weather station. Danielle was angry at me for the same reason. We were both scared of freezing to death. **(1)**

Q: What happened next that raised your spirits?

A: We realized we were on a false summit when we saw the weather station on a ridge above us. **(1)**

Q: What happened when you finally got to the weather station?

A: We banged on the door, but nobody answered. At first we thought no one was there, but then we heard faint music coming from inside. **(1)**

48   Theme 1: **Courage**
Assessment Tip: Total **6** Points

Copyright © Houghton Mifflin Company. All rights reserved.

Name _____

Then What Happened?

Read the passage. Then complete the activity on page 50.

A Day Hike

"I'm so glad you're okay!" Elaine's dad said as he hugged her close. "But what were you thinking, wandering off like that?"

The events of the past hour came rushing back to Elaine. She had been hiking along behind her mom and dad, enjoying the mountain scenery and warm summer day. Then she had stopped to look at some wildflowers. The flowers spread away from the path and down into a meadow. Elaine had wandered off the trail and into the meadow. While her parents had continued hiking up the trail, Elaine had lain on her stomach, peering at hundreds of pink, yellow, and blue blossoms.

A few minutes later she had heard a sound. When she looked up, she couldn't believe her eyes. Fifty yards away stood a mountain lion, staring straight at her! Elaine had frozen, her heart pounding. Should she lie still? Should she run? Then she remembered what her parents had told her the summer before. "If you ever see a mountain lion," they had said, "stay as still as you can. Sudden moves could cause the lion to attack."

Elaine had stayed as still as she could. The lion had watched her for a moment, and then had begun to edge closer. At that moment, her mom and dad had rushed up. As they ran into the meadow, the lion turned and slipped away into the woods. That was when Elaine had collapsed into her father's arms.

Copyright © Houghton Mifflin Company. All rights reserved.

Name _____

Then What Happened? continued

Complete the sequence chart to show the order of events in the passage on page 49. Begin the chart with an event that happened the year before the events described in the passage.

Last summer, Elaine's parents tell her to stay still if she ever
sees a mountain lion. **(2 points)**

↓

The next summer, Elaine goes hiking in the mountains with her
parents. **(2)**

↓

She wanders into a meadow to look at wildflowers while her parents
hike up the trail. **(2)**

↓

Elaine sees a mountain lion fifty yards away. **(2)**

↓

She remembers her parents' advice and lies very still. **(2)**

↓

Her parents return and the mountain lion slips away. **(2)**

↓

Elaine's father hugs her. **(2)**

Now go back to the passage and underline the sentences that tell where two different events happened at the same time. Circle the sequence words that helped you to figure this out. (4 points)

Assessment Tip: Total **18** Points

Copyright © Houghton Mifflin Company. All rights reserved.

Name _____

Prefix Clues

**Underline the word in each sentence that has the prefix *un-* or *re-*.
Then write a meaning for the word on the line below the sentence.**

Prefix	Meaning
un-	not
re-	again, back, backward

1. The hikers agreed to <u>reassemble</u> at the summit. **(1 point)**

   assemble, or meet together, again **(1)**

2. Some of them were <u>unprepared</u> for such a long hike. **(1)**

   not prepared **(1)**

3. They <u>reconsidered</u> their plan and turned back. **(1)**

   considered, or thought about, again **(1)**

4. Jake felt <u>unsteady</u> on the narrow ledge. **(1)**

   not steady **(1)**

5. He had <u>renewed</u> energy after eating a banana. **(1)**

   made new again **(1)**

6. Danielle <u>rearranged</u> the contents of her bag, looking for the map. **(1)**

   arranged again, or in a different way **(1)**

7. Only when the bag was completely <u>unpacked</u> did she find the map. **(1)**

   not packed **(1)**

8. When they <u>reexamined</u> the map, they saw that they did not have far to go. **(1)**

   examined, or looked carefully at, again **(1)**

9. Since the day was clear, they had an <u>unobscured</u> view of the valley. **(1)**

   not hidden, clear **(1)**

10. Despite the <u>unusually</u> warm weather, it was cold on the summit. **(1)**

    not what is usual or expected **(1)**

Copyright © Houghton Mifflin Company. All rights reserved.

More Vowel Spellings

Remember these less common spellings for some long and short vowel sounds:

/ē/ *i*-consonant-*e* (rout**ine**)   /ī/ *y* (c**y**cle)

/ĕ/ *ea* (sw**ea**t)   /ĭ/ *y* (rh**y**thm)   /ŭ/ *o*-consonant-*e* (sh**ove**)

Write each Spelling Word under its vowel sound.
Order of answers for each category may vary.

Spelling Words

1. cycle
2. sweat
3. rhythm
4. rely
5. pleasant
6. routine
7. cleanse
8. shove
9. reply
10. meant
11. sponge
12. apply
13. threat
14. myth
15. deny
16. leather
17. rhyme
18. thread
19. meadow
20. ravine

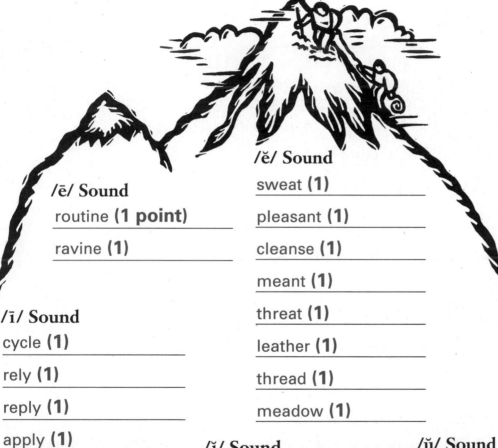

/ē/ Sound
routine **(1 point)**
ravine **(1)**

/ī/ Sound
cycle **(1)**
rely **(1)**
reply **(1)**
apply **(1)**
deny **(1)**
rhyme **(1)**

/ĕ/ Sound
sweat **(1)**
pleasant **(1)**
cleanse **(1)**
meant **(1)**
threat **(1)**
leather **(1)**
thread **(1)**
meadow **(1)**

/ĭ/ Sound
rhythm **(1)**
myth **(1)**

/ŭ/ Sound
shove **(1)**
sponge **(1)**

Assessment Tip: Total **20** Points

Copyright © Houghton Mifflin Company. All rights reserved.

Spelling Spree

Word Changes Write a Spelling Word to fit each clue.

1. Drop two letters from *really* to write a word meaning "to depend."
2. Change a letter in *moth* to write a synonym for *legend*.
3. Drop a consonant from *shovel* to write a word meaning "to push."
4. Replace a consonant in *great* with two letters to write a synonym for *danger*.
5. Change a letter in *repay* to write a synonym for *respond*.
6. Replace two letters in *circle* with one to write a shorthand word for riding a bike.
7. Add a consonant to *peasant* to write a word meaning "enjoyable."
8. Replace a consonant in *leader* with two letters to write a word that names a clothing material.

Spelling Words

1. cycle
2. sweat
3. rhythm
4. rely
5. pleasant
6. routine
7. cleanse
8. shove
9. reply
10. meant
11. sponge
12. apply
13. threat
14. myth
15. deny
16. leather
17. rhyme
18. thread
19. meadow
20. ravine

1. rely **(1 point)**
2. myth **(1)**
3. shove **(1)**
4. threat **(1)**
5. reply **(1)**
6. cycle **(1)**
7. pleasant **(1)**
8. leather **(1)**

Word Addition Write a Spelling Word by adding the beginning of the first word to the end of the second word.

9. throne + bread = thread **(1)**
10. deal + funny = deny **(1)**
11. approach + fly = apply **(1)**
12. swing + defeat = sweat **(1)**
13. rat + thyme = rhyme **(1)**
14. spoke + range = sponge **(1)**

 + = **?**

Theme 1: **Courage**   53
Assessment Tip: Total **14** Points

Copyright © Houghton Mifflin Company. All rights reserved.

Name _____

Proofreading and Writing

Proofreading Circle the six misspelled Spelling Words in this
travel poster. Then write each word correctly.

Spelling Words

You Need a Vacation!

Get away from the daily (routeen) and head for the
mountains! You will (clenz) your body and your mind
with a week of restful hiking and climbing. Follow
well-marked trails to a pleasant (meddow.) Test your
climbing skills as you explore a scenic (ravene.) Delight
in the beauty and (rythm) of nature. You'll discover that
the mountains are the place you were (ment) to be!

1. cycle	11. sponge
2. sweat	12. apply
3. rhythm	13. threat
4. rely	14. myth
5. pleasant	15. deny
6. routine	16. leather
7. cleanse	17. rhyme
8. shove	18. thread
9. reply	19. meadow
10. meant	20. ravine

1. routine **(1 point)**   4. ravine **(1)**

2. cleanse **(1)**   5. rhythm **(1)**

3. meadow **(1)**   6. meant **(1)**

✏️ **Write a Comparison and Contrast** How does the
portrayal of hiking and climbing in the poster above compare
with the experience that Danielle and Jake had in the selection?
Is one more realistic than the other? Is there anything missing
from both accounts?

**On a separate piece of paper, write a paragraph in which
you compare and contrast the two descriptions. Use Spelling
Words from the list.** Responses will vary. **(6)**

Assessment Tip: Total 12 Points

Copyright © Houghton Mifflin Company. All rights reserved.

Name _____

Dictionary Deciphering

Read the dictionary entries. Follow each numbered instruction.
Sample answers shown.

> **des•o•late** (dĕs′ ə lĭt) *adj.* Having few or no inhabitants; deserted: *an abandoned shack on a desolate road.* —*v.* (dĕs′ ə lāt′). des•o•lat•ed, des•o•lat•ing, des•o•lates. To make lonely, forlorn, or wretched: *The loss of our old dog desolated us.* —**des′o•late•ly** *adv.*
>
> **im•pro•vise** (ĭm′ prə vīz′) *v.* im•pro•vised, im•pro•vis•ing, im•pro•vis•es. **1.** To invent or perform without preparation: *The comics improvised several scenes based on audience suggestions.* **2.** To make on the spur of the moment from materials found nearby: *The hikers improvised a bridge out of fallen logs.* —**im′pro•vis′•er** *n.*
>
> **stag•ger** (stăg′ ər) *v.* stag•gered, stag•ger•ing, stag•gers. **1.** To move or stand unsteadily; totter. **2.** To begin to lose confidence or sense of purpose; waver.
>
> **tex•ture** (tĕks′ chər) *n.* **1.** The structure of the interwoven threads or strands of a fabric: *Burlap has a coarse texture.* **2.** The appearance and feel of a surface: *The plaster gives the wall a rough texture.*

1. Write a sample sentence for the first definition of *stagger*.

   The injured animal staggered to its feet. **(2 points)**

2. Write a sentence using the noun *improviser.*

   My cousin is an improviser of dance routines. **(2)**

3. Write a sentence using the second definition of *texture*.

   The cook was pleased with the creamy texture of the dessert. **(2)**

4. Write a sentence using the adjective *desolate*.

   The house seemed desolate after my older sister went off to college. **(2)**

Copyright © Houghton Mifflin Company. All rights reserved.

Assessment Tip: Total **8 Points**

After I Prepared, I Climbed the Mountain

Complex Sentences A clause contains both a subject and a predicate. An independent clause can stand by itself as a sentence. A subordinate clause cannot stand by itself as a sentence. A **complex sentence** has at least one subordinate clause and one independent clause.

A subordinate clause contains a subordinating conjunction. Here are some subordinating conjunctions:

after	because	since	when
although	before	unless	whenever
as	if	until	while

Join the two sentences using the subordinating conjunction shown in parentheses. Write the new complex sentence on the line.

1. You should not try to climb a mountain. You have prepared properly. (until)

   You should not try to climb a mountain until you have prepared properly. **(2)**

2. They begin climbing. Skilled climbers check their equipment. (before)

   Before they begin climbing, skilled climbers check their equipment. **(2)**

3. They reached the peak. They enjoyed the view. (when)

   When they reached the peak, they enjoyed the view. **(2)**

4. Danielle and Jack reached their goal. They could improvise. (because)

   Danielle and Jack reached their goal because they could improvise. **(2)**

5. I want to visit the weather station. I climb Mount Washington. (if)

   I want to visit the weather station if I climb Mount Washington. **(2)**

Assessment Tip: Total **10** Points

Copyright © Houghton Mifflin Company. All rights reserved.

Name _____

Before I Climbed

Correcting Fragments A **sentence fragment** does not express a complete thought. Correct a fragment by adding a subject or a predicate or both.

A **run-on sentence** expresses too many thoughts without correct punctuation. Correct a run-on sentence by creating separate sentences, a compound sentence, or a complex sentence.

Read the following sentence fragments or run-on sentences. Correct the problem, and write a new sentence on the line. There is more than one way to fix each sentence.

Answers will vary.

1. Because the weather can change quickly.

   Bring a warm jacket because the weather can change

   quickly. **(2 points)**

2. Meteorologists predict the daily weather, they make long-range forecasts.

   Meteorologists predict the daily weather and make

   long-range forecasts. **(2)**

3. This weather station has recorded the highest wind speeds. And the coldest temperatures in the state.

   This weather station has recorded the highest wind

   speeds and the coldest temperatures in the state. **(2)**

4. Visitors learn how a barometer works they get a tour of the weather station.

   Visitors learn how a barometer works, and they get a tour

   of the weather station. **(2)**

5. When the next storm comes.

   When the next storm comes, I will be prepared. **(2)**

Copyright © Houghton Mifflin Company. All rights reserved.

Name _____

Will It Rain?

Avoiding Run-Ons A **run-on sentence** expresses too many thoughts without correct punctuation. Correct a run-on sentence by creating separate sentences, a compound sentence, or a complex sentence.

A student visited a weather station and wrote the following. Revise it by correcting run-on sentences. You might need to add punctuation, a conjunction, or both. Here are two examples: Answers will vary.

> **Incorrect:** The sky is cloudy I think it will rain.
> **Correct:** The sky is cloudy. I think it will rain.

> **Incorrect:** The sun came out it was still cold.
> **Correct:** The sun came out, **but** it was still cold.

                                                        . A

I want to be a weather forecaster someday a big

storm would be exciting. A snowstorm can cause traffic
             and
accidents high winds can bring down power lines. I
                        . An
would want to be accurate an accurate forecast helps

people prepare for bad weather. I might be a scientist at
                  , or
a weather station I might work at a television station.

Because I want to be a weather scientist I will study

science. (**2 points** for each corrected sentence)

Assessment Tip: Total **10** Points

Copyright © Houghton Mifflin Company. All rights reserved.

Name _____

Writing a Friendly Letter

A **friendly letter** is a letter that you write to a friend to share news about what is happening in your life.

Use this page to help you plan and organize a friendly letter. Either write a letter that Jake or Danielle might have written to a friend about climbing to the Mount Remington weather station, or write a letter to a friend of yours in which you share a recent experience or adventure of your own. Follow these steps: (10 points)

1. Write a **heading** (your address and the date) and a **greeting** (*Dear* and the person's name followed by a comma).

2. Write the **body** of your letter below the greeting. Begin by writing something that shows you care about the friend to whom you are writing. At the end of the letter, ask your friend to write back soon.

3. Write an informal **closing** such as *Love* or *Your friend* followed by a comma in the lower right corner. Then sign your name under the closing.

Heading _____

_____

_____

Greeting _____

Body _____

_____

_____

_____

_____

Closing _____

Signature _____

When you finish your friendly letter, copy it onto a clean sheet of paper. If you wrote your letter to a friend, address an envelope and mail it!

Copyright © Houghton Mifflin Company. All rights reserved.

Assessment Tip: Total **10** Points

Name _____

Voice

Every writer has a **voice**, or a unique way of saying things. This voice reflects the writer's personality and manner of expression. You can express your own personal voice in writing by using the following techniques:

► Make what you say sound like you.

► Include expressions and figures of speech you might use when speaking. When Danielle reaches the summit of Mount Remington and does not see the weather station, for example, she tells Jake "We're dead" to express her feelings of hopelessness.

► Write in a way that reflects your thoughts and feelings.

Think about how you express yourself in different situations. What do you usually say if you are upset or frustrated? On the lines below, write expressions and figures of speech that you might use to convey different feelings.

My Personal List of Expressions and Figures of Speech

(1 point) _____

(to express fear)

(1) _____

(to express relief)

(1) _____

(to express joy)

(1) _____

(to express doubt)

(1) _____

(to express sympathy)

(1) _____

(to express worry)

(1) _____

(to express confusion)

(1) _____

(to express surprise)

(1) _____

(to express helplessness)

(1) _____

(to express excitement)

When you revise your friendly letter, use several of these expressions and figures of speech to reflect your personal voice. By adding some of these expressions, you can make what you say sound more like you — as if you are speaking directly to your friend. (5)

Assessment Tip: Total **15** Points

Copyright © Houghton Mifflin Company. All rights reserved.

Name _____

A Test of Courage

Use these words to complete the sentences below.

Vocabulary

1. Are you a ___seasoned **(1 point)**___ sailor, or is this your first voyage?

2. To prove that you will be an able sailor, you must climb to the top of the ___rigging **(1)**___ .

3. To start your climb, grab one of the ___ratlines **(1)**___ , the small ropes that form a ladder.

4. As you continue your ___ascent **(1)**___ upward, be careful not to become entangled in the ropes.

5. Rain and wind make the climb even more ___treacherous **(1)**___ than it usually is.

6. I have ___endeavored **(1)**___ to give you guidance, but you must find courage within yourself to make the climb.

Vocabulary

ascent
entangled
seasoned
endeavored
rigging
ratlines
treacherous

Use two vocabulary words in a short description of what it might feel like to make the climb described above.

(2 ponts) _____

_____

_____

Copyright © Houghton Mifflin Company. All rights reserved.

Name _____

Predictions Chart

selection details + personal knowledge + THINKING = prediction

Selection Details page 99	**Personal Knowledge**
▶ Charlotte must climb the tallest mast to prove her worth. The climb is dangerous. Charlotte is steady, though nervous. **(1 point)**	Example: Courageous people will face challenges, despite danger. **(1 point)**

Prediction: Example: Charlotte will go through with the test. **(1)**

Selection Details page 105	**Personal Knowledge**
▶ Charlotte makes it to just below the top gallant spar. It took her thirty minutes to do what a seasoned sailor could do in two. **(1)**	Accept reasonable responses. **(1)**

Prediction: It will take Charlotte a very long time to complete the climb. **(1)**

Selection Details page 107	**Personal Knowledge**
▶ Charlotte begins her climb down. She nearly falls because she can't see where to put her feet. **(1)**	Accept reasonable responses. **(1)**

Prediction: Charlotte will probably make it down. **(1)**

Selection Details page 105	**Personal Knowledge**
▶ Captain Jaggery appears on deck. He is not cheering like everyone else.	Accept reasonable responses. **(1)**

Prediction: Captain Jaggery will not want Charlotte to become a crew member. **(1)**

Assessment Tip: Total **12** Points

Copyright © Houghton Mifflin Company. All rights reserved.

Name _____

A Day on the *Seahawk*

Answer the questions about the setting, characters, and plot of
The True Confessions of Charlotte Doyle.

1. Where is Charlotte when the story begins?
   below deck on the *Seahawk* **(1 point)**

2. What does she have to do to become a member of the crew?
   climb to the top of the royal yard **(1)**

3. Why doesn't Charlotte start over again after she realizes she has
   begun to climb the wrong set of rigging?
   She doesn't want the crew to think she is retreating. **(1)**

4. After the ship dips, how does Charlotte feel about her decision
   to climb?
   She worries she will not will make it down alive. **(1)**

5. How long does it take Charlotte to climb to a point on the mast
   that a seasoned sailor could reach in two minutes?
   thirty minutes **(1)**

6. Why is climbing near the top of the mast more difficult than climbing
   closer to the bottom?
   The swaying motion of the ship increases at the top of the mast. **(1)**

7. Why is climbing down the rigging more difficult than climbing up?
   Charlotte can't see where she's putting her feet. **(1)**

8. How does the crew react when Charlotte finally returns safely to
   the deck?
   They cheer for her. **(1)**

Copyright © Houghton Mifflin Company. All rights reserved.

Name _____

You Guessed It!

Read the story. Then complete the activity on page 65.

The Deep End

Manning flopped around in his bed like a fish. A moment before, he had been sinking to the bottom of a swimming pool. He heard muffled shouts coming from above. He flailed his arms, but it was no use. He just kept sinking. His father's voice roused him from his dream. "Are you ready for your first day of lifeguard training?" Manning groaned.

Rough and Ready Summer Camp was just about the only place around that gave summer jobs to teenagers younger than eighteen. Manning needed money for a backpacking trip to the Rocky Mountains in the fall. He needed to buy a train ticket to Montana. He needed a new backpack and new hiking boots. He needed a job!

He had applied for the position of assistant counselor. He got the job, but was then dismayed to find out that, like all counselors at the camp, he needed to go through lifeguard training. He was a capable swimmer, but he had one discomfort that had been with him all his life: he did not like to be in deep water. In fact, being in water over his head terrified him.

At ten o'clock training began at Taft Pool. The trainer announced that first they would take a swimming test—ten laps of freestyle. "When I blow my whistle, dive in and start swimming," he said. "This is not a race," he added, "it's a test of your endurance."

Manning's heart was pounding. He knew he'd be fine in the shallow water, but what would happen when he reached the deep end? "Swimmers, on your mark!" the trainer called. Manning got into diving position. At the shrill sound of the whistle, he took a deep breath and dove. His body hit the water smoothly, and he fell into an even stroke.

"Just breathe," he told himself as he swam toward the deep end. He concentrated on his stroke. To his relief, he didn't panic as he passed the five-foot marker on the side of the pool. Nor did he panic when he passed the eight-foot marker. By the time he reached the far side of the pool, he was just hitting his best rhythm. He flipped himself around and started back toward the shallow end.

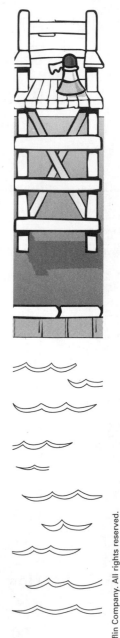

Copyright © Houghton Mifflin Company. All rights reserved.

Name _____

You Guessed It! continued

Answer these questions about the passage on page 64.

1. Do you think Manning will successfully complete lifeguard training? Why or why not?

   Yes. He is a capable swimmer and stays calm in the deep water.

   (2 points)

2. What information in the story might lead you to predict that Manning will not complete the training?

   He is terrified of deep water. He is nervous and doubts his own

   ability. **(2)**

3. At which point in the story might you change your prediction?

   I might change my prediction when Manning does not panic in the

   deep water. **(2)**

4. What do you think Manning will do with the money he earns as assistant counselor?

   He will buy new camping equipment and a train ticket to Montana.

   (2)

5. The following statements are generally true in real life. Which statement helps you predict that Manning will most likely succeed in lifeguard training? Circle it.

   A. People often avoid what they fear.

   B. People will often face a difficult challenge to get something they really want. **(2)**

   C. Good friends help each other through hard times.

Copyright © Houghton Mifflin Company. All rights reserved.

Assessment Tip: Total **10** Points

Name _____

Book Report Rewrite

Underline each contraction or possessive in this book report. Then, on the lines below, rewrite the report, replacing each contraction or possessive with its longer form. (1 point for each underlined word)

> The True Confessions of Charlotte Doyle
> by Avi
>
> Charlotte dresses in <u>sailor's</u> garb and asks to be accepted as a crew member. "<u>You're</u> a girl" is <u>Dillingham's</u> reply. "<u>What'll</u> the captain say?" Charlotte <u>doesn't</u> want to think about the task she must perform, but <u>she's</u> determined. <u>Charlotte's</u> climb is terrifying, but <u>it's</u> nothing compared to her descent. <u>I'd</u> highly recommend this book to adventure lovers. The <u>book's</u> author has also written many other entertaining stories.

Charlotte dresses in the garb of a sailor **(1 point)** and asks to be accepted as a crew member. "You are **(1)** a girl" is the reply of Dillingham **(1)**. "What will **(1)** the captain say?" Charlotte does not **(1)** want to think about the task she must perform, but she is **(1)** determined. The climb of Charlotte **(1)** is terrifying, but it is **(1)** nothing compared to her descent. I would **(1)** highly recommend this book to adventure lovers. The author of the book **(1)** has also written many other entertaining stories.

Assessment Tip: Total **20** Points

Copyright © Houghton Mifflin Company. All rights reserved.

Name _____

The /ou/, /ŏŏ/, /ô/, and /oi/ Sounds

Remember these spelling patterns for the /ou/, the /ŏŏ/, the /ô/, and the /oi/ sounds:

/ou/ *ou* st**ou**t   /ô/ *au, aw, ough, augh*

/ŏŏ/ *oo* bl**oo**m   v**au**lt, squ**aw**k, s**ough**t, n**augh**ty

                        /oi/ *oi, oy* av**oi**d, ann**oy**

Write each Spelling Word under its vowel sound.

Order of answers for each category may vary.

Copyright © Houghton Mifflin Company. All rights reserved.

/ou/ Sound

stout **(1 point)**

crouch **(1)**

mound **(1)**

foul **(1)**

trout **(1)**

noun **(1)**

/ŏŏ/ Sound

bloom **(1)**

droop **(1)**

groove **(1)**

gloom **(1)**

roost **(1)**

/ô/ Sound

vault **(1)**

squawk **(1)**

sought **(1)**

naughty **(1)**

clause **(1)**

/oi/ Sound

annoy **(1)**

avoid **(1)**

hoist **(1)**

appoint **(1)**

Spelling Words

1. bloom
2. stout
3. droop
4. crouch
5. annoy
6. vault
7. squawk
8. avoid
9. sought
10. naughty
11. mound
12. groove
13. foul
14. hoist
15. gloom
16. trout
17. noun
18. roost
19. clause
20. appoint

Name _____

Spelling Spree

Find a Rhyme Write a Spelling Word that rhymes with the
underlined word.

1. If you _____ down, you can see the kangaroo's <u>pouch</u>.

2. The baseball player <u>found</u> his glove near the pitcher's
   _____.

3. Please <u>pause</u> while I find the _____ in this sentence.

4. I think I can see this bird's _____, if you give me a <u>boost</u>.

5. Every plant in the gardener's <u>room</u> was starting to _____.

6. Don't <u>pout</u> just because you didn't catch a _____ today.

1. crouch **(1 point)**   4. roost **(1)**

2. mound **(1)**   5. bloom **(1)**

3. clause **(1)**   6. trout **(1)**

Word Search Find nine Spelling Words in the Word Search
below. Circle each word as you find it, and then write the
words in order.

S H O I S T E R N O U N I N G A V O I D A N
S F O U L S T E G R O O V E D U N V A U L T R U
G L O O M D I A P P O I N T A N A U G H T Y A R N

7. hoist **(1)**   12. vault **(1)**

8. noun **(1)**   13. gloom **(1)**

9. avoid **(1)**   14. appoint **(1)**

10. foul **(1)**   15. naughty **(1)**

11. groove **(1)**

1. bloom
2. stout
3. droop
4. crouch
5. annoy
6. vault
7. squawk
8. avoid
9. sought
10. naughty
11. mound
12. groove
13. foul
14. hoist
15. gloom
16. trout
17. noun
18. roost
19. clause
20. appoint

Assessment Tip: Total **15** Points

Copyright © Houghton Mifflin Company. All rights reserved.

Name _____

Proofreading and Writing

Proofreading Circle the five misspelled Spelling Words in this part of a letter. Then write each word correctly.

Copyright © Houghton Mifflin Company. All rights reserved.

Dear Mother,

   A most unusual event took place onboard today. Miss Charlotte Doyle, a young woman who saught to join the crew, managed to hoist herself to the top of the royal yard. Many of the crew had expected her to fail, and her success seemed to anoy more than a few of them. One sailor's response was to let his shoulders droup noticeably. Another let loose a rude squak and said, "She was just lucky." Personally, I think Miss Doyle has a stout heart and will be a valuable addition to the ship.

Spelling Words

1. bloom
2. stout
3. droop
4. crouch
5. annoy
6. vault
7. squawk
8. avoid
9. sought
10. naughty
11. mound
12. groove
13. foul
14. hoist
15. gloom
16. trout
17. noun
18. roost
19. clause
20. appoint

1. sought **(1 point)**
2. annoy **(1)**
3. droop **(1)**
4. squawk **(1)**
5. stout **(1)**

✏➤ **Write a Character Sketch** What does Charlotte Doyle's behavior tell you about her? What do you think about her ability to make herself climb to the top of the royal yard?

On a separate piece of paper, write a character sketch in which you describe Charlotte. Use Spelling Words from the list. Responses will vary. **(5)**

Name _____

Word Family Matters

Decide which word best completes each sentence. Write the word in the blank.

Vocabulary

1. The puppy barked <u>horribly **(1 point)**</u> when our older dog was let out at night.

2. My <u>advice **(1)**</u> to you is to hike with a friend.

3. I hope you <u>enjoy **(1)**</u> your school vacation.

4. I don't <u>normally **(1)**</u> eat six cookies at lunchtime.

5. Why does my brother <u>oppose **(1)**</u> everything I say?

Now write a sentence using two words you haven't used yet.
Sample answer shown.

To my horror, my school bus went in the opposite

direction. **(3)**

Vocabulary list:

joyous
rejoice
enjoy

advice
advise
adviser

opposite
oppose
opposition

horror
horribly
horrify

normal
normally
normalize

Assessment Tip: Total **8** Points

Copyright © Houghton Mifflin Company. All rights reserved.

Name _____

Charlotte and the Navy

Common and Proper Nouns A **common noun** names a person, a place,
a thing, or an idea. A **proper noun** names a particular person, place,
thing, or idea. Each important word in a proper noun is capitalized.

**Determine which nouns in the following sentences are proper nouns
and which are common nouns. List the nouns in the proper columns
below the sentences.**

> **Example:** New Mexico is a state in the United States.
>
> | **Proper Nouns** | **Common Nouns** |
> |---|---|
> | New Mexico | state |
> | United States | |

1. Charlotte Doyle wanted to be a sailor.
2. My big sister joined the U.S. Navy.
3. Her ship is called *The Piedmont*.
4. Last year, she sailed to Hawaii.
5. The crew is sailing in the Atlantic Ocean now.

Proper Nouns	**Common Nouns**
Charlotte Doyle **(1 point)**	sailor **(1)**
U.S. Navy **(1)**	sister **(1)**
The Piedmont **(1)**	ship **(1)**
Hawaii **(1)**	year **(1)**
Atlantic Ocean **(1)**	crew **(1)**

Copyright © Houghton Mifflin Company. All rights reserved.

Name _____

Foxes and Deer

Singular and Plural Nouns A **singular noun** names one person, place, thing, or idea. A **plural noun** names more than one person, place, thing, or idea. To form the plural of most nouns, simply add -*s* or -*es* to the singular form. Some nouns have the same singular and plural forms, and some nouns have unusual plural forms. Study the examples below.

Singular	Plural	Singular	Plural
ship	ships	chur**ch**	churches
walt**z**	waltz**es**	d**ay**	day**s**
Jone**s**	Jones**es**	di**sh**	dish**es**
sol**o**	solo**s**	scar**f**	scar**ves**
bo**ss**	boss**es**	fo**x**	fox**es**
coun**ty**	count**ies**	deer	**deer**

Compare the spelling pattern of each singular noun below to the ones in the list above. Then write the correct plural form. You may use a dictionary.

Singular	Plural
1. box	boxes **(1)**
2. city	cities **(1)**
3. toss	tosses **(1)**
4. leaf	leaves **(1)**
5. watch	watches **(1)**
6. cap	caps **(1)**
7. ash	ashes **(1)**
8. yes	yeses **(1)**
9. zoo	zoos **(1)**
10. toy	toys **(1)**

Copyright © Houghton Mifflin Company. All rights reserved.

Assessment Tip: Total **10** Points

Name _____

Ms. Doyle and President Kim

Capitalization and Punctuation of People's Titles A title before a
person's name is capitalized. When a title is abbreviated, it is followed
by a period.

> **Examples:** I will introduce **Ms.** Clara Kindowsky.
>   The press interviewed **President** Carter.

**Rewrite each sentence below. Use correct punctuation and
capitalization for titles.**

1. The sailors saluted captain Smith and lieutenant Lee.

   The sailors saluted Captain Smith and Lieutenant Lee. **(2 points)**

   _____

2. A member of the crew approached Capt Smith and dr. Tilton.

   A member of the crew approached Capt. Smith and Dr. Tilton. **(2)**

   _____

3. Dr Tilton visited ensign Johnson, who was sick.

   Dr. Tilton visited Ensign Johnson, who was sick. **(2)**

   _____

4. I recommend either mr. Kim or Mrs Ortiz for the position.

   I recommend either Mr. Kim or Mrs. Ortiz for the position. **(2)**

   _____

5. Mrs Ellison and principal Lesnikoski stood in the hallway.

   Mrs. Ellison and Principal Lesnikoski stood in the hallway. **(2)**

   _____

Copyright © Houghton Mifflin Company. All rights reserved.

Theme 1: **Courage**   73
Assessment Tip: Total **10** Points

Name _____

Writing an Opinion Paragraph

An **opinion** is a strong belief or conclusion that may or may not be supported by facts and reasons. For example, Zachariah in *The True Confessions of Charlotte Doyle* expresses his opinion of Charlotte, saying, "You're as steady a girl as ever I've met." As you read a story, you will form your own opinions about its characters.

As you read *The True Confessions of Charlotte Doyle*, think about this question: *Do you think Charlotte should have been allowed to prove her competence as a sailor by climbing to the top of the royal yard, or should someone have stopped her from performing this hazardous feat?*

Then use this diagram to record your opinion and to write facts and examples that support it.

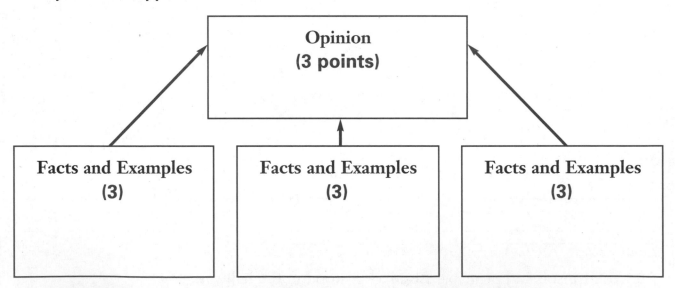

Opinion
(3 points)

Facts and Examples
(3)

Facts and Examples
(3)

Facts and Examples
(3)

Using the information you recorded in the diagram, write an opinion paragraph on a separate sheet of paper. In the first sentence, state your opinion in response to the question above. In the body of the paragraph, write two to three reasons why you think and feel the way you do. Support your opinion with facts and examples. Then end your paragraph with a concluding sentence that restates your opinion. (4)

74   Theme 1: **Courage**

Assessment Tip: Total **16** Points

Copyright © Houghton Mifflin Company. All rights reserved.

Name _____

Combining Sentences with Appositives

One way to improve your writing is to combine two short sentences into one by using an appositive. An **appositive** is a word or group of words that immediately follows a noun and identifies or explains it. Appositives are usually set off from the rest of the sentence by commas. Here is an example of before and after:

Charlotte Doyle was a thirteen-year-old girl. She joined the crew of the *Seahawk*.

Charlotte Doyle, **a thirteen-year-old girl,** joined the crew of the *Seahawk*.

Revise the following sentences from Captain Jaggery's ship's log. Combine each pair of short, choppy sentences into a single sentence with an appositive.

Charlotte Doyle is a young passenger. She wants to work aboard the Seahawk.

Charlotte Doyle, a young passenger, wants to work aboard the *Seahawk*. **(3 points)**

Today two members of the crew described a test of worth that Charlotte had to pass. Zachariah and Foley are the crew members who described the test.

Today Zachariah and Foley, two members of the crew, described a test of worth that

Charlotte had to pass. **(3)**

The men asked Charlotte to climb to the top of the royal yard. The royal yard is the tallest mast of the ship.

The men asked Charlotte to climb to the top of the royal yard, the tallest mast of

the ship. **(3)**

Ewing gave Charlotte some helpful advice. He is a seasoned sailor.

Ewing, a seasoned sailor, gave Charlotte some helpful advice. **(3)**

Happily, Charlotte passed the test with flying colors. The test was a difficult physical and mental challenge.

Happily, Charlotte passed the test, a difficult physical and mental challenge, with

flying colors. **(3)**

Copyright © Houghton Mifflin Company. All rights reserved.

Assessment Tip: Total **15** Points

Name _____

Words for Change

Write the letter to match each word with its definition.

f (1 point)

_____ boycott

e **(1)** petition

d **(1)** reproach

a **(1)** activists

b **(1)** segregation

c **(1)** civil rights

a. people who work hard for a cause they believe in

b. separating people by race

c. the rights belonging to a citizen

d. disapproval

e. a document that requests something

f. a protest that involves refusing to deal with a certain business or person

Write a sentence for each vocabulary word in the spaces provided.
Answers will vary. **(1 point** each**)**

1. activists:

_____

2. petition:

_____

3. boycott:

_____

4. reproach:

_____

5. segregation:

_____

6. civil rights:

_____

Copyright © Houghton Mifflin Company. All rights reserved.

Assessment Tip: Total **12** Points

Name _____

Making a Difference

**After reading each selection, complete the chart below to show what
you learned.** Wording of answers will vary. Details may vary; sample details are given

	Rosa Parks: My Story	*Making a Difference*
What challenge does the main character face?	Rosa Parks has to decide whether or not to stand up to the unfair law of segregation. **(2 points)**	Gloria has to give a speech in front of her class, even though she is very afraid to do so. **(2)**
Details that show the main character's courage	1. She does not give up her seat even when the bus driver threatens to have her arrested. **(1)** 2. She worries that she might be beaten, but she stays seated. **(1)**	1. She frees the bird, even though her sister is frightened by it. **(1)** 2. She gives a speech, even though she is scared. **(1)**

Assessment Tip: Total **8** Points

Copyright © Houghton Mifflin Company. All rights reserved.

Compare and Contrast Judgments

In *Rosa Parks: My Story*, what beliefs and opinions mattered deeply to Rosa Parks? Choose one quotation to copy into the chart below. Make a judgment about that belief or opinion. In the second block indicate on a scale of 1 (strongly disagree) to 10 (strongly agree) whether you agree with the statement or not. In the third block give at least one reason to support your judgment. Sample answers are provided. Then fill out the next column of the chart using a quotation from another selection in this theme.

	Selection Title: *Rosa Parks: My Story*	**Selection Title:** _____
Quotation That States an Opinion or Belief	"I had decided that I would not go anywhere with a piece of paper in my hand asking white folks for favors." (page 116) **(2 points)**	**(2)**
Check Scale	Disagree ___10_____ Agree **(1)**	**(1)** Disagree _____ Agree
Supporting Reason	I agree with Rosa Parks. What she wants is her rights as an American citizen. No one should have to beg for that. **(3)**	**(3)**

Copyright © Houghton Mifflin Company. All rights reserved.

Name _____

Outdoor Words

Use the words from the box to complete the sentences below.

Vocabulary

frantic
fluttering
stealthily
lunged
biodegradable

1. "Make sure to throw your cups in the trash can,"

   Mrs. Newsom said. "Plastic is not a

   biodegradable **(2 points)**
   _____ substance."

2. The cat crept stealthily **(2)**
   _____ toward the

   unsuspecting robin.

3. The robin escaped, fluttering **(2)**
   _____

   its wings as it flew off.

4. Andy lunged **(2)**
   _____ forward as he

   tried to catch a butterfly in his net.

5. A rabbit tangled in a piece of wire hopped back and forth,
   frantic **(2)**
   _____ to get loose.

Use at least two vocabulary words in a short description of what it might be like to spend a day cleaning up a park, lake, or other natural area.

Answers will vary. **(2 points)**
_____

_____

_____

_____

Assessment Tip: Total **12** Points

Copyright © Houghton Mifflin Company. All rights reserved.

Name _____

Test Practice

Use the three steps you've learned to choose the best answer for these questions about *Making a Difference.* Fill in the circle for the best answer in the answer row at the bottom of the page.

1. What is the main idea of *Making a Difference?*

   A A girl has a picnic on her favorite island.

   B A girl inspires her classmates with a speech.

   C A girl helps her sister free a pelican.

   D A girl fears speaking in front of others.

2. Where does the first part of *Making a Difference* take place?

   F on an island   **H** in a classroom

   G in a boat   **J** near a picnic table

3. Why do you think the pelican lunges at Elena but not at Gloria?

   A Elena walks loudly but Gloria walks quietly.

   B Elena tries to take the string off the bird while Gloria takes the string off the roots.

   C Elena screams "Ay!" but Gloria speaks softly.

   D Elena accidentally hits the bird with a stick, but Gloria strokes its head.

4. **Connecting/Comparing** Think about *Making a Difference* and *Hatchet.* In what way are Gloria and Brian alike?

   F Both work with others to improve the environment.

   G Both help others by their actions.

   H Both are stranded in the wilderness.

   J Both bravely face their fears.

ANSWER ROWS   1 (A) ● (C) (D) **(5 points)**   3 (A) ● (C) (D) **(5)**
              2 ● (G) (H) (J) **(5)**   4 (F) (G) (H) ● **(5)**

Copyright © Houghton Mifflin Company. All rights reserved.

Continue on page 82.

Theme 1: **Courage**   81

Name _____

Test Practice   continued

5. Why does Gloria give the first speech?

   A   Ms. Acosta asks Gloria to go first.

   B   Gloria feels that she has something important to say.

   C   Gloria wants to get the speech over fast.

   D   Gloria's classmates ask her to go first.

6. What is one result of Gloria's speech?

   F   Gloria's classmates want to help her clean up the island.

   G   Gloria learns that no one cares about brown pelicans.

   H   Gloria decides to give more speeches about saving wildlife.

   J   Gloria's teacher gives her an A$^+$ for the speech.

7. What was the author's purpose in writing *Making a Difference*?

   A   to tell a story about a brave girl who inspired others to act

   B   to give information about students who work to protect wildlife

   C   to convince people who fish not to use fishing line

   D   to suggest topics for speeches about wildlife

8. **Connecting/Comparing** In what way is Gloria like Danielle in
   Climb or Die?

   F   Gloria gives up on trying to solve a problem.

   G   Gloria argues with a family member about a solution.

   H   Gloria figures out how to solve a serious problem.

   J   Gloria describes a problem and her solution to her classmates.

Copyright © Houghton Mifflin Company. All rights reserved.

ANSWER ROWS   5 Ⓐ ● Ⓒ Ⓓ **(5 points)**   7 ● Ⓑ Ⓒ Ⓓ **(5)**
              6 ● Ⓖ Ⓗ Ⓙ **(5)**   8 Ⓕ Ⓖ ● Ⓙ **(5)**

Assessment Tip: Total 40 Points

Name _____

What Do You Think?

**Read the details below about Rosa Parks and the important actions
she took. Then answer the questions.**

- Rosa Parks didn't join those who took a petition to the bus
  company and city officials.
- She didn't want to ask anyone for favors.
- She made decisions herself, as an individual.
- She didn't sit in the bus seat with the intention of getting arrested.
- She remained in the bus seat because she was tired of giving in.

Answers will vary. Sample responses shown.

1. What does her decision not to give up her seat on the bus tell you
   about Rosa Parks? Make three judgements about Rosa Parks' personality.

   She wanted to accomplish things as a result of her own actions rather than

   through favors from other people. **(2 points)**

   She is an independent thinker. **(2)**

   _____

   She is willing to stand up for things she believes in. **(2)**

2. Explain why you believe your judgements about Rosa Parks to be true.
   Use details from the selection.

   Rosa Parks thought that the busing situation was unjust. She didn't think that

   the way other people were trying to change it made sense. When she found

   herself in a situation that could lead to change, she did not back away from it. **(6)**

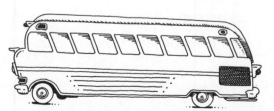

Theme 1: **Courage**   83

Assessment Tip: Total 12 Points

Copyright © Houghton Mifflin Company. All rights reserved.

Name _____

What Would They Do If...?

**Read each situation below and answer the questions that follow it.
Look in the Anthology if you need help remembering details.**

Situation 1: Think about *Making a Difference* on Anthology pages
116H–116L. Imagine that Gloria finds out that a seal at a
nearby beach was injured after it swallowed the type of
plastic holder that holds six cans of soft-drinks.

Answers will vary. Samples shown.

1. How do you predict Gloria might react?

    Gloria will try to convince her friends and others to clean up the beach. **(2 points)**

2. What story details helped you make this prediction?

    Gloria responded to her encounter with the pelican by giving a speech urging

    others to help protect wildlife. **(2)**

3. What personal knowledge or experiences helped you with your prediction?

    People who try to protect certain animals usually care about all sorts of wildlife. **(2)**

Situation 2: Think about *Climb or Die* on Anthology pages 74–86. Imagine
that Danielle and Jake discover that the men at the weather station
cannot help them and that the nearest town is on the other side
of Mount Remington.

4. What do you predict Jake and Danielle might do?

    Jake and Danielle will gather useful materials from the weather station and then

    head off for the town. **(2)**

5. What story details helped you make this prediction?

    Jake and Danielle were resourceful and determined in their efforts to get to the

    weather station. **(2)**

6. What personal knowledge or experiences helped you with your prediction?

    People like Jake and Danielle do not give up when people they care about need

    help. **(2)**

Assessment Tip: Total **12** Points

Copyright © Houghton Mifflin Company. All rights reserved.

Name _____

Word Division Decision

**Read each sentence. Rewrite each underlined word with slashes
to divide the syllables.**

1. The <u>pilot</u> kept the little plane on a <u>steady</u> course.

   pi | lot, stead | y **(2 points)** _____

2. The wind <u>buffeted</u> the plane a bit as it dropped in <u>altitude</u>.

   buf | fet | ed, al | ti | tude **(2)** _____

3. Annie had <u>taken</u> the seat <u>closest</u> to the window.

   tak | en, clos | est **(2)** _____

4. She watched as seven brown pelicans <u>glided</u> below with <u>outspread</u> wings.

   glid | ed, out | spread **(2)** _____

5. The <u>ungainly</u> birds flew in a V <u>formation</u>.

   un | gain | ly, for | ma | tion **(2)** _____

6. The birds quickly <u>vanished</u> in the <u>distance</u>.

   van | ished, dis | tance **(2)** _____

7. Annie <u>wondered</u> how far they might <u>travel</u>.

   won | dered, trav | el **(2)** _____

8. Then she noticed a <u>passenger</u> ship on the <u>horizon</u>.

   pas | sen | ger, ho | ri | zon **(2)** _____

9. Annie's <u>secret</u> dream was to become a cruise ship <u>captain</u>.

   se | cret, cap | tain **(2)** _____

Theme 1: **Courage**   85

Assessment Tip: Total 16 Points

Copyright © Houghton Mifflin Company. All rights reserved.

Name _____

Identifying Dictionary Entries

Choose the correct label for each part of the dictionary entry. Write the labels in the spaces provided.

adjectival form	part of speech
adverbial form	pronunciation
entry word	sample sentence or phrase
first definition	second definition

entry word **(1 point)** _____

part of speech **(1)** _____

pronunciation **(1)** _____

adjectival form **(1)** _____

numb (nŭm) *adj.* **-er, -est 1.** Deprived of the power to feel or move normally. *My fingers were numb with cold.* **2.** Stunned or paralyzed, as from shock. *He was numb from the terrible news.*
—**numbly** *adv.* —**numbness** *n.*

sample sentence **(1)** _____

second definition **(1)** _____

adverbial form **(1)** _____

first definition **(1)** _____

Assessment Tip: Total **8** Points

Copyright © Houghton Mifflin Company. All rights reserved.

Spelling Review

Write Spelling Words from the list to answer the questions.
Order of answers in each category may vary.

1–8. Which eight words have the /ă/, /ĕ/, /ĭ/, /ŏ/, or /ŭ/ sound?

1. wince **(1 point)**
2. bulk **(1)**
3. depth **(1)**
4. prompt **(1)**
5. meant **(1)**
6. craft **(1)**
7. rhythm **(1)**
8. sponge **(1)**

9–30. Which twenty-two words have the /ā/, /ē/, /ī/, /ō/, /yōō/, /ou/, /ōō/, /ȯ/, or /oi/ sound?

9. ravine **(1)**
10. squawk **(1)**
11. gaze **(1)**
12. league **(1)**
13. vault **(1)**
14. avoid **(1)**
15. theme **(1)**
16. sought **(1)**
17. throne **(1)**
18. hoist **(1)**
19. strive **(1)**
20. routine **(1)**
21. stout **(1)**
22. mute **(1)**
23. reply **(1)**
24. strain **(1)**
25. oam **(1)**
26. annoy **(1)**
27. naughty **(1)**
28. sleeve **(1)**
29. foul **(1)**
30. bloom **(1)**

Copyright © Houghton Mifflin Company. All rights reserved.

Spelling Words

1. ravine
2. wince
3. squawk
4. gaze
5. league
6. vault
7. bulk
8. avoid
9. thome
10. sought
11. depth
12. throne
13. hoist
14. strive
15. routine
16. prompt
17. stout
18. mute
19. reply
20. strain
21. roam
22. meant
23. annoy
24. craft
25. naughty
26. rhythm
27. sponge
28. sleeve
29. foul
30. bloom

Assessment Tip: Total **30** Points

Spelling Spree

Spelling Words

Puzzle Play Write a Spelling Word to fit each clue.

1. a plant's flower | b | l | o | o | m | **(1 point)**

2. a muscle injury   s | t | r | a | i | n | **(1)**

3. screech   s | q | u | a | w | k | **(1)**

4. a jacket's arm covering   s | l | e | e | v | e | **(1)**

5. a steady look   g | a | z | e | **(1)**

6. a recurring pattern of sound or movement   r | h | y | t | h | m | **(1)**

7. disobedient   n | a | u | g | h | t | y | **(1)**

Now write the boxed letters in order. They will spell a mystery word that is a synonym for *courage*.

Mystery Word: b | r | a | v | e | r | y

Spelling Words

1. vault
2. theme
3. sleeve
4. squawk
5. meant
6. throne
7. rhythm
8. stout
9. strain
10. hoist
11. sponge
12. bloom
13. naughty
14. annoy
15. gaze

Word Switch Write a Spelling Word to replace each underlined word or word group in these sentences.

8. The gold coins were kept in a locked storage area for valuables. __vault **(1)**__

9. The ruler's chair was inlaid with gems. __throne **(1)**__

10. Movers used a crane to haul up the piano to the top floor. __hoist **(1)**__

11. We discussed the subject of the book. __theme **(1)**__

12. I intended to give her your message, but I forgot. __meant **(1)**__

13. The ship was tied to the dock with strong and sturdy ropes. __stout **(1)**__

14. The fly's constant buzzing began to irritate me. __annoy **(1)**__

15. Please wipe off the table. __sponge **(1)**__

Buzz!

Copyright © Houghton Mifflin Company. All rights reserved.

Assessment Tip: Total 15 Points

Name _____

Proofreading and Writing

Proofreading **Circle the six misspelled Spelling Words in this letter to the editor. Then write each word correctly.**

As a usual (routene,) I don't write letters to newspapers. (The (bulck) of my writing is reserved for homework!) I must, though, tell the public about a very special person.

Last Saturday, the weather was really (fowle) Since my baseball (leage) practice was canceled, I decided to test my new hiking rain gear. In the hills near town, I slipped and fell into a deep gully. Gushing rainwater swept me along, and I was struck (muete) with terror! Suddenly, a stranger's arms grabbed me and began to hoist me to solid ground. I can never thank that person enough for my rescue. From now on, I will (stryve) to be as courageous as he is!

Spelling Words

1. bulk
2. mute
3. prompt
4. craft
5. league
6. avoid
7. roam
8. ravine
9. reply
10. foul
11. depth
12. routine
13. wince
14. sought
15. strive

1. routine **(1)**   3. foul **(1)**   5. mute **(1)**

2. bulk **(1)**   4. league **(1)**   6. strive **(1)**

Just the Opposite **Write the Spelling Word that means almost the opposite of each word or words.**

7. to grin wince **(1)**   12. confront avoid **(1)**

8. stand still roam **(1)**   13. late prompt **(1)**

9. found sought **(1)**   14. lack of ability craft **(1)**

10. hilltop ravine **(1)**   15. to ask reply **(1)**

11. width depth **(1)**

➤ **Write an Interview Script** **On a separate sheet of paper, write the script of an interview with a real or imagined hero. Use the Spelling Review Words.** Responses will vary. **(5)**

Copyright © Houghton Mifflin Company. All rights reserved.

Classifying and
Rewriting Sentence Types

**Write what kind of sentence each is—*declarative, interrogative,
imperative,* or *exclamatory*.**

1. Why was Rosa Parks arrested? <u>interrogative **(1 point)**</u>

2. She challenged an unfair law. <u>declarative **(1)**</u>

3. How courageous she was! <u>exclamatory **(1)**</u>

4. Make a timeline of the civil rights movement. <u>imperative **(1)**</u>

**Read the sentences. Rewrite each as the sentence type indicated
in parentheses. Use correct end punctuation.**

5. Did Ms. Parks work in Montgomery, Alabama? (declarative)
   <u>Ms. Parks worked in Montgomery, Alabama. **(2)**</u>

6. She was determined to eliminate segregation on city buses. (interrogative)
   <u>Was she determined to eliminate segregation on city buses? **(2)**</u>

7. You should read this biography of Rosa Parks. (imperative)
   <u>Read this biography of Rosa Parks. **(2)**</u>

8. Stories of heroism inspire me. (exclamatory)
   <u>Stories of heroism inspire me! **(2)**</u>

90   Theme 1: **Courage**
Assessment Tip: Total 12 Points

Copyright © Houghton Mifflin Company. All rights reserved.

Identifying and Writing Conjunctions and Compound Sentences

**Circle each conjunction in the sentences below. After each
compound sentence, write *compound sentence*.**

1. Birds try to avoid humans, (but) sometimes they need some human help.
   compound sentence **(2 points)** _____

2. Sometimes a bird will get entangled in string (or) wire.
   (1) _____

3. One helper must calm the bird, (and) the other must free it from the tangles.
   compound sentence **(1)** _____

**Rewrite each pair of sentences as a compound sentence. Use correct
end punctuation.** Answers will vary.

4. My brother saw a baby bird. He did not touch it.
   My brother saw a baby bird, but he did not touch it. **(2)**

5. It was in a nest. Its mother was nowhere around.
   It was in a nest, and its mother was nowhere around. **(2)**

6. Soon the mother returned. We were glad we had left the baby bird alone.
   Soon the mother returned, and we were glad we had left the baby bird alone. **(2)**

Copyright © Houghton Mifflin Company. All rights reserved.

Name _____

Words About a Poem

Read the first stanza of a poem by Henry Wadsworth Longfellow. Then use words from the box to complete the statements about it.

Vocabulary

figurative language

lines

repetition

rhyme

rhythm

sensory language

> The day is cold, and dark, and dreary;
> It rains, and the wind is never weary;
> The vine still clings to the moldering wall,
> But at every gust the dead leaves fall,
>   And the day is dark and dreary.

1. There are five ___lines **(1 point)**___ in this stanza.

2. The poet uses ___figurative language **(1)**___ when he compares the wind to a person who is "never weary."

3. The beats of syllables suggest a heavy, sad, plodding ___rhythm **(1)**___.

4. The poet uses ___repetition **(1)**___ by making the last line almost the same as the first line.

5. The poet ends the first pair of lines and the second pair of lines with ___rhyme **(1)**___.

6. Words such as *clings, gust, cold, dark,* and *moldering* help readers see, touch, and even smell the scene. The words are examples of ___sensory language **(1)**___.

Copyright © Houghton Mifflin Company. All rights reserved.

Name _____

Literary Devices in Poetry

Sample answers are shown. Students may find other poems and

Device	Poem Title	Examples
Sensory Language: words that describe how things look, smell, feel, taste, and sound <u>Example:</u> *tiny pawprints in the wet sand* **(4 points)**	"Good Hotdogs" "Losing Livie" "Child Rest"	"splash on/ . . . yellow mustard and onions" "little burnt tips/ of french fries" "an apple halfway to my mouth" details describing what Livie did to "clean up her own party" "Her red and yellow flower blossoms, beadwork complete"
Figurative Language: imaginative comparisons between unlike things <u>Examples:</u> *a voice as calm as moonlight* (simile); *icicles were dripping fangs* (metaphor); *breezes danced playfully* (personification) **(4)**	"Losing Livie" "Oranges" "Sundays"	"where the wind takes a rest sometimes." "Fog hanging like old/ Coats between the trees." "with cuffs stiff/ as the ace of spades" "hands as tough and smooth/ as the underside of a tortoise" "as slowly as bread rising,/ he rolled up his sleeves"
Rhyme: similar end sounds <u>Examples:</u> *friend/end; pale/detail* **(4)**	"The Pasture" "My Own Man"	"away/may; young/tongue" "busy/spicy"
Repetition: repeated use of words, phrases, or lines <u>Example:</u> *A happy bird/Am I, am I.* **(4)**	"The Pasture" "Family Photo"	"You come too." "One last"

Copyright © Houghton Mifflin Company. All rights reserved.

Assessment Tip: Total **16** Points

Name _____

Describing Poetry

Complete each statement about the poem indicated.

Sample answers for both poems are given.

1. In the poem "Child Rest," the poet tells about

   a memory of feeling secure and peaceful as a child beside a great grandmother

   who is beading   .

   An example of sensory language in the poem is

   "She half whistles, half hums an old song for me" **(4 points)**

   _____.

2. In "Poem," the poet uses repetition when he says

   "I loved my friend" as the first and last lines **(4)**

   _____.

   The poet may have decided to use repetition because

   he wanted to emphasize how much he misses his friend **(4)**

   _____.

3. In the poem "The People, Yes," the poet tells about

   opposite pieces of advice that a father might give a son about how to live

   _____.

   An example of figurative language is

   "Life is a soft loam" **(4)**

   _____.

Copyright © Houghton Mifflin Company. All rights reserved.

Name _____

Comparing Poems

Choose two poems from this section. Compare and contrast them by answering the questions in the chart. Add questions of your own to the chart too.

	Poem #1 Title: _____	**Poem #2** Title: _____
What is the poet's main point?	Answers will vary. **(20 points** for chart**)**	
What words in the poem help you imagine and feel?		
Does the poem remind you of something from your own life? Explain.		
What is the mood or tone?		

Which poem did you like more? Why?

Answers will vary. **(5)**

_____

_____

_____

Assessment Tip: Total **25** Points

Copyright © Houghton Mifflin Company. All rights reserved.

What Makes a Good Poem?

Reread the poem "Oranges" on pages 126–127. Fill in the blanks below to complete a summary of the story that the poem tells.

The narrator is a twelve-year-old boy who describes a time in December when he goes on his <u>first date **(1 point)**</u> with a girl. After he meets her at her house, they both walk to a <u>drugstore **(1)**</u>. He brings her to the <u>candies **(1)**</u> and tells her to pick what she wants. She picks a chocolate that costs a <u>dime **(1)**</u> and he has only a <u>nickel **(1)**</u>. The boy then places the nickel and an orange from his pocket on the counter. Fortunately, the saleslady understands that the boy wants to <u>impress **(1)**</u> the girl but doesn't have the <u>money **(1)**</u>. After that, the boy and the girl walk <u>hand in hand **(1)**</u>.

Answer these questions. Include quotations from the poem. Sample answers given below. Try to use names of literary devices too.

1. How does the poet make the time of year come alive?

   <u>Sample answer: uses imagery and sensory language: hearing the "frost</u>
   <u>cracking beneath my steps," seeing "breath before me, then gone," and "the</u>
   <u>gray of December." **(4 points)**</u>

2. How does the poet show the narrator's feelings about the girl?

   <u>Sample answer: The author shows what the narrator does when he's with her.</u>
   <u>"I smiled, touched her shoulder"; "I took my girl's hand/ in mine for two blocks"</u>
   <u>**(4)**</u>

3. What is a particularly vivid image in the poem?

   <u>Sample answers: "A few cars hissing past,/ Fog hanging like old/ coats between</u>
   <u>the trees" **(4)**</u>

Copyright © Houghton Mifflin Company. All rights reserved.

Name _____

Prefixes and Suffixes

The words in the box have the prefixes *re-* and *un-* and the suffixes *-less, -ful,* and *-ly.* Find the word that matches each clue. Write it in the letter spaces.

reunited	priceless	unaware	carelessly	plentiful
completely	unknown	fearfully	breathless	retelling

1. in a total way: c o m p l e <u>t</u> e l y **(1 point)**

2. without taking in air: b r e a t <u>h</u> l e s s **(1)**

3. not seeing or feeling something: u n <u>a</u> w a r e **(1)**

4. explaining again: r e <u>t</u> e l l i n g **(1)**

5. like a treasure: p r i c e l e <u>s</u> s **(1)**

6. more than enough: <u>p</u> l e n t i f u l **(1)**

7. together again: r <u>e</u> u n i t e d **(1)**

8. not at all bravely: f e <u>a</u> r f u l l y **(1)**

9. not familiar: u n <u>k</u> n o w n **(1)**

10. in a sloppy way: c a r e l e <u>s</u> s l y **(1)**

Write the boxed letters in order on the spaces below to complete the quotation.

An ancient Greek once wrote, "Painting is silent poetry, and poetry painting

t h a t s p e a k s ."

Assessment Tip: Total **10** Points

Copyright © Houghton Mifflin Company. All rights reserved.

Name _____

Silent to Sounded

You can sometimes remember how to spell a word with a silent consonant by thinking of a related word in which the letter is pronounced.

silent consonant: soften

sounded consonant: soft

Write a pair of related Spelling Words in each row. For each pair, underline the letter that is silent in one word and pronounced in the other. Order of word pairs may vary.

Spelling Words

1. autumn
2. autumnal
3. muscle
4. muscular
5. crumb
6. crumble
7. sign
8. signal
9. bomb
10. bombard
11. haste
12. hasten
13. column
14. columnist
15. heir
16. inherit
17. hymn
18. hymnal
19. design
20. designate

Silent Consonant	Sounded Consonant
autumn **(2 points)**	autumnal **(2)**
muscle **(2)**	muscular **(2)**
crumb **(2)**	crumble **(2)**
sign **(2)**	signal **(2)**
bomb **(2)**	bombard **(2)**
hasten **(2)**	haste **(2)**
column **(2)**	columnist **(2)**
heir **(2)**	inherit **(2)**
hymn **(2)**	hymnal **(2)**
design **(2)**	designate **(2)**

Copyright © Houghton Mifflin Company. All rights reserved.

Name _____

Spelling Spree

Analogies Complete each analogy. Write a Spelling Word so that the second pair of words has the same relationship as the first pair.

Spelling Words

1. *Scream* is to *yell* as *hurry* is to <u>hasten</u> **(1 point)**.

2. *Tune* is to *melody* as *songbook* is to <u>hymnal</u> **(1)**.

3. *Day* is to *Thursday* as *season* is to <u>autumn</u> **(1)**.

4. *Book* is to *novelist* as *newspaper* is to <u>columnist</u> **(1)**.

5. *Heavy* is to *light* as *flabby* is to <u>muscular</u> **(1)**.

6. *Wide* is to *narrow* as *row* is to <u>column</u> **(1)**.

7. *Save* is to *preserve* as *attack* is to <u>bombard</u> **(1)**.

8. *Poem* is to *haiku* as *song* is to <u>hymn</u> **(1)**.

9. *Dry* is to *moisten* as *stick* is to <u>crumble</u> **(1)**.

Phrase Fillers Write the Spelling Word that completes each phrase.

10. to clean up every <u>crumb</u> **(1)**

11. a <u>muscle</u> **(1)** cramp

12. to <u>designate</u> **(1)** a representative

13. the saying that <u>haste</u> **(1)** makes waste

14. to <u>inherit</u> **(1)** a fortune

15. to <u>signal</u> **(1)** for help

Spelling Words

1. autumn
2. autumnal
3. muscle
4. muscular
5. crumb
6. crumble
7. sign
8. signal
9. bomb
10. bombard
11. haste
12. hasten
13. column
14. columnist
15. heir
16. inherit
17. hymn
18. hymnal
19. design
20. designate

Assessment Tip: Total **15** Points

Copyright © Houghton Mifflin Company. All rights reserved.

Name _____

Proofreading and Writing

Proofreading Circle the five misspelled Spelling Words in this poem. Then write each word correctly.

Order of answers may vary.

Of all the lovely seasons,

It's autumn Mom holds dear,

Bright colors splashed on every tree,

And days so cool and clear.

Leaves without haste dance to the ground,

An (autunmal) waltz that makes no sound.

As my mother's (air,) I must agree,

The leaves are a special (sine,)

Like the explosion of a huge paint (bom,)

A unique seasonal (desine.)

1. autumnal **(1 point)**

2. heir **(1)**

3. sign **(1)**

4. bomb **(1)**

5. design **(1)**

1. autumn
2. autumnal
3. muscle
4. muscular
5. crumb
6. crumble
7. sign
8. signal
9. bomb
10. bombard
11. haste
12. hasten
13. column
14. columnist
15. heir
16. inherit
17. hymn
18. hymnal
19. design
20. designate

✎ **Write an Opinion** What kind of poems do you like best? Do you like funny poems or ones that touch your emotions? Do you prefer poems that rhyme or ones that have a free-flowing rhythm?

On a separate sheet of paper, write a paragraph that explains what kind of poems you like. Give reasons why you like that kind of poetry. Use Spelling Words from the list. Responses will vary. **(5)**

Copyright © Houghton Mifflin Company. All rights reserved.

Name _____

Negatives to Positives

Susie Plotkin thinks Artie is a great reporter, but the job recommendation she wrote for him doesn't sound very positive. Fix her letter by replacing each underlined word with one that has either a positive or a neutral connotation. Write the new word on the line that has the same number. Next to each word, write *positive* **or** *neutral* **to describe the connotation of your new word.**
Suggest that students use a thesaurus and a dictionary. Answers will vary.
Sample answers shown.

Artie Shaw is an <u>obsessive</u> worker who never leaves a job unfinished. His
₁
<u>nosiness</u> can sometimes get him into <u>impossible</u> situations, but he always
₂   ₃
manages to <u>barge</u> through any doors that are <u>slammed</u> in his face. His
₄   ₅
<u>cutthroat</u> style guarantees that he always finishes first. Thanks to Artie's
₆
<u>relentless</u> reporting skills, he has <u>stolen</u> many <u>lurid</u> stories from under the noses
₇   ₈   ₉
of other writers on our staff. Needless to say, his coworkers <u>resent</u> him. If you
₁₀
ask me, they all wish they had his <u>devious</u> talent for news gathering. What else
₁₁
can I say about Artie? I'm sure you'll find him a very <u>odd</u> employee, and I
₁₂
mean that in the best possible way.

1. attentive (positive) **(1 point)**

2. curiosity (neutral) **(1)**

3. challenging (neutral) **(1)**

4. go (neutral) **(1)**

5. shut (neutral) **(1)**

6. ambitious (positive) **(1)**

7. determined (positive) **(1)**

8. taken (neutral) **(1)**

9. exciting (positive) **(1)**

10. envy, admire (neutral, positive) **(1)**

11. clever (positive) **(1)**

12. unique (special/positive) **(1)**

Assessment Tip: Total 12 Points

Copyright © Houghton Mifflin Company. All rights reserved.

Name _____

Apple Season

Using Subordinate Clauses Compound sentences can be changed into complex sentences, using subordinating conjunctions.

Rewrite each sentence as a complex sentence, using a subordinating conjunction from the box. Use each conjunction once. Use commas correctly. Answers may vary. Sample answers are given.

after	as	before	when	while

1. The apples in Grandma Wallace's orchard ripen, and everyone in the family helps pick them.

   When the apples in Grandma Wallace's orchard ripen, everyone

   in the family helps pick them. **(2 points)**

2. The apples have been picked, and they must be washed.

   After the apples have been picked, they must be washed. **(2)**

3. Dad spreads newspaper on the floor, and the grandchildren begin peeling the apples.

   Before the grandchildren begin peeling the apples, Dad spreads

   newspaper on the floor. **(2)**

4. Dad cuts each apple into pieces, and he also removes the core with its seeds.

   As Dad cuts each apple into pieces, he also removes the core with

   its seeds. **(2)**

5. The apples simmer slowly in a big pot, and Grandma occasionally stirs them.

   While the apples simmer slowly in a big pot, Grandma

   occasionally stirs them. **(2)**

Copyright © Houghton Mifflin Company. All rights reserved.

Name _____

Farewell to a Friend

Compound-Complex Sentences A compound sentence and a subordinate clause can be combined to form a compound-complex sentence.

Rewrite each pair of sentences as a compound-complex sentence, using a subordinating conjunction from the box. Use each conjunction once. Use commas correctly. (Answers may vary. Sample answers are given.)

> although   while   because   before   when

1. My best friend Jamie told us she was moving. I felt very sad, and we both cried.

   When my best friend Jamie told us she was moving, I felt very
   sad, and we both cried. **(2 points)**

2. Jamie's father has a new job. Her family will move to Idaho, and they plan to leave soon.

   Because Jamie's father has a new job, her family will move to
   Idaho, and they plan to leave soon. **(2)**

3. Jamie leaves next month. Our class will make a memory poster, and Jerome will write a funny poem for her.

   Before Jamie leaves next month, our class will make a memory
   poster, and Jerome will write a funny poem for her. **(2)**

4. We will miss Jamie. We hope she will be happy in her new school, and we want her to write to us.

   Although we will miss Jamie, we hope she will be happy in her
   new school, and we want her to write to us. **(2)**

5. We still have some time. She and I will go to some movies, and she will sleep over at my house.

   While we still have some time, she and I will go to some movies,
   and she will sleep over at my house. **(2)**

Assessment Tip: Total 10 Points

Copyright © Houghton Mifflin Company. All rights reserved.

Name _____

Poetry in Motion

Using Commas with Long Sentences Use a comma before the conjunction to separate the two parts of a compound sentence. Use a comma after a subordinate clause when the clause begins a sentence. A comma is usually not used before a subordinate clause at the end of a sentence.

Use proofreading marks to correct the ten errors in punctuation and capitalization in this journal entry.

1 point for each correction

Example: before I walked, to the gym I went to my poetry class?

Proofreading Marks

⊬	Indent
∧	Add
⊰	Delete
＝	Capital letter
/	Small letter
⊙	Add Period
∧	Add Comma
ᵛᵛ ᵛᵛ	Add Quotes
∽	Transpose

May 2

While I was playing basketball I had a terrific idea for a poem. The first part would have the rhythm of dribbling and the second part would have the soaring grace of a great leap when the game was over I dashed back to my locker. I grabbed my favorite pen with green ink and quickly wrote eight short lines. After I read those lines to myself I added two long lines, and then I read the poem to my friend Anton. Anton said that I should submit my poem to the school newspaper because it was so clever. Who knows maybe I'll be a published author?

Copyright © Houghton Mifflin Company. All rights reserved.

Planning a Poem About a Person

The person I have chosen is _____.

What the Person Looks Like (3 points)
What the Person Sounds Like (3)
The Person's Gestures and Habits (3)
Meaningful Things the Person Has Done (3)
What the Person Likes and Dislikes (3)
How I Feel About the Person (3)

Copyright © Houghton Mifflin Company. All rights reserved.

Assessment Tip: Total **18** Points

Name _____

Sensory Language

Identify the sensory language in this passage.
Write the words and phrases on the chart in the correct space.

The Creative Chef

I could tell by the smoky odor and sizzling hiss that my brother Paul had invaded the kitchen. I walked in. A pot was spilling over with thick red sauce. On the counter was a pan heaped with drooping slices of eggplant. Paul smiled weakly. "Hi," he said. "I call this dish Eggplant Madness. It will be ready in an hour. I bet you can't wait to try some." Then he raced to the pot and stirred furiously. "Don't worry, I threw away the burned part. Here, taste this sauce."

I'm a sport. I took the spoon Paul offered and slid the warm, smooth sauce into my mouth. I recognized a zingy garlic flavor and a tinge of sweet basil. Believe it or not, I was starting to look forward to Eggplant Madness.

Sight	spilling over with thick red sauce; heaped with drooping slices; smiled weakly; raced; stirred furiously **(3 points)**
Hearing	sizzling hiss **(1)**
Taste	zingy garlic flavor; tinge of sweet basil **(1)**
Smell	smoky odor **(1)**
Touch	slid the warm, smooth sauce **(1)**

Write a sentence of your own that could belong in "The Creative Chef." Use sensory language. (3)

_____

_____

Copyright © Houghton Mifflin Company. All rights reserved.

Name _____

What Really Happened?

Each selection in this theme attempts to explain a mystery. After reading each selection, complete the chart below and on the next page to show what you learned about these mysteries.

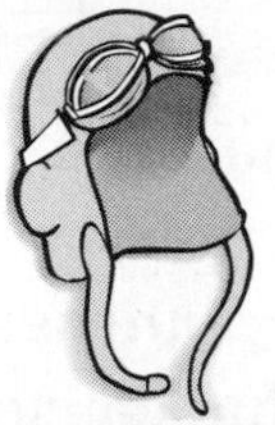

	Amelia Earhart: First Lady of Flight	The Girl Who Married the Moon	Dinosaur Ghosts
What mystery does the selection attempt to explain?	what happened to Amelia Earhart when her plane crashed **(2 points)**	what causes the moon to move across the sky and to seem to change shape **(2)**	what caused the dinosaurs at Ghost Ranch to die out **(2)**
What do you think the author's purpose was in writing the selection?	The author wanted to teach readers about Amelia Earhart and to fascinate them with the mystery of her disappearance. **(2)**	The author wanted to entertain readers by retelling a folktale about the moon. **(2)**	The author wanted to inform readers about Ghost Ranch, the dinosaurs that once lived there, and the theories about their disappearance. **(2)**
What kind of writing is the selection an example of?	nonfiction **(2)**	folktale **(2)**	nonfiction **(2)**

Copyright © Houghton Mifflin Company. All rights reserved.

Name _____

What Really Happened? continued

	Amelia Earhart: First Lady of Flight	The Girl Who Married the Moon	Dinosaur Ghosts
How did the author attempt to explain the mystery?	The author gave several different explanations and discussed why each one might or might not be reasonable. **(2)**	The author retold a traditional story. **(2)**	The author offered several hypotheses about what caused the dinosaurs to die out, and then gave scientific facts that might help prove or disprove each theory. **(2)**
Why do you think the mystery fascinates people?	Amelia Earhart was a hero to many Americans, and people want to know what happened to her. Her disappearance was a mystery because she vanished without a trace. **(2)**	People have wondered about the sky, the moon, and the stars since the beginning of time. **(2)**	No one really knows why the dinosaurs died out. The fact that there were so many dinosaurs at Ghost Ranch and that they appeared to die suddenly makes their disappearance very mysterious. **(2)**

What are some different ways in which people try to explain mysterious events?

People sometimes try to explain mysteries by looking at facts and thinking of

several possible explanations that could be based on facts. Storytellers once

explained mysteries by telling folktales and myths. **(2)**

Assessment Tip: Total **10** Points per selection and **2** points for the final question

Copyright © Houghton Mifflin Company. All rights reserved.

Name _____

A Tragic Disappearance

Use these words to complete the paragraph below.

Vocabulary

accounting
journal
runway
disappearance
aviation
taxied
inspiration
accomplish
navigator
transmission

One of the greatest mysteries in the history of
aviation **(1 point)** is the disappearance **(1)** of
famed pilot Amelia Earhart and her navigator **(1)**
Fred Noonan. When Amelia taxied **(1)** down
the runway **(1)** and took off toward Howland
Island on the second of July, 1937, she seemed certain to
accomplish **(1)** her goal of flying around the world at
the equator. She had been giving an accounting **(1)**
of her experiences to newspapers, and her words were an
inspiration **(1)** to millions of people everywhere.
She was also keeping a journal **(1)**, in which she
recorded her thoughts. During that day's flight, radio operators
lost contact with Amelia after she sent a confusing
transmission **(1)** over the radio. She and Noonan
never reached their goal. It may never be known for sure
what happened.

Copyright © Houghton Mifflin Company. All rights reserved.

Name _____

Fact and Opinion Chart

Passage	Fact or Opinion?	How I Can Tell
Page 148: She had read the note but believed Noonan had made an error.	Fact **(1 point)**	This statement is a fact, although Earhart's belief that Noonan made an error is her personal opinion. **(1)**
Page 148: Noonan had been right that it was necessary to turn south in order to get to Dakar.	Fact **(1)**	This fact was proven: they ended up north of Dakar because Earhart turned north instead of south. **(1)**
Page 151: Earhart's plane ran out of gas and crashed at sea.	Opinion **(1)**	No one has proven that this is true. **(1)**
Page 152: Amelia Earhart was spying for the U.S. government.	Opinion **(1)**	Some people say that there are facts to back up this claim, but nothing has ever been proven. **(1)**
Page 153: The Japanese did not let the U.S. search party into their waters, or onto the islands they controlled, to look for Amelia and Fred.	Fact **(1)**	This can be proven. **(1)**
Page 154: When Goerner showed the islanders photographs of several women, all of them picked Earhart as the woman they had seen.	Fact **(1)**	This can be proven. **(1)**
Page 154: Amelia had been brainwashed and was "Tokyo Rose."	Opinion **(1)**	This was some people's opinion, but there are not enough facts to back it up. **(1)**
Page 156: Amelia was "a tragedy of the sea."	Opinion **(1)**	This was Amelia's sister's opinion. It can't be proven that everyone would agree with her. **(1)**

Assessment Tip: Total **16** Points

Copyright © Houghton Mifflin Company. All rights reserved.

Name _____

Mystery Fact Sheet

Fill in the fact sheet below with important information from the selection.

The pilot: Amelia Earhart **(1 point)**

The navigator: Fred Noonan **(1)**

The goal: to fly around Earth at its widest point, the equator **(1)**

Where their plane disappeared: over the South Pacific, between New Guinea and Howland Island **(1)**

What Happened?

The Theories	Supporting Evidence	Evidence Against
1. They ran out of gas and crashed into the ocean.	They did not take off with very much fuel. **(1 point)**	The plane would not have sunk right away. It would have left an oil slick. **(1)**
2. They were spies for the United States.	Earhart was friends with President Roosevelt. The U.S. Navy organized the largest search in history. **(1)**	The United States government denies Earhart and Noonan were spies. **(1)**
3. Amelia was still alive.	More than 100 residents of Saipan claimed to have seen Earhart after the crash. **(1)**	Two skeletons were found, but tests showed they were not those of Earhart and Noonan. **(1)**
4. Amelia crashed on Nikumaroro.	Remains of a shoe and a piece of metal were found. Both could have belonged to Amelia. **(1)**	No one can be sure that these items belonged to Earhart. **(1)**

Copyright © Houghton Mifflin Company. All rights reserved.

Name _____

Focus on Facts

Read the passage. Then complete the activity on page 115.

Jacqueline Cochran, American Aviator

Jacqueline Cochran was a record-breaking female aviator. Though not as famous as Charles Lindbergh or Amelia Earhart, she certainly deserves to be.

Jacqueline was born in the early 1900s in Pensacola, Florida. She had a poor childhood in a lumber mill town. By age thirteen, she was working as a hair cutter in a beauty salon. Eventually, she moved to New York City and started her own cosmetics company. This was a courageous and admirable achievement. So that she could sell her products in more places, she learned to fly. "At that moment, when I paid for my first lesson," Cochran said, "a beauty operator ceased to exist and an aviator was born."

Soon Jacqueline was the leading female pilot in the United States. In September of 1938, with just enough gas for another few minutes of flying, she won the transcontinental Bendix Race. This was a truly incredible feat: the former beautician flew the 2,042 miles from Los Angeles to Cleveland in an amazing 8 hours, 10 minutes, and 31 seconds. She was the first person to finish the course nonstop. More than once, she was awarded the women's Harmon Trophy, the highest honor given then to American women aviators. She also broke the women's altitude record and several speed records. "I might have been born in a hovel," Jacqueline said, "but I was determined to travel with the wind and the stars."

In 1943, during World War II, Jacqueline became the leader of the Women's Airforce Service Pilots, or WASPs. These pilots did jobs such as ferrying planes, training B-17 turret gunners, testing planes at repair depots, and teaching staff pilots at navigator schools. By the end of 1944, however, Congress unfairly refused to admit the WASPs into the military and ended the program. Despite her disappointment, Jacqueline continued to fly and set records until the 1970s, when health problems forced her to stop flying. She died in 1980.

Copyright © Houghton Mifflin Company. All rights reserved.

Name _____

Focus on Facts continued

Answer these questions about the passage on page 114.

1. What opinion about Jacqueline Cochran does the author give in the first paragraph?

   She deserves to be as famous as Charles Lindbergh or Amelia Earhart. **(2 points)**

2. The author includes several facts and one opinion in the second paragraph. Write them here.

   Facts: Jacqueline was born in the early 1900s in Pensacola, Florida. By age 13, she was working as a hair cutter. She moved to New York and started her own cosmetics company. She learned to fly to sell her products in more places. **(2)**

   Opinion: Opening her own cosmetics company was courageous and admirable. **(2)**

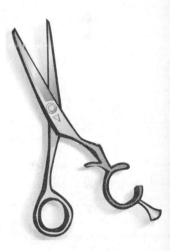

3. What opinion about Jacqueline's victory in the transcontinental Bendix Race does the author give in the third paragraph?

   It was a truly incredible feat. **(2)**

4. The author uses facts to support an opinion about Jacqueline's victory in the Bendix Race. What are they?

   She flew 2,042 miles in 8 hours, 10 minutes, and 31 seconds.

   She was the first person to finish the course nonstop. **(2)**

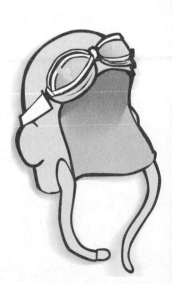

5. What opinion does the author give in the fourth paragraph?

   Congress was unfair when it refused to admit the WASPs into the military and ended the program. **(2)**

6. Rewrite the following sentence so it states a fact and not an opinion:
   Jacqueline Cochran was an amazing female aviator.

   Jacqueline Cochran was a female aviator who set many records and won several awards. **(2)**

Copyright © Houghton Mifflin Company. All rights reserved.

Theme 2: **What Really Happened?**   115
Assessment Tip: Total **14** Points

Name _____

Be a Searcher!

Amelia Earhart's plane has words on it. Circle each word that has a suffix meaning "someone who." Then use those words to complete the sentences. (1 point for each circled word)

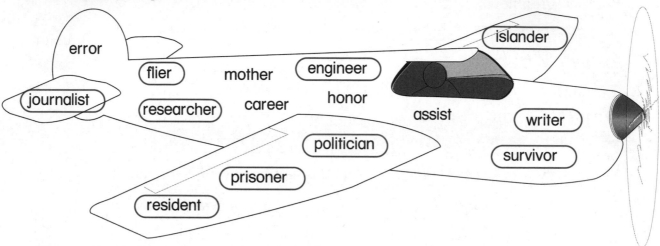

1. Years of training in how to handle a plane have made him an excellent <u>flier **(1 point)**</u>.

2. The <u>politician **(1)**</u> thanked everyone who voted for her.

3. When the war was over, each <u>prisoner **(1)**</u> was set free.

4. Every <u>resident **(1)**</u> in the town had lived there at least five years.

5. The <u>islander **(1)**</u> took a boat to school every day.

6. The <u>writer **(1)**</u> had always liked to make up stories when she was a child.

7. The <u>researcher **(1)**</u> is experimenting to find out how trees make oxygen.

8. The <u>journalist **(1)**</u> reported on the record-breaking blizzard.

9. My grandfather was the only <u>survivor **(1)**</u> of a house fire when he was young.

10. The <u>engineer **(1)**</u> designed a new plan for the factory.

Assessment Tip: Total **20** Points

Copyright © Houghton Mifflin Company. All rights reserved.

Name _____

Vowel + /r/ Sounds

Remember the following spelling patterns for these vowel + /r/ sounds:

/ûr/	ear, ur, ir	**ear**th, **ur**ge, sk**ir**t
/ôr/	or, our	sc**or**n, m**our**n
/är/	ar	sn**ar**l
/îr/	ier	fi**er**ce

Spelling Words

1. fierce
2. sword
3. court
4. snarl
5. thorn
6. earth
7. skirt
8. chart
9. urge
10. yarn
11. whirl
12. mourn
13. rehearse
14. curb
15. earnest
16. starch
17. purse
18. birch
19. pierce
20. scorn

Write each Spelling Word under its vowel + /r/ sounds.

Order of answers for each category may vary.

/ûr/ Sounds
earth **(1 point)**

skirt **(1)**

urge **(1)**

whirl **(1)**

rehearse **(1)**

curb **(1)**

earnest **(1)**

purse **(1)**

birch **(1)**

/ôr/ Sounds
sword **(1)**

court **(1)**

thorn **(1)**

mourn **(1)**

scorn **(1)**

/är/ Sounds
snarl **(1)**

chart **(1)**

yarn **(1)**

starch **(1)**

/îr/ Sounds
fierce **(1)**

pierce **(1)**

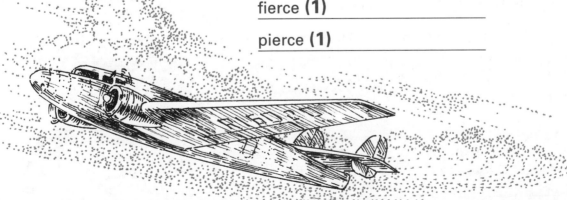

Copyright © Houghton Mifflin Company. All rights reserved.

Spelling Spree

Clues Write a Spelling Word for each clue.

1. You do this to prepare for a performance.
2. A judge presides there.
3. You step off this to cross a street.
4. A woman may wear one with a blouse.
5. A unfriendly dog may do this.
6. Some people ask the cleaner to add it to their laundry.
7. Its bark may be white and papery.
8. Kittens get tangled up in it.
9. You might find change in this.

1. rehearse **(1 point)**
2. court **(1)**
3. curb **(1)**
4. skirt **(1)**
5. snarl **(1)**

6. starch **(1)**
7. birch **(1)**
8. yarn **(1)**
9. purse **(1)**

Word Search Write the Spelling Word that is hidden in each sentence.

    Example: How is a <u>pear</u> like an apple? *pearl*

10. Everybody loves corn on the cob!
11. Did you hear that moaning sound?
12. The people at the pier celebrated the yacht's victory.
13. He gave me his word of honor.
14. The gardener will trim our new rosebushes.

10. scorn **(1)**
11. earth **(1)**
12. pierce **(1)**
13. sword **(1)**
14. mourn **(1)**

Spelling Words

1. fierce
2. sword
3. court
4. snarl
5. thorn
6. earth
7. skirt
8. chart
9. urge
10. yarn
11. whirl
12. mourn
13. rehearse
14. curb
15. earnest
16. starch
17. purse
18. birch
19. pierce
20. scorn

Copyright © Houghton Mifflin Company. All rights reserved.

Assessment Tip: Total **14** Points

Proofreading and Writing

Name _____

Proofreading Circle the six misspelled Spelling Words in this message. Then write each word correctly.

Spelling Words

While we were flying toward Howland Island, we ran into some (feirce) winds. The plane began to (wirl) out of control. It came to earth on an island that Fred and I can't find on our (choart.) Our supplies are running low, and the only plants on the island are (thourn) bushes that bear no fruit. We (earge) anyone who finds this message to contact the United States government. A rescue operation must be organized immediately. This is in (ernest.) It is not a prank!

Spelling Words

1. fierce
2. sword
3. court
4. snarl
5. thorn
6. earth
7. skirt
8. chart
9. urge
10. yarn
11. whirl
12. mourn
13. rehearse
14. curb
15. earnest
16. starch
17. purse
18. birch
19. pierce
20. scorn

1. fierce **(1 point)**

2. whirl **(1)**

3. chart **(1)**

4. thorn **(1)**

5. urge **(1)**

6. earnest **(1)**

✏️ **Write a Journal Entry** Amelia was a unique individual who attempted a daring feat. Have you ever tried something that may have had some element of risk to it? Did anyone try to discourage you? Did you have doubts? How did you resolve the doubts? Use your own or someone else's experience to think about the idea of taking risks.

On a separate sheet of paper, write a journal entry about taking risks. Use Spelling Words from the list. Responses will vary. **(4)**

Copyright © Houghton Mifflin Company. All rights reserved.

Name _____

Stress on Syllables

Read each dictionary entry. Sound out the word several times, placing stress on a different syllable each time. Circle the choice with the correct stress.

1. **ap•proach** (ə **prōch′**) *v.* To come near or nearer in place or time.

   AP•proach (ap•PROACH) **(1 point)**

2. **a•vi•a•tion** (ā′ vē **ā′** shən) *n.* The art of operating and navigating aircraft.

   A•vi•a•tion   a•VI•a•tion (a•vi•A•tion) a•vi•a•TION **(1)**

3. **cal•cu•late** (kăl′ kyə lāt′) *v.* To find or determine an answer by using mathematics.

   (CAL•cu•late)   cal•CU•late   cal•cu•LATE **(1)**

4. **con•ti•nent** (kŏn′ tə nənt) *n.* One of the seven great land masses of the earth.

   (CON•ti•nent)   con•TI•nent   con•ti•NENT **(1)**

5. **ex•haust•ed** (ĭg zôst′ əd) *adj.* Completely worn-out; tired.

   EX•haust•ed (ex•HAUST•ed)   ex•haust•ED **(1)**

6. **fre•quen•cy** (frē′ kwən sē) *n.* The number of complete cycles of a wave, such as a radio wave, that occur per second.

   (FRE•quen•cy)   fre•QUEN•cy   fre•quen•CY **(1)**

7. **re•fu•el** (rē fyoō′ əl) *v.* To provide with fuel again.

   RE•fu•el (re•FU•el)   re•fu•EL **(1)**

8. **re•verse** (rĭ vûrs′) *v.* To turn around to the opposite direction.

   RE•verse (re•VERSE) **(1)**

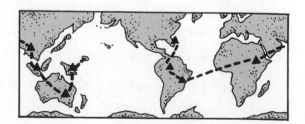

Copyright © Houghton Mifflin Company. All rights reserved.

Name _____

Amelia's Plane

Singular and Plural Possessive Nouns Possessive nouns show ownership or possession. To form the possessive of a singular noun, add an apostrophe and an -*s* (*'s*). To form the possessive of a plural noun that ends in -*s*, add only an apostrophe ('). To form the possessive of a plural noun that does not end in -*s*, add an apostrophe and an -*s* (*'s*).

---

singular noun: dog   **singular noun**: James
possessive: dog's   **possessive**: James's
plural noun: boys   **plural noun**: deer
possessive: boys'   **possessive**: deer's

Write the possessive form of each noun in parentheses.

1. the (plane) <u>plane's **(1 point)**</u> cockpit

2. the (women) <u>women's **(1)**</u> plane

3. the (planes) <u>planes' **(1)**</u> hangar

4. the (man) <u>man's **(1)**</u> binoculars

5. our (country) <u>country's **(1)**</u> flag

Assessment Tip: Total **5** Points

Copyright © Houghton Mifflin Company. All rights reserved.

Name _____

Amelia Earhart's Disappearance

More Possessive Nouns Remember how to form **possessive nouns**:

1. Add an apostrophe and an -s ('s) to a singular noun.
2. Add an apostrophe and an -s ('s) to a plural noun that does not end in -s.
3. Add an apostrophe (') to a plural noun that ends in -s.

The following sentences use phrases that show possession or ownership. Revise each underlined phrase to use a possessive noun.

> **Example:** Lynette visited the home of Amelia Earhart.
>
> Lynette visited **Amelia Earhart's home**.

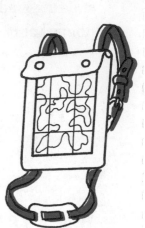

1. No one knows the fate of Amelia Earhart.

   No one knows Amelia Earhart's fate. **(2 points)**

2. Her fate has aroused the interest of many people.

   Her fate has aroused many people's interest. **(2)**

3. The theories of researchers are interesting to read.

   Researchers' theories are interesting to read. **(2)**

4. The fascination of Ross with Earhart's disappearance has led him to read many books.

   Ross's fascination with Earhart's disappearance has led him to

   read many books. **(2)**

5. The planes of early pilots seem primitive today.

   Early pilots' planes seem primitive today. **(2)**

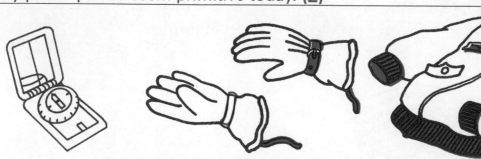

Assessment Tip: Total **10** Points

Copyright © Houghton Mifflin Company. All rights reserved.

Name _____

Write to My Friend

Using Apostrophes Writers use apostrophes in possessives and in contractions. If you leave an apostrophe out, you can confuse your reader. Likewise, if you use an apostrophe incorrectly, you can also confuse your reader. Look at how apostrophes change the meaning in the examples below.

We'll see you.   Well see you.   the dog's food   the dogs' food

Proofread the following draft of a letter Lynette wrote to her friend in Kansas. Underline each error in the use of apostrophes in possessives and contractions. Then rewrite each underlined word correctly above the error.

Dear Carolyn,

　　　　I'm **(2 points)**
　　Im so glad that I had the chance to visit you

　　　　　　　　　can't **(2)**
in Kansas last month. You ca'nt imagine how much

I miss seeing you in school every day, but the town

you now live in is beautiful. It is interesting that
　　　　　　　　　　　　Earhart's **(2)**
your town is also Amelia Earharts hometown. I
　　　　　　　　family's **(2)**
enjoyed visiting her familys' house. Her story
　　　　　haven't **(2)**
inspired me, and I havent stopped thinking about

the mystery. What do you think really happened?

　　　　　　Your friend,
　　　　　　Lynnette

Copyright © Houghton Mifflin Company. All rights reserved.

Name _____

Writing a News Article

Amelia Earhart's disappearance over the Pacific Ocean during her 1937 flight around the world was front-page news. Imagine you are a reporter for the *World News and Recorder*. Use the chart below to gather facts and details for a *news article* about the disappearance of Earhart's plane or about another historic event. Answer these questions: Who was involved? What happened? When, where, and why did this event occur? How did it happen?

Who? (2 points)
What? (2)
When? (2)
Where? (2)
Why? (2)
How? (2)

Now use the details and facts you gathered to write your news article on a separate sheet of paper. Write a beginning that gives the facts, yet captures the reader's attention. Present the facts you recorded in the chart in the order of most to least important. Use quotations where possible to bring this news event to life, and include a headline that will grab your reader's attention. **(3)**

Assessment Tip: Total **15** Points

Copyright © Houghton Mifflin Company. All rights reserved.

Name _____

Adding Details

A good reporter uses details to hold the interest of readers and satisfy their curiosity, to clearly explain what happened, and to make the people who were involved in the event come alive.

Read the following draft of a news article. Then rewrite it on the lines below, adding details from the list to improve it. Responses may vary slightly.

Aviator Mysteriously Vanishes

American aviator Amelia Earhart and her navigator mysteriously vanished in the skies on July 2, 1937. Earhart and Noonan were attempting a west-to-east flight. Their airplane, which departed from Lae, New Guinea, was headed northeast when it disappeared.

The last radio communication with Earhart occurred in the morning with William Galten, who serves aboard the United States Coast Guard cutter.

American aviator Amelia Earhart and her navigator **Frederick Noonan** mysteriously

vanished in the skies **over the Pacific Ocean** on July 2, 1937. Earhart and Noonan

were attempting a west-to-east flight **around the world**. Their **Lockheed Electra**

airplane, which departed from Lae, New Guinea, was headed northeast **toward tiny**

Howland Island when it disappeared.

The last radio communication with Earhart occurred in the morning **at 8:47** A.M.

with **Radioman Third Class** William Galten, who serves aboard the United States

Coast Guard cutter *Itasca*. **(1 point** per detail)

Details

Lockheed Electra	Frederick Noonan
over the Pacific Ocean	toward tiny Howland Island
Itasca	at 8:47 A.M.
around the world	Radioman Third Class

Copyright © Houghton Mifflin Company. All rights reserved.

Assessment Tip: Total **8 Points**

Name _____

Revising Your Story

Reread your story. Put a checkmark in the box for each sentence that describes your paper. Use this page to help you revise.

Loud and Clear!

☐ My story has a clear beginning, middle, and ending. It is focused on an interesting problem.

☐ Details and dialogue make characters seem real.

☐ I wrote in a way that gets my readers' attention.

☐ Many exact words create vivid pictures.

☐ Sentences flow smoothly. There are few mistakes.

Sounding Stronger

☐ My beginning, middle, or ending is unclear. The plot may not be focused on a problem.

☐ I need more details and dialogue for my characters.

☐ My writing won't always hold my reader's attention.

☐ My words are too vague. I could make them more exact.

☐ Some sentences are choppy. There are some mistakes.

Turn Up the Volume

☐ There is no beginning, middle, or ending. There is no problem.

☐ I didn't use any details. There is no dialogue.

☐ My writing sounds flat.

☐ I use the same word many times.

☐ Most sentences are choppy. There are many mistakes.

Copyright © Houghton Mifflin Company. All rights reserved.

Name _____

Using Exact Nouns

Replace each underlined noun. In exercises 1–4, circle the letter of the noun that best completes each sentence. In exercises 5–8, write in a noun of your own choice.

(2 points for each circled answer)

1. A lion held a mouse in its <u>hands</u> and said, "Tell me why I should not eat you, little one."

   a. legs   b. fingers   (c.) paws   d. jaws

2. "Because one day I may save you from a great <u>situation</u>," said the mouse.

   (a.) peril   b. happiness   c. accident   d. elephants

3. The lion laughed. "How could a tiny mouse such as you ever help a great <u>animal</u> such as myself?" the lion asked.

   a. mammal   (b.) beast   c. critter   d. freak

4. The lion let the mouse go and it escaped into the <u>beyond</u>.

   a. unknown   b. trail   c. cave   (d.) jungle

5. Weeks later, the mouse heard a <u>sound</u> and found a lion caught in a net.

   roar **(2)**

6. "Help me, little mouse," the lion cried. "I am in deep <u>adversity</u>."

   trouble **(2)**

7. With teeth as sharp as <u>pins</u>, the mouse ate through the net and freed the lion. "How can I ever repay you?" said the lion.

   razors **(2)**

8. "You already have," said the mouse. "For I am the same mouse that you caught weeks ago. You let me make an <u>exit</u> then, so I helped you now."

   escape **(2)**

Copyright © Houghton Mifflin Company. All rights reserved.

Spelling Words

Look for familiar spelling patterns to help you remember how to spell the Spelling Words on this page. Think carefully about the parts that you find hard to spell in each word.

Write the missing letters in the Spelling Words below.

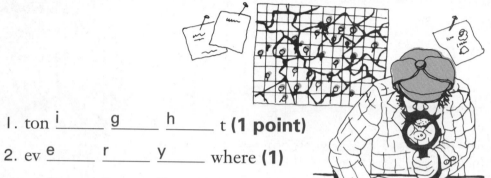

1. ton <u>i</u> <u>g</u> <u>h</u> t **(1 point)**
2. ev <u>e</u> <u>r</u> <u>y</u> where **(1)**
3. ev <u>e</u> <u>r</u> <u>y</u> body **(1)**
4. <u>a</u> <u>n</u> other **(1)**
5. bec <u>a</u> <u>u</u> <u>s</u> e **(1)**
6. <u>w</u> <u>h</u> ole **(1)**
7. p <u>e</u> <u>o</u> ple **(1)**
8. c <u>o</u> <u>u</u> <u>s</u> <u>i</u> n **(1)**
9. clo <u>t</u> <u>h</u> <u>e</u> s **(1)**
10. h <u>e</u> <u>i</u> <u>g</u> <u>h</u> t **(1)**
11. a <u>l</u> <u>w</u> <u>a</u> ys **(1)**
12. r <u>i</u> <u>g</u> <u>h</u> t **(1)**
13. m <u>i</u> <u>g</u> <u>h</u> t **(1)**
14. re <u>a</u> <u>l</u> <u>l</u> y **(1)**
15. ev <u>e</u> <u>r</u> <u>y</u> thing **(1)**

Spelling Words

1. tonight
2. everywhere
3. everybody
4. another
5. because
6. whole
7. people
8. cousin
9. clothes
10. height
11. always
12. right
13. might
14. really
15. everything

Study List On a separate sheet of paper, write each Spelling Word. Check your spelling against the words on the list.
Order of words may vary.

Copyright © Houghton Mifflin Company. All rights reserved.

Name _____

Spelling Spree

Syllable Scramble Rearrange the syllables in each item to write a Spelling Word. There is one extra syllable in each item.

Spelling Words

1. ways al all
2. oth un an er
3. cause be coz
4. ry were eve where
5. nite night to
6. ple pe peo
7. ev thing ry eve
8. bo eve ry in dy

1. always **(1 point)** _____
2. another **(1)** _____
3. because **(1)** _____
4. everywhere **(1)** _____
5. tonight **(1)** _____
6. people **(1)** _____
7. everything **(1)** _____
8. everybody **(1)** _____

Spelling Words

1. tonight
2. everywhere
3. everybody
4. another
5. because
6. whole
7. people
8. cousin
9. clothes
10. height
11. always
12. right
13. might
14. really
15. everything

Find a Rhyme Write a Spelling Word that rhymes with the underlined word and makes sense in the sentence.

9. It looks like we _____ have to find another <u>site</u> for the building.
10. Somebody <u>stole</u> the _____ eight thousand dollars!
11. There's only a <u>slight</u> difference between your _____ and mine.
12. When she gets _____ mad, she gets a <u>steely</u> look in her eyes.
13. My brother really <u>loathes</u> buying new _____.
14. Turn the screw to the _____ until it gets really <u>tight</u>.
15. I'm going to pick up a <u>dozen</u> donuts for my _____.

9. might **(1)** _____
10. whole **(1)** _____
11. height **(1)** _____
12. really **(1)** _____
13. clothes **(1)** _____
14. right **(1)** _____
15. cousin **(1)** _____

Copyright © Houghton Mifflin Company. All rights reserved.

Theme 2: **What Really Happened?**   129

Assessment Tip: Total **15 Points**

Name _____

Proofreading and Writing

Proofreading Circle the five misspelled Spelling Words in this advertisement. Then write each word correctly.

Read all about it!

You (mite) think you've heard the whole story behind last winter's plane crashes, but if you do, you're wrong. Do you want to know what (realy) happened? Then read the book that everyone (everwhere) is talking about! This book tells you (evrything) that you could want to know about why those flights went down. It just goes to show that you can't (allways) believe what you see on television!

Spelling Words

1. tonight
2. everywhere
3. everybody
4. another
5. because
6. whole
7. people
8. cousin
9. clothes
10. height
11. always
12. right
13. might
14. really
15. everything

1. might **(1 point)**
2. really **(1)**
3. everywhere **(1)**
4. everything **(1)**
5. always **(1)**

Write a Tag-Team Mystery Team up with a classmate. Then, taking turns writing sentences, write a mystery story. Use Spelling Words from the list. Responses will vary. **(5)**

130   Theme 2: **What Really Happened?**

Assessment Tip: Total **10** Points

Copyright © Houghton Mifflin Company. All rights reserved.

Name _____

Fishing for the Right Word

Fill in each blank with a word from the box.

Vocabulary

mainland
suspicious
common room
sod
hearth
phases
kayak
sparkling
village

1. If you are in a light, one-person boat traditionally used in the Arctic, you are in a ___kayak **(1 point)**___.

2. If you watch the moon each night for a month, you will observe all its ___phases **(1)**___.

3. If you live in a very small settlement, you live in a ___village **(1)**___.

4. If you had been alive hundreds of years ago, you might have cooked on a ___hearth **(1)**___.

5. If you do not trust someone, you are ___suspicious **(1)**___ of that person.

6. If your roof is made of squares of soil held together with the roots of grasses, it is made of ___sod **(1)**___.

7. If you are on an island, you are not on the ___mainland **(1)**___.

8. If you are looking at waves on which the sun is shining, you are seeing ___sparkling **(1)**___ waters.

9. If you are in the part of a traditional dwelling where family members gather, you are in the ___common room **(1)**___.

Copyright © Houghton Mifflin Company. All rights reserved.

Assessment Tip: Total **9** Points

Name _____

Inferences Chart

Question	Evidence from the Story	Own Knowledge	Inference
Pages 172–173 What does nature mean to the cousins and their culture?	The cousins make hats and baskets from roots. They gather food from the land and ocean. **(1 point)**	Example: It is important to people who get food, clothing, and tools from the out-of-doors. **(1)**	Nature is important to the cousins and the Alutiiq culture. **(1)**
Pages 175–176 Why do you think Moon wants the most patient cousin for his wife?	Moon must work and cannot always be home. His wife gets bored. **(1)**	Example: It takes patience to be alone for a long time without getting bored. **(1)**	His wife will need to be patient in order to wait for him while he is away. **(1)**
Page 176 What is the work Moon must do?	His wife complains that he leaves every night. The cousins saw him in the sky every night. **(1)**	Example: The moon shines in the sky every night. **(1)**	He needs to shine in the sky all night. **(1)**
Pages 178–179 Why are the star people lying facedown?	They each have one sparkling eye. This section of the story takes place on the "other side" of the sky. **(1)**	Example: Stars shine down on Earth. If someone were on the "other side" of the sky, they would have to look down to see Earth. **(1)**	They are looking down so they can make the stars shine down on Earth. **(1)**
Page 180 Why does Moon's wife cover her head with a blanket and say she has a pain on her face?	Moon told her not to go into the storeroom, but she did. Now she has one of Moon's pieces of light stuck to her face. **(1)**	Example: When people do something they're not supposed to do, they usually don't want anyone to know. **(1)**	She doesn't want Moon to know she was in the storeroom trying on his masks. **(1)**

132   Theme 2: **What Really Happened?**

Assessment Tip: Total **15 Points**

Copyright © Houghton Mifflin Company. All rights reserved.

Name _____

Questioning the Answers

Write an answer for each question below.

1. When did the cousins fall in love with the Moon?

   one night when they were sitting on the beach, admiring the

   Moon's beauty **(1 point)**

2. What did the cousins have to do in order to become the Moon's wife?

   Moon told them to keep their eyes closed until he said they

   could open them. **(1)**

3. What happened to the cousin who opened her eye?

   She fell from the sky and lost her long hair. **(1)**

4. What did the Moon tell his wife not to do?

   look behind the blanket and in the storehouse **(1)**

5. Who were the one-eyed people whom the Moon's wife met?

   the stars **(1)**

6. What did the Moon's wife find in the storeroom?

   different masks of light for each phase of the moon **(1)**

7. What happened to Moon's wife when she tried on one of his masks?

   The mask stuck to her face. **(1)**

8. What job did the Moon give his wife?

   He told her she could carry the pieces of the moon for the

   second half of its cycle. **(1)**

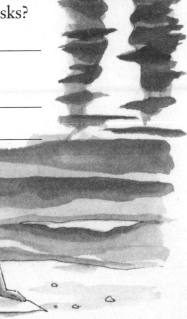

Copyright © Houghton Mifflin Company. All rights reserved.

Theme 2: **What Really Happened?**   133

Assessment Tip: Total **8** Points

Name _____

Putting Clues Together

Read the passage. Then complete the activity on page 135.

Eos and Tithonus, A Greek Myth

It was still dark when Eos, the dawn, awoke. She rose from her pink pillows and pushed her yellow bedcover aside. Pale light glowed from her hair. Eos dipped her rosy fingers into a glass and sprinkled dewdrops over the world. Then she ran outside and threw open the palace gates. She shaded her eyes as four fiery stallions pulled a golden chariot with her brother Helios, the sun, through the gates into the early morning sky. After latching the gates, Eos yawned and strolled back into the palace.

From the bedroom she heard a tiny cough. Tithonus, her husband, must be awake. "Poor dear," Eos thought, hurrying to the bedside. She caught sight of herself in the mirror and couldn't help smiling. She didn't look a day over twenty, although she was far, far older than her husband.

Eos looked everywhere for Tithonus, but she couldn't find him. At last she spied him crouching in a corner, a shriveled, tiny man about the size of a grasshopper. In fact, his wheezing sounded a little like chirping. Eos sighed sadly. "He is quite old — almost 350," she thought. It seemed only yesterday that she had glimpsed him on Earth, the handsomest young man imaginable. She had begged Zeus to make him immortal so she could marry him. Zeus had done his best, but he'd warned her that something like this might happen.

After serving Tithonus a very small breakfast, she had an idea. Why not keep him in her little handkerchief basket? A basket might keep him safe, and it was certainly a better size for him than furniture in the palace. Tithonus did not object to his new home, and Eos set the basket on the windowsill so he could enjoy the sun. That night his sad chirping lulled her to sleep. When Eos peered into the basket next morning, she thought he looked greener than he did the day before.

Copyright © Houghton Mifflin Company. All rights reserved.

Name _____

Putting Clues Together   continued

Answer these questions about the story on page 134.

1. How does Eos feel about Tithonus?
   She loves him, but she feels a little sorry for him. **(2 points)**

2. What clues in the story tell you that Eos loves and pities her
   husband?
   She thinks, "Poor dear," and sighs sadly when she remembers
   his age. She takes care of him. **(2)**

3. What has happened to Tithonus that has not happened to Eos?
   Tithonus has grown old, but Eos has remained young. **(2)**

4. What seems to be happening to Tithonus? How can you tell?
   He seems to be turning into an insect. He has shrunk to the size
   of a grasshopper, chirps, and is greener than he was yesterday. **(2)**

5. What do you think Tithonus might become? Why?
   He might turn into a grasshopper. He is small and green like a
   grasshopper, and he chirps. **(2)**

6. Myths and folktales often do more than entertain. What purpose
   do you think this story has? Circle one answer. Answer shown

   A. to teach a lesson about what is right

   B. to explain how grasshoppers came to be **(2)**

   C. to explain the movement of the sun and moon

Copyright © Houghton Mifflin Company. All rights reserved.

Assessment Tip: Total **12 Points**

Name _____

What's the Ending?

**Read the letter. Circle the ten words with the endings -*s* or -*es*.
Write each word in the first column, and then write the base word
and the ending.**

Dear cousin,

　　We have different (lives) now, and I won't see you again. But there
are many possible (husbands) in the (villages) all around you. Do you still
walk on the (beaches) in the (evenings) to glimpse the moon? If you look up,
you will see me in the (heavens) My husband and I share the (cycles) of the
moon. He (enjoys) his work, and so do I. He (carries) the moon for the first
half of each cycle, and I carry it for the second half. So, whenever the
moon (glimmers) down on you, think of me.

　　　　　　　　　　　　Your loving cousin

(1 point for each part)

	Word	Base word	Ending
1.	lives	life	-s
2.	husbands	husband	-s
3.	villages	village	-s
4.	beaches	beach	-es
5.	evenings	evening	-s
6.	heavens	heaven	-s
7.	cycles	cycle	-s
8.	enjoys	enjoy	-s
9.	carries	carry	-es
10.	glimmers	glimmer	-s

Assessment Tip: Total **30** Points

Copyright © Houghton Mifflin Company. All rights reserved.

Name _____

Homophones

Words that sound alike but have different spellings and meanings are called **homophones**. When you use a homophone, be sure to spell the word that has the meaning you want.

vain	(vān)	unsuccessful, fruitless
vein	(vān)	a blood vessel

**Write the homophone pairs among the Spelling Words.
(2 points for each pair)**

Copyright © Houghton Mifflin Company. All rights reserved.

Spelling Words

1. fir
2. fur
3. scent
4. sent
5. scene
6. seen
7. vain
8. vein
9. principal
10. principle
11. manor
12. manner
13. who's
14. whose
15. tacks
16. tax
17. hangar
18. hanger
19. died
20. dyed

Homophones

fir	fur
scent	sent
scene	seen
vain	vein
principal	principle
manor	manner
who's	whose
tacks	tax
hanger	hangar
died	dyed

Theme 2: **What Really Happened?** 137

Assessment Tip: Total **20** Points

Name _____

Spelling Spree

Homophone Riddles Write a pair of Spelling Words to complete each statement.

1–2. A hook to hang your coat on in an airport storage building is a _____ _____.

3–4. A dog might call the needles of a pine tree _____ _____.

5–6. The most important one in a set of rules or standards is the _____ _____.

7–8. A gift of perfume mailed to a friend is a _____ _____.

1. hangar **(1 point)**
2. hanger **(1)**
3. fir **(1)**
4. fur **(1)**
5. principal **(1)**
6. principle **(1)**
7. sent **(1)**
8. scent **(1)**

Familiar Phrases Write the Spelling Word that completes each phrase or sentence. Remember to capitalize the first word in a sentence.

9. as _____ as a peacock
10. a tie-_____ shirt
11. the _____ of the crime
12. not pushpins, but _____
13. draw blood from a _____
14. federal income _____
15. Knock, knock. _____ there?

9. vain **(1)**
10. dyed **(1)**
11. scene **(1)**
12. tacks **(1)**
13. vein **(1)**
14. tax **(1)**
15. Who's **(1)**

Copyright © Houghton Mifflin Company. All rights reserved.

Assessment Tip: Total **15** Points

Spelling Words

1. fir
2. fur
3. scent
4. sent
5. scene
6. seen
7. vain
8. vein
9. principal
10. principle
11. manor
12. manner
13. who's
14. whose
15. tacks
16. tax
17. hangar
18. hanger
19. died
20. dyed

Name _____

Proofreading and Writing

Proofreading Circle the five misspelled Spelling Words in this e-mail message. Then write each word correctly.

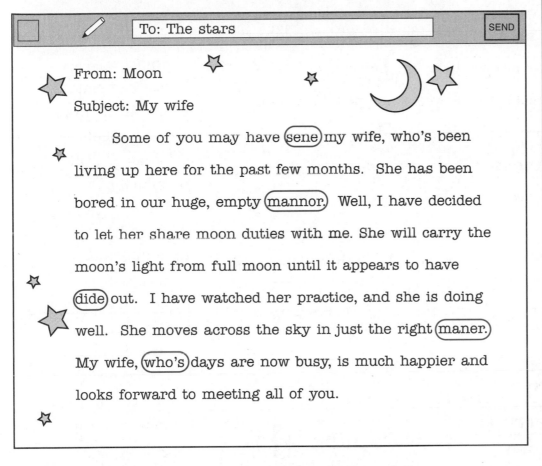

To: The stars   SEND

From: Moon

Subject: My wife

Some of you may have (sene) my wife, who's been living up here for the past few months. She has been bored in our huge, empty (mannor.) Well, I have decided to let her share moon duties with me. She will carry the moon's light from full moon until it appears to have (dide) out. I have watched her practice, and she is doing well. She moves across the sky in just the right (maner.) My wife, (who's) days are now busy, is much happier and looks forward to meeting all of you.

Spelling Words

1. fir
2. fur
3. scent
4. sent
5. scene
6. seen
7. vain
8. vein
9. principal
10. principle
11. manor
12. manner
13. who's
14. whose
15. tacks
16. tax
17. hangar
18. hanger
19. died
20. dyed

1. seen **(1 point)**

2. manor **(1)**

3. died **(1)**

4. manner **(1)**

5. whose **(1)**

Write a Job Description Moon decided to give his wife half of his work to do, but suppose he had wanted to hire someone he didn't know. How would he have described the job in a Help Wanted ad? **(5 points)**

On a separate sheet of paper, write a job description for Moon's work. Use Spelling Words from the list. Responses will vary. **(5)**

Copyright © Houghton Mifflin Company. All rights reserved.

Name _____

Match the Sounds

Match the correct definition to the boldface word. Then complete the homophone pairs below.

_h_ **(1)** 1. We can **see** the moon move through its phases.

_e_ **(1)** 2. The **hare** hopped in the moonlit snow.

_c_ **(1)** 3. In the **past** some people worshiped the moon.

_b_ **(1)** 4. The moon's light **shone** brightly.

_j_ **(1)** 5. They **heard** a wolf call in the distance.

_i_ **(1)** 6. Her **hair** was the color of night.

_f_ **(1)** 7. The raging wind **passed** through the trees.

_a_ **(1)** 8. The **herd** of deer bounded by in the woods.

_d_ **(1)** 9. The path went down to the **sea**.

_g_ **(1)** 10. Have you **shown** anyone that trail?

a. a group of wild animals

b. gave off light

c. the time before the present

d. ocean

e. animal like a rabbit

f. moved

g. pointed out or revealed

h. perceive through the eyes

i. strands that grow on the head

j. perceived by the ears

11. see   sea **(1)**

12. hare   hair **(1)**

13. past   passed **(1)**

14. shone   shown **(1)**

15. heard   herd **(1)**

Assessment Tip: Total 15 Points

Copyright © Houghton Mifflin Company. All rights reserved.

Name _____

We Collect Shells

Action Verbs and Direct Objects An **action verb** tells what the subject does. A **direct object** receives the action of the verb. To find the direct object in a sentence, first find the verb. Then ask who or what receives the action of the verb:

> **Jeff found a shell on the beach.** The action verb is *found*. Jeff found *what* on the beach? He found a shell. *Shell* is the direct object.

The following sentence has a **compound direct object**.

> **Karen wore her jacket and scarf to the beach**. The action verb is *wore*. Karen wore *what* to the beach? She wore her *jacket* and her *scarf*. The compound direct object is *jacket and scarf*.

Find the action verb and the direct object in each sentence below. Circle the verb and underline the direct object.

1. The older girls (collect) shells on the beach. **(2 points)**

2. Grandfather (builds) a blazing fire. **(2)**

3. Earlier, little Anna and Michael (chased) a flock of sandpipers. **(2)**

4. Grandmother (tells) stories in the moonlight. **(2)**

5. Father (wraps) Anna and Michael in a blanket. **(2)**

Assessment Tip: Total **10** Points

Copyright © Houghton Mifflin Company. All rights reserved.

Name _____

Auxiliary Verbs Will Help Us

Main Verbs and Auxiliaries A **verb phrase** is made up of a main verb and an auxiliary. The **main verb** usually shows action. The **auxiliary** works with the main verb.

Common Auxiliary Verbs					
am	were	do	has	must	might
is	be	does	had	will	would
are	being	did	can	shall	should
was	been	have	may	could	

What is the main verb in each sentence below? Is there an auxiliary verb? Fill in the chart below the sentences. If there is no auxiliary verb write *none*.

1. Peggy will tell us fascinating stories.
2. She has told two stories about her life.
3. Joan and Margaret have laughed harder than ever before.
4. Should Peggy repeat that story?
5. Peggy is a great storyteller!

Main Verb	**Auxiliary Verb**
1. tell **(1 point)**	will **(1)**
2. told **(1)**	has **(1)**
3. laughed **(1)**	have **(1)**
4. repeat **(1)**	Should **(1)**
5. is **(1)**	none **(1)**

Assessment Tip: Total **10** Points

Copyright © Houghton Mifflin Company. All rights reserved.

Name _____

Look at the Moon and Stars

Sentence Combining with Compound Direct Objects A good writer avoids writing too many short sentences, which can sound choppy. You can combine two sentences that have the same verb and different direct objects to make one sentence with a **compound direct object**.

> Nora has **binoculars**. She has a **telescope** too.
>
> Nora has **binoculars and a telescope.**

Here is the draft of an essay Nora is writing. Revise the draft by changing short, choppy sentences into sentences with compound direct objects. Write your version below. Answers may vary.

Ancient people told stories about the moon. They told stories about the stars too. Today we have seen people on the moon. We have seen robots on Mars. Giant telescopes in the sky take pictures of Saturn. The telescopes take pictures of other planets too. Every night, I look at the moon through a telescope. I look at stars and planets too. Someday, I'll study Mars at an observatory. I'll also study Venus. I'll be a scientist. I'll be an astronaut. I'm shooting for the stars!

Ancient people told stories about the moon and the stars.

(2 points) Today we have seen people on the moon

and robots on Mars. **(2)** Giant telescopes in the sky take pictures

of Saturn and other planets too. **(2)** Every night, I look at the

moon, the stars, and the planets through a telescope. **(2)**

Someday, I'll study Mars and Venus at an observatory. **(2)** I'll be

a scientist and an astronaut. **(2)** I'm shooting for the stars!

Copyright © Houghton Mifflin Company. All rights reserved.

Name _____

Writing a Journal Entry

A **journal** is a notebook, diary, folder, or file in which you can record and save notes, lists, questions, ideas, thoughts, and feelings. For example, imagine that one of the two cousins in *The Girl Who Married the Moon* keeps a journal. She might write an entry to express her feelings about the Moon, to describe what happened when she received her chin tattoo, or to tell about such activities as weaving a basket from spruce roots or taking a sweat bath.

On the lines below, write your own journal entry for one day's events. Follow these guidelines:

► Write the date at the beginning. You may also want to note the location.

► Write in the first person, using the pronouns *I*, *me*, *my*, *mine*, *we*, and *our*.

► Describe the day's events or experiences.

► Include personal thoughts, feelings, reactions, questions, and ideas.

► Use sequence words when you narrate events.

(5 points)

_____

_____

_____

_____

_____

_____

_____

_____

_____

When you finish your journal entry, you may want to share it with a friend or a classmate.

Assessment Tip: Total **5** Points

Copyright © Houghton Mifflin Company. All rights reserved.

Name _____

Using Exact Verbs

Good writers use exact verbs to bring their experiences to life. For example, exact verbs like *glow* or *sparkle* describe actions more precisely than does a common verb such as *shine*. When you write a journal entry, you can use exact verbs to create a more vivid picture of what happened.

Suppose this journal entry was written by the cousin who became the Moon's wife in *The Girl Who Married the Moon*. Read it and then rewrite it on the lines below, replacing the general verbs that have been underlined with more exact verbs from the list. (1 point each).

May 25, Moon's House

Today I felt incredibly bored, so I looked into Moon's storeroom and then went inside. What a surprise! Moon's storeroom is filled with sparkling pieces of light. I found all the moon phases except for the full moon. Now I know where my husband hides his phases.

The phases shined so temptingly! I took a piece of moon from a shelf and put it on my own face. Now the piece will not come off. What if Moon becomes angry?

May 25, Moon's House

Today I felt incredibly bored, so I peeked into Moon's storeroom and then sneaked inside. What a surprise! Moon's storeroom is crammed with sparkling pieces of light. I discovered all the moon phases except for the full moon. Now I know where my husband conceals his phases.

The phases glittered so temptingly! I plucked a piece of moon from a shelf and placed it on my own face. Now the piece will not come off. What if Moon becomes angry?

Exact Verbs	
conceals	peeked
placed	glittered
sneaked	discovered
plucked	crammed

Copyright © Houghton Mifflin Company. All rights reserved.

Assessment Tip: Total **8** Points

Name _____

Categorizing Vocabulary

Write each word from the box under the correct category.

two kinds of scientists

paleontologist **(1 point)**

geologists **(1)**

two kinds of artifacts

fossils **(1)**

specimens **(1)**

two names for beliefs based on facts and observations

hypotheses **(1)**

theory **(1)**

a word for proof or support

evidence **(1)**

two ways soil can be removed

excavation **(1)**

erosion **(1)**

a word for a vanished species of animals or plants

extinct **(1)**

Vocabulary

theory
erosion
paleontologist
extinct
specimens
geologists
fossils
hypotheses
evidence
excavation

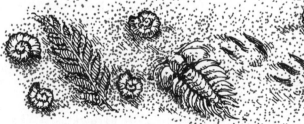

Now choose at least five words from the box. Use them to write a short paragraph about searching for the remains of ancient plants and animals.

one point for each word used correctly **(5 points)**

_____

_____

_____

_____

_____

_____

_____

Copyright © Houghton Mifflin Company. All rights reserved.

Assessment Tip: Total **15** Points

Name _____

Text Organization Chart

Organization: Main Ideas and Details

A Big Find of Small Dinosaurs

What did Dr. Ned Colbert find in 1947 at Ghost Ranch, New Mexico?

dozens of dinosaur skeleton fossils **(1 point)**

What question did Dr. Colbert's discovery make scientists ask themselves?

How and why did the dinosaurs die? **(1)**

What Happened Here?

List two details about the dinosaur bones scientists found.

Accept any of the following: some skeletons complete; some

separated with missing bones; no predator tooth marks; found

among other animal skeletons; in an area 30 feet long and wide;

surrounded by red rock; not cracked from drying in the sun. **(2)**

Organization: Hypothesis and Evidence

Stuck in the Mud? **Hypothesis 1:**

got stuck in the mud while feeding at river **(1)**

Support *For* **or** *Against*:

_____

_____

Volcanic Violence? **Hypothesis 2:**

volcanic eruption buries dinosaurs with ash and mud **(1)**

Support *For* **or** *Against*:

For: many animals killed by Mount St. Helens in 1980.

Against: geologists haven't found smashed silica bubbles,

usually found in volcanic rock. (1)

Copyright © Houghton Mifflin Company. All rights reserved.

Assessment Tip: Total **8 Points**

Name _____

What Happened to *Coelophysis*?

Scientists decided that the hypotheses below were *not* the best explanations for *Coelophysis*'s death. List the evidence *against* each one. Then answer the questions below.

Hypothesis Notes: *Why Coelophysis might have died*
Hypothesis 1: *Stuck in mud*

Evidence Against: Skeletons were found lying down. Animals who die in mud are usually found vertical. **(2 points)**

Hypothesis 2: *Volcanic eruption*

Evidence Against: The rock found around the dinosaurs does not contain the smashed silica bubbles usually found in volcanic rock. **(2)**

Hypothesis 3: *Asteroid fallout caused starvation*

Evidence Against: There is no evidence in the soil of asteroid fallout, plus the skeletons are too close together to have died of starvation. **(2)**

What two new hypotheses did scientists decide best explain

Coelophysis's death? __drought **(1)**__ and __flood **(1)**__

How might these two hypotheses have worked together? Give evidence to support your explanation.

First, a drought killed some dinosaurs, which explains the fish skeletons, mud cracks, and curved necks of some skeletons. Then a flood killed more dinosaurs, which explains the skeletons that were found tangled and in good condition. **(2)**

Assessment Tip: Total **10** Points

Copyright © Houghton Mifflin Company. All rights reserved.

Name _____

Taking Text Apart

Read the article. Then answer the questions on page 150.

Trapped in Amber

A clear golden lump sells for $27,000 at an auction. This lump of *amber*, as the material is called, started out as sap from a tree. What makes it so valuable now? Look closely — inside the amber is a small thirty-million-year-old lizard.

What Is Amber?

Amber is hardened sap from ancient trees. Over millions of years the sap has changed into a rock-hard material. Because it is beautiful and lasts many years, amber is often used in jewelry. Some amber pieces give scientists a rare opportunity to study prehistoric *inclusions* such as leaves, insects, and reptiles preserved in the once-sticky sap.

How Does Amber Form?

Picture this process. Long ago (perhaps as long ago as the age of dinosaurs), sap oozes from a tree. It hardens on the tree trunk and is covered by more sap. After many years, the tree dies and decays. It is swept into a stream and eventually ends up under the sea or beneath layers of rock. If the sap had been left out in the air, it would have rotted. Because the sap is not exposed to oxygen, however, its molecules change, forming stronger and stronger bonds. Eventually, all its oils evaporate, and it becomes hard and shiny, a beautiful golden brown. It becomes amber.

How Is Something Trapped in Amber?

It is possible today to see plants, insects, and even small reptiles from long ago preserved in amber. How did they get there? Here is one way this might have happened: an unlucky insect lands on a tree trunk that is sticky with sap. It gets stuck. More sap flows down the tree, entirely covering the bug. Over the centuries the sap slowly turns to amber. The insect dries out but otherwise stays perfectly preserved.

Copyright © Houghton Mifflin Company. All rights reserved.

Name _____

Taking Text Apart continued

Answer these questions about the passage on page 149.

1. How many sections does the article have? (Don't count the introductory paragraph.)

   three **(2 points)**

2. What feature of the text helps you identify the different sections?

   the headings **(2)**

3. Reread the section under the heading *What Is Amber?* Is it organized by main idea and details, or by sequence of events?

   by main idea and details **(2)**

4. Reread the section under the heading *How Does Amber Form?* Is this section organized by main idea and details, or by sequence?

   by sequence **(2)**

5. What sequence words or phrases can you find in the second section? Write them here.

   long ago, after many years, eventually **(2)**

Assessment Tip: Total **10** Points

Copyright © Houghton Mifflin Company. All rights reserved.

Name _____

Sorting Out Suffixes

Read this field diary page. Underline each word with the suffix *-al*, *-ive*, or *-ous*.

Beginning today, we will use our best <u>investigative</u> methods to figure out why so many dinosaurs died here. The area is one <u>massive</u> <u>burial</u> ground. There are so many skeletons, it looks almost <u>comical</u>, as though the dinosaurs were gathering to watch a <u>famous</u> celebrity when they died. We know that this animal was <u>carnivorous</u> because of the bones of other animals in the skeletons' bellies. Our theories may be <u>experimental</u>, but only if we are <u>creative</u> and <u>inventive</u> can we solve the mystery. Really, it is <u>marvelous</u> work.

Now write the words you underlined. Use the paragraph above to help you find the meaning of each word.

1. investigative: related to investigating **(2 points)**

2. massive: very large **(2)**

3. burial: having to do with burying **(2)**

4. comical: related to comedy; funny **(2)**

5. famous: having fame **(2)**

6. carnivorous: meat-eating **(2)**

7. experimental: related to an experiment **(2)**

8. creative: good at creating **(2)**

9. inventive: good at inventing **(2)**

10. marvelous: full of marvels; wonderful **(2)**

Copyright © Houghton Mifflin Company. All rights reserved.

Name _____

Final /ər/, /ən/, and /əl/

The **schwa sound,** shown as /ə/, is a weak vowel sound often found in an unstressed syllable. Remember the following spelling patterns for the /ə/ sound:

final /ər/	er, or, ar	messeng**er**, direct**or**, simil**ar**
final /n/ or /ən/	on, en	weap**on**, fright**en**
final /l/ or /əl/	le, el, al	strugg**le**, chann**el**, ment**al**

► The spelling of the final /ər/ sound in *acre* differs from the usual patterns. The final /ər/ sound in *acre* is spelled *re*.

Write each Spelling Word under its final sound.

Order of answers for each category may vary.

Spelling Words

1. struggle
2. director
3. weapon
4. similar
5. mental
6. frighten
7. channel
8. messenger
9. familiar
10. acre*
11. error
12. gallon
13. rural
14. calendar
15. elevator
16. stumble
17. youngster
18. kitchen
19. passenger
20. quarrel

Final /ər/ Sound

director **(1 point)**

similar **(1)**

messenger **(1)**

familiar **(1)**

acre **(1)**

error **(1)**

calendar **(1)**

elevator **(1)**

youngster **(1)**

passenger **(1)**

Final /n/ or /ən/ Sound

weapon **(1)**

frighten **(1)**

gallon **(1)**

kitchen **(1)**

Final /l/ or /əl/ Sound

struggle **(1)**

mental **(1)**

channel **(1)**

rural **(1)**

stumble **(1)**

quarrel **(1)**

Assessment Tip: Total 20 Points

Copyright © Houghton Mifflin Company. All rights reserved.

Name _____

Spelling Spree

Match Game Match each word beginning below to an ending to form a Spelling Word. Then write each word correctly.

Spelling Words

Word Beginnings

1. ac
2. quarr
3. weap
4. elevat
5. stumb
6. ment
7. messeng
8. kitch

Word Endings

on
er
le
en
al
re
or
el

1. acre **(1 point)**
2. quarrel **(1)**
3. weapon **(1)**
4. elevator **(1)**
5. stumble **(1)**
6. mental **(1)**
7. messenger **(1)**
8. kitchen **(1)**

Syllable Spot Write the Spelling Word that includes one of the syllables in each word below.

Example: format *matter*

9. frightfully — frighten **(1)**
10. gallery — gallon **(1)**
11. passage — passenger **(1)**
12. correction — director **(1)**
13. tunnel — channel **(1)**
14. calculate — calendar **(1)**
15. fanatic — familiar **(1)**

Spelling Words

1. struggle
2. director
3. weapon
4. similar
5. mental
6. frighten
7. channel
8. messenger
9. familiar
10. acre*
11. error
12. gallon
13. rural
14. calendar
15. elevator
16. stumble
17. youngster
18. kitchen
19. passenger
20. quarrel

Assessment Tip: Total **15** Points

Copyright © Houghton Mifflin Company. All rights reserved.

Name _____

Proofreading and Writing

Proofreading Circle the five misspelled Spelling Words in this journal entry. Then write each word correctly.

July 25

After weeks in this (rurel) area searching for dinosaur skeletons, I have finally had some success. Today, I found several skeletons (similiar) to *Coelophysis*. However, unless I made an (errer) in my measurements, these are larger and have a sturdier bone structure. The smallest, probably a (yongster,) is the most curious. It seems to have died in some sort of (strugle.) The rest of the skeletons are spread over an acre of land, and I have not had time to analyze them in detail. It looks like my work is cut out for me.

1. rural **(1 point)**	4. youngster **(1)**
2. similar **(1)**	5. struggle **(1)**
3. error **(1)**	

Spelling Words

1. struggle
2. director
3. weapon
4. similar
5. mental
6. frighten
7. channel
8. messenger
9. familiar
10. acre*
11. error
12. gallon
13. rural
14. calendar
15. elevator
16. stumble
17. youngster
18. kitchen
19. passenger
20. quarrel

✏️ **Write an Explanation** What do you think about the answer put forward in the selection for why so many dinosaur skeletons have been found at Ghost Ranch? Do you think the conclusions match the evidence? What about the possibility of new evidence suggesting another explanation?

On a separate piece of paper, write a short description of how you think the dinosaur skeletons wound up at Ghost Ranch. Use Spelling Words from the list. Responses will vary. **(5)**

Assessment Tip: Total **10** Points

Copyright © Houghton Mifflin Company. All rights reserved.

Name _____

Discovering the Key

Use the spelling table/pronunciation key below to figure out how to pronounce each underlined vowel sound. Find a word in the vocabulary box with a similar vowel sound, and write that word after the sentence.

Spellings	Sample Words
a, ai, ei, ey	made, plait, vein, they
e, ee, ie, y	these, fleet, chief, bumpy
o, oe, ou, ow	fold, toe, boulder, slow
o, u, ou, oo	stomach, cut, rough, flood

Vocabulary

blow
late
nut
reel
sail
ton

1. Shoulder bones were found among the fossils.

   blow **(2 points)** _____

2. The scientists found dozens of skeletons of the little dinosaur.

   nut or ton **(2)** _____

3. Each specimen was carefully weighed and recorded.

   late or sail **(2)** _____

4. The dinosaurs hunted for prey along rivers and lakes.

   late or sail **(2)** _____

5. Red blood cells were made in the marrow cavity.

   nut or ton **(2)** _____

6. These dinosaurs had no armor to shield themselves from predators.

   reel **(2)** _____

Copyright © Houghton Mifflin Company. All rights reserved.

Name _____

Dinosaurs Eat . . .

Transitive and Intransitive Verbs A **transitive verb** is an action verb with a **direct object**, which receives the action. An **intransitive verb** has no direct object. See the examples below.

Verb	Transitive	Intransitive
read	I **read** the book.	I **read** quickly.
sit	(none)	They **sit** on the bus.
visit	He **visits** the ranch.	He **visits** often.

Underline the verb or verb phrase in each sentence below. Then write *transitive* or *intransitive* after the sentence.

1. Maurice <u>saw</u> a movie about dinosaurs. <u>transitive **(2 points)**</u>

2. I <u>researched</u> prehistoric times. <u>transitive **(2)**</u>

3. My friend <u>went</u> to the La Brea Tar Pits. <u>intransitive **(2)**</u>

4. Some dinosaurs <u>ate</u> meat. <u>transitive **(2)**</u>

5. We <u>will see</u> dinosaur bones at the museum. <u>transitive **(2)**</u>

6. Dinosaurs <u>lived</u> during the Mesozoic era. <u>intransitive **(2)**</u>

7. Some dinosaurs <u>hunted</u> other animals. <u>transitive **(2)**</u>

8. Still other dinosaurs <u>munched</u> plants. <u>transitive **(2)**</u>

9. Birds <u>may have evolved</u> from dinosaurs. <u>intransitive **(2)**</u>

10. Not all dinosaurs <u>grew</u> to become giants. <u>intransitive **(2)**</u>

Assessment Tip: Total **20** Points

Copyright © Houghton Mifflin Company. All rights reserved.

Name _____

Dinosaurs Are Extinct

Being Verbs and Linking Verbs A **being verb** shows a state of being, not action. A **being verb** is called a **linking verb** when it links the subject to a predicate noun or a predicate adjective. A **predicate noun** identifies or renames the subject. A **predicate adjective** describes the subject.

Common Being and Linking Verbs				
am	was	be	become	feel
is	were	being	look	taste
are	seem	been	appear	smell

Underline the linking verb in each sentence below. After each sentence, write whether the verb links to a predicate noun or predicate adjective.

Example: Some dinosaurs <u>were</u> giants. _predicate noun_____

1. The paleontologist <u>seems</u> excited by that stone. _predicate adjective_ **(2)**_____

2. That stone <u>is</u> a fossil of a dinosaur. _predicate noun_ **(2)**_____

3. The work of a paleontologist <u>looks</u> interesting to me. _predicate adjective_ **(2)**_____

4. Fossils of ferns <u>are</u> common here. _predicate adjective_ **(2)**_____

5. A paleontologist <u>is</u> a scientist. _predicate noun_ **(2)**_____

Copyright © Houghton Mifflin Company. All rights reserved.

Name _____

Dinosaurs Was/Were . . .

Using Forms of the Verb *be* A good writer uses the correct form of the verb *be*, especially when writing sentences with linking verbs. Study the present and past tense forms of the verb *be* in the chart below.

	Present Tense	**Past Tense**
Singular	I am	I was
	You are	You were
	She/he/it is	She/he/it was
Plural	We are	We were
	You are	You were
	They are	They were

Below is the beginning of a report written by a student who found a fossil. Write the correct form of the verb *be* above any incorrect verbs. (2 points each)

            was
Example: I were tired.
           ^

                  are
My brother and I is interested in dinosaurs. Yesterday,

were
we was at the creek looking for fossils. My brother showed

                  was
me a good place to look. It were a place with a lot of slate.

                                        are
I didn't think we'd find anything because fossils is hard

am
to find. I are happy to tell you that I was wrong. I found

a fossil impression of a tiny snail in a piece of slate.

Copyright © Houghton Mifflin Company. All rights reserved.

Assessment Tip: Total **10** Points

Name _____

Writing a Business Letter

When Ned Colbert in *Dinosaur Ghosts* began to study *Coelophysis* skeletons in 1947, he probably wrote business letters to ask paleontologists at other museums and universities around the United States for help. You write a **business letter** to request or persuade someone to do something, to apply for a job, to order a product from ads or catalogs, to ask for information, to complain about a product or service, or to express an opinion to a newspaper, radio, or TV station.

Use this page to plan and organize a business letter in which you write to either a company or a government agency requesting information. Follow these steps: (2 points each)

1. Write a **heading** (your own address and the date) in the upper right corner.
2. Write the **inside address** (the address of the person or business you are writing to) at the left margin.
3. Write a **greeting** (*Dear Sir or Madam:* or *Dear [business name]:*) at the left margin below the inside address.
4. Write the **body** of your letter below the greeting. Be brief and direct, but present all of the necessary details. If you state an opinion, support it with details. Make sure to use a formal and polite tone.
5. Write a formal **closing** such as *Sincerely, Cordially,* or *Yours truly* in the lower right corner.
6. Sign your full name under the closing. Then print or type your name below your **signature**.

When you finish your business letter, copy it onto a clean sheet of paper. Then share it with a classmate.

Copyright © Houghton Mifflin Company. All rights reserved.

Assessment Tip: Total **12** Points

Name _____

Using the Right Tone

The attitude that a writer has toward a subject is called the **tone**. A writer's choice of words and details conveys his or her tone. When you write a business letter, you want to create a good impression by using the right tone. Here are some tips to follow: Use polite language. Use a more formal tone than you would use in a friendly letter. Use correct grammar, complete sentences, and well-formed paragraphs. Avoid the use of slang. Do not include personal information.

Read the following business letter from a college student to Ned Colbert. Fill in the chart below with examples of language and details that are *not* businesslike.

Dear Ned,

   Wow! I seen the cool photographs of your project in Life magazine. I do not have anything better to do, so I am interested in coming to New Mexico this summer to help with the Coelophysis excavation at Ghost Ranch. Would you tell me how to join your field crew?

   I am fascinated by the Ghost Ranch skeletons. Since I will be studying history and geology next semester, this job would give me some excellent firsthand knowledge. I am a hard worker. Ask anyone at the Ribs Palace on Route 120 where I used to work. Keep in touch.

   Sincerely,
   Dennis Sauer

Slang	Wow!, cool
Impolite Language	I do not have anything better to do
Informal Tone	Dear Ned, Keep in touch
Personal Information	Ask anyone at the Ribs Palace on Route 120 where I used to work.
Incorrect Grammar	I seen the cool photographs.

Assessment Tip: Total **8** Points

Copyright © Houghton Mifflin Company. All rights reserved.

Name _____

Key Vocabulary

Use the words in the box to complete the sentences below.

Vocabulary

steward
jostled
tremor
pumice
throng
rubble

1. A large group of people gathered together
   is a throng **(1 point)** _____.

2. One type of lightweight volcanic rock
   is called pumice **(1)** _____.

3. Someone who has been pushed or
   elbowed has been
   jostled **(1)** _____.

4. A shaking or vibrating motion is a
   tremor **(1)** _____.

5. Broken pieces of rock and stone are
   rubble **(1)** _____.

6. A servant in charge of a household is a
   steward **(1)** _____.

**Use four of the words from the sentences above
to write a short paragraph describing what it
might be like to experience a natural disaster.**

Answers will vary. **(4 points** total: **1 point** for each word)

_____

_____

_____

_____

Copyright © Houghton Mifflin Company. All rights reserved.

Infer and Compare

As you read each selection, use the chart below to write down details about Eros and Giuseppe Fiorelli. Then use your own experience to make an inference about each person. Answers will vary. Sample answers are given.

	Eros	Giuseppe Fiorelli
Details	While the volcano erupts, he worries about his master's house; he is concerned about the treasure in the cellar. **(2 points)**	He pays attention to all of Pompeii, not just valuable items; he takes time to record everything he finds. **(2)**
I know that	In an emergency, I focus on important things. **(2)**	It is hard to turn down a chance to make money; and that writing records takes time **(2)**
Inference	Eros's job is very important to him. **(2)**	Giuseppe Fiorelli cares a lot about excavating the city carefully. **(2)**

Assessment Tip: Total **12** Points

Copyright © Houghton Mifflin Company. All rights reserved.

Name _____

Connecting and Comparing

Think about the setting of *Pompeii.* **How has the author helped you put yourself in that time and place? Fill out the chart with information about the setting of** *Pompeii.* **Then choose another selection in this theme in which the setting is important, and complete the chart.** Answers will vary. Sample answers are shown.

	Selection Title: *Pompeii*	Selection Title: _____
The Setting	in the streets of Pompeii, the day Mt. Vesuvius erupts **(2 points)**	**(2)**
Descriptive Language About the Setting	"odd yellowish cast to the air"; "enormous black cloud billowed from the summit"; "Tiny white pellets of pumice began to fall like a soft hail storm." **(2)**	**(2)**
Why the Setting Is Important	The whole story is about a natural disaster that occurs in this setting. **(2)**	**(2)**

Copyright © Houghton Mifflin Company. All rights reserved.

Assessment Tip: Total **12** Points

Excavation Word Match-up

Match the words with their definitions.

1. spewed **(2 points)** ——————— a huge group of rocks moving down a hill

2. avalanche **(2)** ——————— to send out violently

3. glimpse **(2)** ——————————— a quick look at something

Use each of the words below in a sentence. Answers will vary. (2 points each)

4. spewed:

_____

5. avalanche:

_____

6. glimpse:

_____

164   Theme 2: **What Really Happened?**

Assessment Tip: Total **12** Points

Copyright © Houghton Mifflin Company. All rights reserved.

Test Practice

Use the three steps you've learned to choose the best answer to complete these sentences about *Epilogue.* Fill in the circle for the best answer in the answer row at the bottom of the page.

1. The author's main purpose for writing *Epilogue* was to _____.

   A provide more information about Eros

   B tell what scientists learned about the eruption

   C explain the warning signs of a volcano eruption

   D compare two ways of excavating ancient cities

2. Giuseppe Fiorelli improved the way Pompeii was being excavated by _____.

   F looking for valuable artifacts

   G punishing sloppy archeologists

   H using an organized system for the excavation

   J destroying artifacts that were not important

3. One reason that people returned to Pompeii just after the eruption was to _____.

   A begin construction of new buildings

   B seek shelter from the extreme heat

   C find food to eat

   D search for valuables

4. **Connecting/Comparing** The descriptions of the eruption in *Pompeii* and *Epilogue* are based partly on _____.

   F information from Pliny's uncle   H a written account by Eros

   G the letters of Pliny   J writings found in Pompeii

ANSWER ROWS   1 Ⓐ ● Ⓒ Ⓓ (5 points)   3 Ⓐ Ⓑ Ⓒ ● (5)
              2 Ⓕ Ⓖ ● Ⓙ (5)   4 Ⓕ ● Ⓗ Ⓙ (5)

Continue on page 166.

Theme 2: **What Really Happened?**   165

Copyright © Houghton Mifflin Company. All rights reserved.

Test Practice continued

5. Objects that have been buried for centuries in volcanic pumice and ash are most likely _____

   A well preserved

   B highly valuable

   C completely crushed

   D extremely hot

6. In the late 1700s, statues, coins, and other valuable items were uncovered by _____.

   F Giuseppe Fiorelli

   G Amedeo Maiuri

   H treasure hunters

   J survivors of the eruption

7. Some of the objects found in the House of the Menander show that _____.

   A the house was owned by Eros

   B some people of Pompeii farmed

   C the house had just been built

   D houses in Pompeii were small

8. **Connecting/Comparing** The scientists in both *Epilogue* and *Dinosaur Ghosts* are working to _____.

   F understand events that occurred long ago

   G prove that life is less dangerous today than long ago

   H gain wealth and fame

   J prevent a new disaster

ANSWER ROWS 5 Ⓐ Ⓑ Ⓒ Ⓓ **(5 points)** 7 Ⓐ Ⓑ Ⓒ Ⓓ **(5)**
               6 Ⓕ Ⓖ Ⓗ Ⓙ **(5)**   8 Ⓕ Ⓖ Ⓗ Ⓙ **(5)**

Copyright © Houghton Mifflin Company. All rights reserved.

Assessment Tip: Total **40** Points

Name _____

Facts or Opinions?

**Read each sentence. Label each Fact or Opinion. If an opinion
is supported by a fact, write the fact on the line below it.**

1. Perhaps most of the people in Pompeii first thought that the
   eruption of Vesuvius was another earthquake.

   Opinion **(1 point)** Sample answer: City had an earthquake seventeen years before. **(1)**
   _____

2. The people who remained in Pompeii died from the extreme heat or
   were suffocated by hot ash.

   Fact **(1)**
   _____

3. Pompeii was buried under a thick blanket of pumice and ash.

   Fact **(1)**
   _____

4. Heat from the eruption of Vesuvius probably caused Pliny's uncle to die.

   Opinion **(1)** Sample answer: The eruption of Vesuvius produced a lot of heat. **(1)**
   _____

5. Amedeo Maiuri discovered the house of Menander between 1927
   and 1932.

   Fact **(1)**
   _____

6. We believe that the house of Menander was one of the finest
   in Pompeii.

   Opinion **(1)** Sample answer: found chests full of gold and silver, jewelry, silver dishes **(1)**
   _____

7. I think that putting Giuseppe Fiorelli in charge of the excavation of Pompeii was a
   good decision.

   Opinion **(1)** Sample answer: He made detailed maps, recorded new finds, restored

   art and buildings. **(1)**
   _____

8. The buildings and objects uncovered in Pompeii allow us to see what life was like
   long ago.

   Fact **(1)**
   _____

Copyright © Houghton Mifflin Company. All rights reserved.

Assessment Tip: Total **12** Points

Looking Closely at Text

Read the article. Then answer the questions.

Volcanoes, Volcanoes, Volcanoes

Volcanoes have formed in various places, but most are found along the edges of the Earth's plates. Volcanoes have many different shapes and sizes. One classification system separates them into three main types, based on their shape and the materials from which they are formed: cinder cones, shield volcanoes, and composite volcanoes.

Cinder Cone Volcanoes

These volcanoes are formed when rock fragments, made of sticky magma, erupt through an opening or vent. When the fragments or cinders fall back to the ground around the vent, they form a mountain shaped like a cone.

Shield Volcanoes

These volcanoes are formed when lava flows from a vent. The lava spreads out and slowly builds up to form a low, dome-shaped mountain.

Composite Volcanoes

These volcanoes are formed when both rock fragments and lava flow from a vent. The materials pile up to form a tall mountain in the shape of a cone. Mount Vesuvius is one example of this type of volcano.

1. What are the different sections of this article about? kinds of volcanoes,
cinder cones, shield volcanoes, and composite volcanoes **(4 points)**

2. What text feature helped you answer the first question? the headings **(1)**

3. What text feature helps you know what the different types of volcanoes look like? the illustrations **(1)**

4. How do you know which type of volcano is represented by each illustration? the captions **(1)**

5. How are the sections of this article organized—by main ideas and details, by sequence of events, or by cause and effect? main ideas and details **(3)**

Assessment Tip: Total 10 Points

Copyright © Houghton Mifflin Company. All rights reserved.

Name _____

Sentences with Suffixes

**Read the sentences. Underline each word with the
suffix *-ous*, *-ive*, or *-al*.**

1. The eruption of Mount Vesuvius is a <u>famous</u> event. **(1 point)**

2. The force of the eruption was so <u>explosive</u> that it destroyed
   many buildings. **(1)**

3. The ash cloud was <u>disruptive</u> to life even many miles away from
   the volcano. **(1)**

4. Gases from the volcano were <u>hazardous</u> to all people and animals. **(1)**

5. Despite the destruction, the eruption was a <u>natural</u> event. **(1)**

6. Archaeologists found many <u>cultural</u> artifacts buried in the rubble. **(1)**

**Now write the words you underlined along with their meanings.
Use the meanings of the base word and suffix along with sentence
context to help you.**

1. famous **(2 points)** _____

2. explosive **(2)** _____

3. disruptive **(2)** _____

4. hazardous **(2)** _____

5. natural **(2)** _____

6. cultural **(2)** _____

Copyright © Houghton Mifflin Company. All rights reserved.

Name _____

Pronunciation Practice

**Read each sentence below. Use the pronunciation key to figure out
how to pronounce each underlined vowel sound. Then list a sample
word that uses the same spelling for that vowel sound.**

ŭ	pat, laugh	ŏ	horrible, pot
ā	ape, aid, pay	ō	go, row, toe, though
ĕ	pet, pleasure, wear	ô	all, caught, paw
ē	be, bee, easy, piano		

Sample answers are shown.

1. The light str<u>ea</u>med through the wind<u>ow</u>.

2. The man s<u>aw</u> the l<u>ea</u>ther purse.

3. He l<u>ay</u> on a narr<u>ow</u> bed.

4. The m<u>a</u>n's d<u>augh</u>ter was found nearby.

5. A bl<u>a</u>nket of ash covered the w<u>a</u>lls.

6. Esc<u>a</u>pe was n<u>o</u>t possible.

7. She could not s<u>ee</u> the dog b<u>e</u>l<u>ow</u> her feet.

8. <u>We</u> took shelter from the r<u>ai</u>n of ash.

easy; row **(2 points)**

paw; pleasure **(2)**

pay; row **(2)**

pat; caught **(2)**

pat; all **(2)**

ape; pot **(2)**

bee; row **(2)**

be; aid **(2)**

Assessment Tip: Total **16** Points

Copyright © Houghton Mifflin Company. All rights reserved.

Name _____

Spelling Review

Write Spelling Words from the list to answer the questions.
Order of answers in each category may vary.

1–24. Which twenty-four words contain the /ûr/, /ôr/, /är/, or
/îr/ sounds, or have the final /ər/, /ən/, or /əl/ sounds?

1. channel **(1 point)**
2. familiar **(1)**
3. hanger **(1)**
4. chart **(1)**
5. calendar **(1)**
6. rehearse **(1)**
7. starch **(1)**
8. purse **(1)**
9. hangar **(1)**
10. curb **(1)**
11. mourn **(1)**
12. director **(1)**
13. frighten **(1)**
14. manor **(1)**
15. thorn **(1)**
16. messenger **(1)**
17. pierce **(1)**
18. struggle **(1)**
19. manner **(1)**
20. sword **(1)**
21. similar **(1)**
22. whirl **(1)**
23. gallon **(1)**
24. rural **(1)**

25–30. Which six one-syllable words are homophones?

25. who's **(1)**
26. whose **(1)**
27. vain **(1)**
28. vein **(1)**
29. sent **(1)**
30. scent **(1)**

Copyright © Houghton Mifflin Company. All rights reserved.

Spelling Words

1. channel
2. familiar
3. hanger
4. who's
5. chart
6. calendar
7. rehearse
8. starch
9. purse
10. whose
11. hangar
12. curb
13. mourn
14. director
15. frighten
16. manor
17. thorn
18. vain
19. messenger
20. pierce
21. struggle
22. sent
23. vein
24. manner
25. sword
26. similar
27. scent
28. whirl
29. gallon
30. rural

Nikumaroro

Assessment Tip: Total **30** Points

Name _____

Spelling Spree

Syllable Scramble Rearrange the syllables in each item to write a Spelling Word. There is one extra syllable in each item.

Example: er for sid con   *consider*

1. sen ger mes ize   messenger **(1 point)**

2. en cal men dar   calendar **(1)**

3. ger iar mil fa   familiar **(1)**

4. hearse in re   rehearse **(1)**

5. rec na tor di   director **(1)**

Spelling Words

1. familiar
2. calendar
3. mourn
4. frighten
5. gallon
6. rehearse
7. starch
8. purse
9. director
10. vain
11. messenger
12. scent
13. curb
14. vein
15. manner

Word Maze Begin at the arrow and follow the Word Maze to find ten Spelling Words. Write the words in the order you find them.

Start ⟶ r o s s t a r c h q p u r s e y u v a i n i t
q u p o m o u r n w a t
p y p o m a n n e r
e f r i g h t e n o p e c u r b i f g a l l o n
y t d s c e n t l a v e i n g o v

6. starch **(1)**

7. purse **(1)**

8. vain **(1)**

9. scent **(1)**

10. vein **(1)**

11. frighten **(1)**

12. curb **(1)**

13. gallon **(1)**

14. manner **(1)**

15. mourn **(1)**

Assessment Tip: Total **15** Points

Copyright © Houghton Mifflin Company. All rights reserved.

Name _____

Proofreading and Writing

Proofreading Circle the six misspelled Spelling Words in this detective's journal. Then write each word correctly.

Spelling Words

The case of Mrs. VanCash's jewels has put me into a (whurl.) At first I didn't know how to (chaurt) a course. It's been a real (struggel) for me, Sherlock McGillicuddy, to find the truth. The mystery was truly a (thorne) in my side! When the maid swore the jewels were hers, I wondered (whos) they really were. Then I solved the mystery! The maid was telling the truth. Her jewels were (simalar) to the stolen ones, but hers were fakes.

Spelling Words

1. channel
2. hanger
3. who's
4. chart
5. whose
6. hangar
7. thorn
8. pierce
9. struggle
10. sword
11. similar
12. sent
13. whirl
14. manor
15. rural

1. whirl **(1 point)**

2. chart **(1)**

3. struggle **(1)**

4. thorn **(1)**

5. whose **(1)**

6. similar **(1)**

Reporting the Facts Write the Spelling Words that best complete this television news report.

An ancient, long-bladed 7. sword **(1)** has been found in a 8. rural **(1)** area outside town. The weapon was found in an old airplane 9. hangar **(1)**. A worker picked it up, thinking it was a coat 10. hanger **(1)**. Experts believe this may be the blade used centuries ago to 11. pierce **(1)** a stone near the 12. manor **(1)** house of Sir Percy. The blade will be 13. sent **(1)** to a lab for testing. Now the question is, 14. who's **(1)** going to claim this treasure? Stay tuned to this 15. channel **(1)**!

✏ **Write a Plot Outline** On a separate sheet of paper, write a plot outline for a story about an unsolved mystery. Responses will vary. **(5)**

Copyright © Houghton Mifflin Company. All rights reserved.

Working with Possessive Nouns

Draw a line under each possessive noun. Write whether it is a singular possessive noun or a plural possessive noun.

1. An <u>earthquake's</u> rumble is terrifying.

   singular possessive noun **(2 points)**

2. The tremors can frazzle <u>residents'</u> nerves.

   plural possessive noun **(2)**

3. A <u>volcano's</u> eruption is an awesome event.

   singular possessive noun **(2)**

4. <u>Children's</u> parents rush them to safe places.

   plural possessive noun **(2)**

5. Even a minor <u>eruption's</u> effects can cause devastation.

   singular possessive noun **(2)**

Write the possessive form of each noun in parentheses.

6. the (tree) tree's **(1)** _____ branches

7. the (lava) lava's **(1)** _____ heat

8. the (rescuers) rescuers' **(1)** _____ equipment

9. the (geese) geese's **(1)** _____ cries

10. the (reporters) reporters' **(1)** _____ descriptions

Copyright © Houghton Mifflin Company. All rights reserved.

Name _____

Finding Action Verbs and Direct Objects

Find the action verb and the direct object in each sentence below. Circle the verb and underline the direct object or direct objects. Not every sentence has a direct object.

1. Guiseppe Fiorelli (led) the first organized <u>excavation</u> of Pompeii. **(1 point)**

2. This archaeologist (developed) a sensible <u>plan</u>. **(1)**

3. He (made) accurate <u>maps</u> and detailed <u>lists</u>. **(1)**

4. Workers (restored) <u>buildings</u> under his guidance. **(1)**

5. Looting of art treasures (diminished) significantly. **(1)**

6. Another archaeologist (made) a wonderful <u>discovery</u> in

   Pompeii in the late 1920s. **(1)**

7. He (uncovered) an ancient <u>mansion</u>. **(1)**

8. Diggers (found) two <u>chests</u> with gold and silver treasures. **(1)**

9. The workers (discovered) several <u>bodies</u> among the ruins there. **(1)**

10. Many unfortunate people (perished) in the terrible eruption. **(1)**

Copyright © Houghton Mifflin Company. All rights reserved.

Name _____

Playing It Up

Use the words in the box to complete the description of a play below.

Vocabulary

actors
audience
cast
character
comedy
dialogue
drama
perform
stage directions
tragedy

    I saw a wonderful play last night. It was a very funny <u>comedy</u> **(2 points)** about two twin brothers on a Kansas farm who always get mistaken for each other. My favorite <u>character</u> **(2)** in the play was their mother, who like everyone else in the story couldn't tell her sons apart!

    All the <u>actors</u> **(2)** in the <u>cast</u> **(2)** did a good job making their words and actions believable. I'll bet they were happy to <u>perform</u> **(2)** in such an amusing play. I think the playwright did an excellent job with the <u>dialogue</u> **(2)** because everyone in the <u>audience</u> **(2)** laughed at all the jokes. From the way the actors moved and spoke, the <u>stage directions</u> **(2)** seemed pretty funny also.

    There was a lot of <u>drama</u> **(2)** and emotion in the play as well as laughs, although no one would ever mistake it for a <u>tragedy</u> **(2)**. The show is still playing for one more week, so I suggest you and your family go see it. To miss such a fun night at the theater would be a disaster!

Copyright © Houghton Mifflin Company. All rights reserved.

Name _____

Understanding a Play: "The Diary of Anne Frank"

Character	Personality Traits	Examples in Dialogue and Action
Anne	outgoing, direct, curious **(2 points)**	starts conversation with Peter; picks up cat without asking; asks lots of questions; was always in the middle of the action at schoolyard **(2)**
Peter	a loner, observant, independent **(2)**	tells how he "watched from the sidelines" at school and observed Anne; takes back his cat, hinting that Anne is still a stranger; had no plans to see anyone that day; dares to cut off star **(2)**
Mr. Frank	kind, responsible, strict **(2)**	sets up a bed for Peter's cat; brings some of Anne's favorite belongings to the hiding place; sternly reminds Anne and Peter of the limits of activity while in hiding **(2)**

Relationship	Description	Examples in Dialogue and Action
Anne and Mr. Frank	respectful, positive, affectionate, shared love of learning **(2)**	Mr. Frank encourages Anne to enjoy the things that are possible in hiding: learning, writing, avoiding things she didn't like; she heeds his warning about going downstairs; they communicate clearly and kindly. **(2)**

Copyright © Houghton Mifflin Company. All rights reserved.

Assessment Tip: Total **16** Points

Name _____

Compare and Contrast

Two of the characters in these plays learn more about themselves.
Complete the chart to compare and contrast their searches and what
they find out.

	The Diary of Anne Frank	*A Better Mousetrap*
What challenges do Anne Frank and the Woman face?	Anne must adjust to being in hiding, never going outdoors. **(4 points)**	The Woman is frightened by the Mouse and asks for her husband's help in getting rid of it. **(4)**
How do Anne and the Woman change?	When Anne writes in her new diary, she starts to feel things are going better. **(4)**	The Woman discovers that her husband is useless, and she independently leaves for her sister's house. **(4)**

Copyright © Houghton Mifflin Company. All rights reserved.

Assessment Tip: Total **16** Points

Name _____

Critic's Corner

Think about one of the plays you have read in the *Focus on Plays* section. Think about the characters, the setting, the plot, and other details. Write a critical review of the play, telling what you liked and didn't like about it. Be specific. Use examples from the play to support your points. **(10 points)**

Copyright © Houghton Mifflin Company. All rights reserved.

Assessment Tip: Total **10** Points

Name _____

Understanding a Play: "A Better Mousetrap"

Sample answers are shown.

Character	Personality Traits	Examples in Dialogue and Action
Man	classic conflict avoider; wants to please woman yet not hurt mouse; creative in finding ways to appear determined to kill mouse while saving it **(2 points)**	calls woman silly pet names; talks in friendly way to mouse, which he is supposedly about to kill; builds crazy, ineffective mousetrap **(2)**
Woman	silly, helpless, and demanding; unable to solve problem or put it in perspective **(2)**	overreacts to mouse ("Eek!"); complains but never takes action; actually thinks the silly mousetrap might work **(2)**
Mouse	smart enough not to go after the cheese; has enough sense of humor to enjoy the prank **(2)**	jokes with man, showing that mouse has the trap figured out; talks in witty way to man at the end, showing they understand each other **(2)**

What is funny about this play?

Sample answers: Many characters are silly inventions—not people at all but pieces

of a trap. The various versions of the mousetrap and the noises it makes are funny.

The woman is ridiculously helpless. When the mouse asks the man for a cracker

with his cheese, it's funny. **(3 points)**

Copyright © Houghton Mifflin Company. All rights reserved.

Confounding Compounds

Circle the ten words that are compound words in the dialogue below. Write each word in the first column. Then write the two smaller words that make up the compound words in the second and third columns. After you have written each compound word and its parts, use three of these compound words in a sentence of your own.

Solomon: You've left another mess in the (hallway) (upstairs.) We were

supposed to split the chores (fifty-fifty,) but I'm doing all of

the work by myself. I refuse to clean up after you.

John: Don't get so (upset.) I'll fix (everything) right after I finish

eating my (hot dog) and reading the (newspaper.) I promise,

by the end of the (weekend,) this house will look (brand-new.)

Compound Word	First Word Part	Second Word Part
hallway **(1 point)**	hall **(1)**	way **(1 point)**
upstairs **(1)**	up **(1)**	stairs **(1)**
fifty-fifty **(1)**	fifty **(1)**	fifty **(1)**
upset **(1)**	up **(1)**	set **(1)**
everything **(1)**	every **(1)**	thing **(1)**
hot dog **(1)**	hot **(1)**	dog **(1)**
newspaper **(1)**	news **(1)**	paper **(1)**
weekend **(1)**	week **(1)**	end **(1)**
brand-new **(1)**	brand **(1)**	new **(1)**

(2 points for each compound word used.)

_____

Assessment Tip: Total **33** Points

Copyright © Houghton Mifflin Company. All rights reserved.

Compound Words

A **compound word** is made up of two or more smaller words.

    ship + yard = shipyard

To spell a compound word correctly, you must remember whether it is written as one word, as a hyphenated word, or as separate words.

Write each Spelling Word under the heading that tells how the compound word should be written.

Order of words in each category may vary.

Copyright © Houghton Mifflin Company. All rights reserved.

Spelling Words

1. headache
2. warehouse
3. cupboard
4. old-fashioned
5. teammate
6. rattlesnake
7. blueberry
8. headquarters
9. space shuttle
10. baby-sit
11. handwriting
12. nighttime
13. self-respect
14. shipwreck
15. penknife
16. mother-in-law
17. wristwatch
18. handkerchief
19. bulletin board
20. software

One Word

headache (**1 point**)

warehouse (**1**)

cupboard (**1**)

teammate (**1**)

rattlesnake (**1**)

blueberry (**1**)

headquarters (**1**)

handwriting (**1**)

nighttime (**1**)

shipwreck (**1**)

penknife (**1**)

wristwatch (**1**)

handkerchief (**1**)

software (**1**)

With a Hyphen

old-fashioned (**1**)

baby-sit (**1**)

self-respect (**1**)

mother-in-law (**1**)

Separate Words

space shuttle (**1**)

bulletin board (**1**)

Theme 2: **Focus on Plays**   183
Assessment Tip: Total **20** Points

Name _____

Spelling Spree

Clue Addition Add the clues to create a Spelling Word.

Example: group of workers + friend = teammate

Spelling Words

1. headache
2. warehouse
3. cupboard
4. old-fashioned
5. teammate
6. rattlesnake
7. blueberry
8. headquarters
9. space shuttle
10. baby-sit
11. handwriting
12. nighttime
13. self-respect
14. shipwreck
15. penknife
16. mother-in-law
17. wristwatch
18. handkerchief
19. bulletin board
20. software

1. not day + 3:00 p.m. =   nighttime **(1 point)**

2. a color + a small fruit =   blueberry **(1)**

3. where the hand meets the arm + small clock =   wristwatch **(1)**

4. large boat + terrible accident =   shipwreck **(1)**

5. infant + to rest in a chair =   baby-sit **(1)**

6. container for liquid + flat wooden plank =   cupboard **(1)**

7. sits on top of your neck + pain =   headache **(1)**

8. something to write with + something that cuts =   penknife **(1)**

9. can be a fist + printed or cursive =   handwriting **(1)**

10. female parent + not out + a formal rule =   mother-in-law **(1)**

11. not young + made or formed =   old-fashioned **(1)**

12. houses your mind + place to live =   headquarters **(1)**

13. announcement + plank =   bulletin board **(1)**

14. baby's toy + kind of reptile =   rattlesnake **(1)**

Assessment Tip: Total **14** Points

Copyright © Houghton Mifflin Company. All rights reserved.

Name _____

Proofreading and Writing

Proofreading **Circle the six misspelled Spelling Words in this critic's review of a play. Then write each word correctly.**
Order of answers may vary.

Spelling Words

1. headache
2. warehouse
3. cupboard
4. old-fashioned
5. teammate
6. rattlesnake
7. blueberry
8. headquarters
9. space shuttle
10. baby-sit
11. handwriting
12. nighttime
13. self-respect
14. shipwreck
15. penknife
16. mother-in-law
17. wristwatch
18. handkerchief
19. bulletin board
20. software

Space Hackers a Bust

I am sorry to report that attending the play *Space Hackers* will be a waste of your time. The plot is so bizarre that I am still recovering from the headache of trying to sort it all out.

The story takes place in an abandoned whearhouse in Silicon Valley. Cornelius Dingleberry, who plays the part of a brilliant soft ware developer, must work with his teamate to save a runaway space-shuttle. The dialogue is so poorly written that it would have been better for the actors to improvise their lines rather than to follow the script.

The only time that you will need a hankerchief at this flick is when you cry over the money you spent for the ticket. I hope veteran director Paul Blackadder directs another play soon to restore his self respect.

1. warehouse **(1 point)**
2. software **(1)**
3. teammate **(1)**
4. space shuttle **(1)**
5. handkerchief **(1)**
6. self-respect **(1)**

Write a Review Suppose that you are another newspaper critic who liked the play *Space Hackers*.

On a separate sheet of paper, write a few paragraphs that give a positive review of *Space Hackers*. Use Spelling Words from the list. (4)

Copyright © Houghton Mifflin Company. All rights reserved.

Assessment Tip: Total **10** Points

Name _____

Brand-Name Words

The diary entry below contains ten words that started out as trademarked brand names. As you read, circle each one you find. (1 point each)

Dear Diary,

I had a really great day today! I think it was all thanks to my new breakfast routine, which involves eating a big bowl of shredded wheat with hot sauce. That's right, hot sauce. It's my secret to waking up in the morning. Some people prefer coffee and cornflakes, but to each his own! After breakfast, I put on my Walkman, swept the linoleum, and rollerbladed off down the street to Teddy's house. When I got there, Teddy was taking aspirin and rubbing ice on his knee. He had a big rip in his Levi's and a bruise on his head. Teddy explained that he'd fallen while trying to skate backward down some stairs. His kneepads and helmet had fallen off because their velcro straps didn't stick. We rested for a minute and had a glass of Kool-Aid. Then I asked him if he felt well enough to go skating again, and he said yes. But when he suggested skating down an escalator, I gently talked him out of it.

Think of three other brand name words. Write a sentence for each new word.

(2 points for each sentence)

_____

_____

_____

_____

_____

_____

Assessment Tip: Total **16** Points

Copyright © Houghton Mifflin Company. All rights reserved.

Name _____

Lion's Tale

Using Introductory Words Interjections, introductory words, and nouns in direct address can make dialogue in a play more realistic.

Write a word or a phrase from the box to begin each sentence, and follow it with the correct punctuation mark. (2 points each)

Lion	Oh no	Hurrah	Rabbit
Well	Hey	Grrr	Absolutely not

Answers may vary. Sample answers are shown.

Rabbit is hopping through the forest. Suddenly a lion appears.

Lion: Rabbit, _____ I'm going to eat you.

Rabbit: Hurrah! _____ I'm glad I'll be eaten by a small, quiet beast instead of a big, loud one.

Lion: Grrr! _____ What are you talking about?

Rabbit leads Lion to a well, leaps onto the edge, and points down into it.

Rabbit: There's someone bigger and louder than you. Look!

Lion (*seeing his reflection*): Hey! _____ Who do you think you are?

The lion's words echo from the well.

Lion: Well, _____ I'm the biggest, loudest beast in the forest!

The lion again hears his words echoed from the well.

Lion: Absolutely not! _____ I'll show you!

The furious lion bares his teeth and leaps into the well to attack his reflection. A splash is heard.

Lion: Oh no! _____

Rabbit: Lion, _____ you may be the biggest, loudest beast in the forest, but I don't think you are the smartest one.

Copyright © Houghton Mifflin Company. All rights reserved.

Theme 2: **Focus on Plays**   187
Assessment Tip: Total **16** Points

Of Mice and Cats

Points of Ellipsis Unfinished thoughts or pauses can help make play dialogue more realistic and lively. Use points of ellipsis, or three spaced dots, to show a pause or an unfinished thought.

Rewrite this dialogue. Make it more realistic and lively by adding five pauses or unfinished thoughts. Use points of ellipsis. (2 points each)

The mice are talking inside a mouse hole. Just outside, a cat is sleeping.

Mousely: That cat is giving me a headache!

Cheeser: Me, too. Every time I go out he sneaks up and tries to catch me. I can't go on this way!

Nibbles: You're right. We must do something.

Mousely: I have an idea. Let's put a bell on the cat so he can't sneak up on us.

Cheeser: That's a great plan. Do it now!

Mousely: Wait a minute! I'm a slow runner.

Nibbles: This was *your* idea.

Answers will vary. Sample sentences:

Mousely: That cat is giving me a headache!
Cheeser: Me, too. Every time I go out he sneaks up and tries to catch me. I can't . . . I won't go on this way!

Nibbles: You're right. We must do something. . . but what?
Mousely: Hmmm . . . I have an idea. Let's put a bell on the cat so he can't sneak up on us.

Cheeser: That's a great plan. You can do . . .

Mousely: Wait a minute! I'm a slow runner. Nibbles, you could . . .

Nibbles: No way! This was your idea.

Assessment Tip: Total 10 Points

Copyright © Houghton Mifflin Company. All rights reserved.

Name _____

The Water Hole

Punctuating Play Dialogue Use an exclamation point with strong interjections. Use commas with introductory words, mild interjections, and nouns in direct address. Use points of ellipsis to show a pause or an incomplete thought.

Use proofreading marks to correct the twelve errors in punctuation in this play dialogue.
(**1 point** for each correction)
Example: Wart Hog: Well, This looks like a nice water hole.

Proofreading Marks

⊢ Indent
∧ Add
y Delete
= Capital letter
/ Small letter
⊙ Add Period
∧ Add Comma
ꞌꞌ ꞌꞌ Add Quotes
∿ Transpose

Wart Hog: Hey, you! This is my water hole.

Lion: Grrr! I am the king, everyone makes way for me.

Wart Hog: No, stay away! My tusks are the sharpest in the land.

Lion: Wart Hog, I am going to chew you up, and then I'll . . .

Wart Hog: Lion, I am going to stomp you down, and then I'll . . .

Lion: Wait! Do you see those vultures?

Wart Hog: Yes, I see them.

Lion: They're waiting for one of us to die . . . and one of us will, if we fight.

Wart Hog: Hmm . . . maybe we should share this water hole.

Lion: Good idea!

Copyright © Houghton Mifflin Company. All rights reserved

Name _____

Writing a Funny Play

Silly Character		
Appearance	**Habits, Gestures**	**Style of Speaking**

Other Characters	
Setting	

Plot	
Problem	**Solution**

Copyright © Houghton Mifflin Company. All rights reserved.

Name _____

Writing Stage Directions

This passage from a play has vague stage directions. Revise each numbered item so that an actor would clearly understand what to do.

Characters: Mom, Dad, Ed, Liz, Furhead the dog
Setting: the family car, on a long drive to Grandma's house

Ed: (1. *Looking somewhere*): I'm so bored, I can hardly breathe.

Mom: (2. *Seeing someone*): Why don't we all play a game? That will help pass the time! I love games! Guess which one is my favorite.

Liz: Please, Mom, not the license plate game. (3. *Liz makes an expression.*)

Dad: We used to play the license plate game when I traveled to visit my grandmother, with my parents. It must be a great family tradition! That will help us pass the next four hours, all right. (4. *Liz and Ed look at each other.*)

Furhead: Arf, arf! (5. *The dog moves.*)

Liz: Furhead! What are you doing? (6. *Liz does something to the dog.*)

Ed: See, Mom and Dad, even Furhead can't bear the license plate game. (7. *Ed speaks quietly to Furhead.*) Furhead, good dog, good dog.

Mom: Never mind about the game. I'll sing all my favorite Broadway show tunes to keep everyone from being bored! Which shall I sing first?

Dad: (8. *His voice changes.*): All of them, dear? Um, how about just one or two?

Sample answers

1. Staring out the window **(2 points)**

2. Smiling at her family **(2)**

3. Liz grimaces. **(2)**

4. Liz and Ed roll their eyes. **(2)**

5. The dog leaps onto Liz's lap, knocking her book away. **(2)**

6. Liz pushes the dog back onto its blanket. **(2)**

7. Ed whispers gently to Furhead. **(2)**

8. His voice cracks because he's afraid Mom will really start singing show tunes. **(2)**

Copyright © Houghton Mifflin Company. All rights reserved.

Assessment Tip: Total **16** Points

Name _____

Growing Up

How do the characters in this theme grow? Add to this chart and the one on the next page after you read each story.

Answers will vary. (**10 Points** per selection)

	Where the Red Fern Grows	**Last Summer with Maizon**
Who is the main character or characters?	Billy	Margaret
What problem does the main character have?	Billy needs to save money for a pair of hound pups. This is very difficult because he lives during the Great Depression and money is scarce.	Margaret is having a hard time because her father died and her best friend moved away.
What does the main character learn about himself or herself in the story?	Billy learns that he is resourceful and that he can get what he wants if he tries. He learns that he is different from town kids.	Margaret learns that she can cope with her losses. She learns that writing can help her express her feelings.

Copyright © Houghton Mifflin Company. All rights reserved.

Assessment Tip: Total **20 Points**

Name _____

Growing Up continued

(**10 Points** per selection)

	The Challenge	The View from Saturday
Who is the main character or characters?	José, Estela	Nadia
What problem does the main character have?	José likes Estela, but he can't get her to notice him.	Nadia must cope with a new family member she doesn't like and with her parents' divorce.
What does the main character learn about himself or herself in the story?	José learns that girls can beat boys at sports. He learns not to brag about his abilities, especially about skills he doesn't have.	Nadia learns that she and her father are alike and that they must help each other get through the storm in their private lives.

Sometimes struggle leads to growth. How do the stories in this theme support this statement? **(2)**

All the characters grow as a result of a challenge or struggle.

_____

Assessment Tip: Total **22** Points

Copyright © Houghton Mifflin Company. All rights reserved.

Name _____

Going to Market

Use the words in the box to complete the paragraph below.

Vocabulary

provisions
determination
depot
urgency
wares
cheap

Several times a year, people who live in the mountains load up their wagons and travel to town to sell homemade pies, jars of jam, and other <u>wares **(2 points)**</u>. It takes <u>determination **(2)**</u> to rise before dawn and ride such a long distance.   Restaurants in town are not <u>cheap **(2)**</u>, so the mountain people usually bring their own food.   They carry strips of dried mcat and other <u>provisions **(2)**</u> in their packs.   The travelers feel a sense of <u>urgency **(2)**</u> as they approach the town because they must hurry to set up their displays before shoppers from the city begin arriving at the train <u>depot **(2)**</u>.

Copyright © Houghton Mifflin Company. All rights reserved.

Assessment Tip: Total **12** Points

Name _____

Generalization Chart

Sample answers are shown. Generalizations	Information from the Story	Information from My Own Life
Page 247 It can take a lot of hard work to reach a goal. **(1 point)**	Page 247 Billy works hard to earn money to buy the hound pups. He traps, fishes, and gathers. **(1)**	Example: When I wanted a new bicycle, I had to save my money for almost a year. **(1)**
Pages 248–252 When people work hard to do something difficult, their family members are proud. **(1)**	Pages 248–252 Grandpa cries after he learns how Billy earned and saved the fifty dollars. **(1)**	(Answers will vary.) **(1)**
Pages 253–254 People who are focused on a goal sometimes behave strangely. **(1)**	Pages 253–254 Billy walks around as if he is lost. He misses getting a haircut. He goes off alone without telling anyone. **(1)**	(Answers will vary.) **(1)**
Page 254 Most people raised in a particular area will feel comfortable there even if they are alone. **(1)**	Page 254 Billy is not afraid to be by himself at night because he was raised in the mountains. **(1)**	(Answers will vary.) **(1)**
Pages 257–260 Some people make fun of outsiders without bothering to get to know them. **(1)**	Pages 257–260 Several people in Tahlequah tease Billy. **(1)**	(Answers will vary.) **(1)**
Pages 262–264 After people wait for something for so long, they sometimes don't know what to do when it finally arrives. **(1)**	Pages 262–264 When Billy gets to the depot he is scared. **(1)**	(Answers will vary.) **(1)**

Assessment Tip: Total **16** Points

Copyright © Houghton Mifflin Company. All rights reserved.

Name _____

A Conversation with Papa

Suppose that Billy returns from Tahlequah, and must tell his parents where he's been and why. Below is a conversation he might have with his father. Use details from the story to help you fill in the words Billy might say.

Papa: Billy, where've you been? Your mother and I have been worried about you.

Billy: I went to Tahlequah. **(1 point)** _____

Papa: Why did you go there?

Billy: *(showing the bag with the hound pups)* to get these hound pups **(1)** _____

Papa: Hound pups! Who'd you buy them from?

Billy: I got them from a kennel in Kentucky. They sent them to the train depot in _____

Tahlequah. **(2)**

Papa: Those pups must be worth 30 dollars apiece! How'd you pay for them?

Billy: They only cost 20 dollars each. I used money I've been saving for the past _____

two years. **(2)**

Papa: Where'd you get that much money?

Billy: I earned it by selling bait and vegetables to the fishermen, collecting berries _____

selling them to Grandpa for his store, and trapping animals for their furs. **(3)**

Papa: Now wait a minute. How'd you order the puppies?

Billy: Grandpa did it for me. **(1)** _____

Papa: Why did you walk to Tahlequah by yourself? Did Grandpa tell you to?

Billy: No, that was my idea. I couldn't wait for a ride into town. **(2)** _____

_____

Copyright © Houghton Mifflin Company. All rights reserved.

Name _____

Broadly Speaking . . .

Read the passage. Then complete the activity on page 199.

Dot and the Turkeys

All families were poor during the Great Depression. Dot's family was no exception. Even after selling milk and butter from the dairy farm, Ma and Pa struggled to keep food on the table for themselves and their seven children. The family's meals usually consisted of cornbread and buttermilk. Only on holidays did the children get treats such as nuts or a piece of fresh fruit. For children during the Depression, oranges were a particularly special treat. In general, families had little money for clothes, and often made their clothes by hand. Dot had no shoes and only owned one dress to wear to school, a homemade dress her older sister outgrew.

For a while Pa tried to make ends meet by raising turkeys. Ma had warned six-year-old Dot to stay away from the turkey pen. "Most turkeys are just plain mean," she said. Dot, however, was fascinated with the big birds and their drooping red wattles. She listened for hours to their clucking and gobbling and watched them strut about proudly. One day she slipped inside the pen to pet the huge, soft-looking birds. The turkeys, however, were not amused by the small girl inside their pen. The flock rushed at her and nearly smothered her. Dot's terrified screaming brought Ma and her brothers to her rescue. She never went near the turkeys again.

Copyright © Houghton Mifflin Company. All rights reserved.

Name _____

Broadly Speaking . . . continued

Answer these questions about the passage on page 198.

1. The underlined sentence in the first paragraph states a generalization. Do you think it is valid or invalid? Why?

   Invalid. Some families were not poor during the Depression.

   (2 points)

2. How could you rewrite this sentence so that it states a valid generalization?

   Many families were poor during the Great Depression. **(2)**

3. What two generalizations about food are made in the first paragraph?

   A. The family's meal usually consisted of cornbread and

   buttermilk. **(1)**

   B. For children during the Depression, oranges were a particularly

   special treat. **(1)**

4. What two generalizations about clothes are made in the first paragraph?

   A. In general, families had little money for clothes. **(1)**

   B. Families often made their clothes by hand. **(1)**

5. How do the details about Dot's clothes support these generalizations?

   Dot has no shoes and only owns the dress her sister outgrew. **(2)**

6. What other generalization could you make about life during the Depression?

   Answers will vary. **(2)**

_____

_____

Copyright © Houghton Mifflin Company. All rights reserved.

Name _____

Word Patterns in Writing

Add slashes between the syllables of each underlined word.
Then write another sentence using the word correctly. Answers will vary. Samples are shown.

1. My hands were <u>calloused</u> after raking leaves all day.
   <u>cal/loused **(1 point)** His mother's hands were calloused</u>

   <u>from years of hard farm work. **(2)**</u>

   _____

2. The girl was <u>dumbfounded</u> by the sight of the vast prairie.
   <u>dumb/found/ed **(1)** I wanted to speak to the president,</u>

   <u>but I was dumbfounded by his presence. **(2)**</u>

   _____

3. My sister and I like to tease our <u>grandfather</u> about his beard.
   <u>grand/fa/ther **(1)** My grandfather traveled to</u>

   <u>Europe as a young man. **(2)**</u>

   _____

4. At the first light of dusk, the <u>mosquitoes</u> begin biting.
   <u>mos/qui/toes **(1)** Mosquitoes make fishing on the pond</u>

   <u>almost impossible. **(2)**</u>

   _____

5. The boys saw a <u>shadowy</u> figure move in the window of the house.
   <u>shad/ow/y **(1)** My room becomes shadowy in late afternoon. **(2)**</u>

   _____

Assessment Tip: Total **15** Points

Copyright © Houghton Mifflin Company. All rights reserved.

Name _____

VCV, VCCV, and VCCCV Patterns

Copyright © Houghton Mifflin Company. All rights reserved.

To spell a two-syllable word, divide the word into syllables. Look for spelling patterns, and spell the word by syllables.

Divide a VCV word after the consonant if the first syllable has the short vowel pattern. Divide the word before the consonant if the first syllable ends with a vowel sound.

VC/V **bal / ance**   V/CV **mi / nus**

VCCV words are usually divided between the consonants. They can be divided before or after two consonants that together spell one sound.

VC/CV **law / yer**   V/CCV **au / thor**   VCC/V **meth / od**

VCCCV words are often divided after the first of the three successive consonants.

When *y* spells a vowel sound, it is considered a vowel.

VC/CCV **sup / ply**

Write each Spelling Word under its syllable pattern.

Order of answers for each category may vary

VCV
balance **(1 point)**

sheriff **(1)**

minus **(1)**

item **(1)**

require **(1)**

spirit **(1)**

adopt **(1)**

poison **(1)**

deserve **(1)**

relief **(1)**

VCCV
lawyer **(1)**

author **(1)**

method **(1)**

whisper **(1)**

tennis **(1)**

rescue **(1)**

journey **(1)**

VCCCV
supply **(1)**

instant **(1)**

laundry **(1)**

Spelling Words

1. balance
2. lawyer
3. sheriff
4. author
5. minus
6. method
7. item
8. require
9. supply
10. whisper
11. spirit
12. tennis
13. adopt
14. instant
15. poison
16. deserve
17. rescue
18. journey
19. relief
20. laundry

Theme 3: **Growing Up**   201
Assessment Tip: Total **20** Points

Name _____

Spelling Spree

The Third Word Write the Spelling Word that belongs with each group of words.

1. police chief, marshal, sheriff **(1 point)**

2. save, recover, rescue **(1)**

3. demand, insist, require **(1)**

4. editor, publisher, author **(1)**

5. venom, toxin, poison **(1)**

6. earn, merit, deserve **(1)**

7. liveliness, energy, spirit **(1)**

8. ping pong, badminton, tennis **(1)**

9. way, technique, method **(1)**

10. object, article, item **(1)**

Syllable Scramble Rearrange the syllables in each item to write a Spelling Word. An extra syllable is in each item.

11. jour di ney journey **(1)**

12. nus mi less minus **(1)**

13. yer pre law lawyer **(1)**

14. dol ance bal balance **(1)**

15. lief re ant relief **(1)**

16. a com dopt adopt **(1)**

17. ex ply sup supply **(1)**

18. dry im laun laundry **(1)**

19. per whis un whisper **(1)**

20. in port stant instant **(1)**

Spelling Words

1. balance
2. lawyer
3. sheriff
4. author
5. minus
6. method
7. item
8. require
9. supply
10. whisper
11. spirit
12. tennis
13. adopt
14. instant
15. poison
16. deserve
17. rescue
18. journey
19. relief
20. laundry

Copyright © Houghton Mifflin Company. All rights reserved.

Assessment Tip: Total **20** Points

Name _____

Proofreading and Writing

Proofreading Circle the five misspelled Spelling Words in this advertisement. Then write each word correctly.

NEEDED: People needed to (addopt) one or more puppies. They are playful and full of (spirrit,) and they require lots of love and attention. They have been living in our (londry) room, but they still need to be housebroken. We will (suply) the first two weeks of food. These are great dogs, and they (desserve) a good home. Call 555-3647.

Copyright © Houghton Mifflin Company. All rights reserved.

1. adopt **(1 point)** _____
2. spirit **(1)** _____
3. laundry **(1)** _____
4. supply **(1)** _____
5. deserve **(1)** _____

Spelling Words

1. balance
2. lawyer
3. sheriff
4. author
5. minus
6. method
7. item
8. require
9. supply
10. whisper
11. spirit
12. tennis
13. adopt
14. instant
15. poison
16. deserve
17. rescue
18. journey
19. relief
20. laundry

✏➤ **Write Guidelines for Pet Care** Dogs, cats, and other pets need a great deal of care. What kinds of guidelines would a new pet owner need?

Choose a type of pet. Then, on a separate sheet of paper, write a list of guidelines for caring for that pet. Use Spelling Words from the list. Responses will vary. **(5 points)**

Name _____

Synonym Sampler

Read each entry word, its definition, and its synonyms on the thesaurus page below. Then rewrite the numbered sentences using synonyms to replace the words in bold print. Sample answers shown.

> **happiness** *n.* The state or quality of feeling joy or pleasure.
>
> > **joy** A feeling of great happiness or delight.
> >
> > **gladness** The state or quality of feeling joy or pleasure.
> >
> > **bliss** Extreme happiness; joy.
>
> **courage** *n.* The quality of spirit that enables one to face danger or hardship; bravery.
>
> > **spirit** A mood marked by vigor, courage, or liveliness.
> >
> > **mettle** Spirit; daring; courage.
> >
> > **bravery** The quality or condition of showing courage.

1. Billy's **courage** helped him to reach his goal.

   Billy's spirit helped him to reach his goal. **(2 points)**

2. As he touched the pups, **happiness** welled up in Billy's heart.

   As he touched the pups, bliss welled up in Billy's heart. **(2)**

3. Billy's **happiness** was hardly contained when he knew that the pups were about to come.

   Billy's gladness was hardly contained when he knew that the pups were

   about to come. **(2)**

4. Billy needed extra **courage** to carry out his plan.

   Billy needed extra mettle to carry out his plan. **(2)**

5. Billy's **courage** as he hiked through the hills was matched by his **happiness** when he arrived.

   Billy's bravery as he hiked through the hills was matched by his joy

   when he arrived. **(2)**

Assessment Tip: Total **10** Points

Copyright © Houghton Mifflin Company. All rights reserved.

Name _____

Summer Days

Verb Tenses The **tense** of a verb tells when the action takes place. The **present tense** is used when something is happening now, or happens regularly over time. The **past tense** is used when something has already happened. Here is how the verb *walk*, a regular verb, looks in these two tenses:

Present Tense	**Past Tense**
I **walk**.	I **walked**.
You **walk**.	You **walked**.
She/He/It **walks**.	She/He/It **walked**.
We **walk.**	We **walked**.
You **walk.**	You **walked**.
They **walk.**	They **walked**.

Circle the verb in each of the following sentences. Decide whether the verb is in the past tense or the present tense, and write *past* or *present* on the line.

1. He (lived) in the Ozark Mountains. past **(1)**

2. Celia (fishes) in the river. present **(1)**

3. I (strolled) through the grass in my bare feet. past **(1)**

4. They (played) with Kelly's new puppy. past **(1)**

5. You (like) the outdoors. present **(1)**

Now rewrite the five sentences above. If the original verb was in the past tense, change it to the present tense. If the original verb was in the present tense, change it to the past tense.

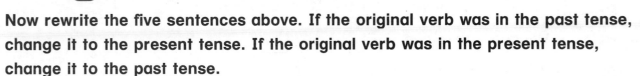

1. He lives in the Ozark Mountains. **(1)**

2. Celia fished in the river. **(1)**

3. I stroll through the grass in my bare feet. **(1)**

4. They play with Kelly's new puppy. **(1)**

5. You liked the outdoors. **(1)**

Copyright © Houghton Mifflin Company. All rights reserved.

Assessment Tip: Total **10** Points

Name _____

Money!

More About Verb Tenses The **present tense** of a verb is used when something is happening now or happens regularly. The **past tense** of a verb is used when something has already happened. The **future tense** of a verb is used when something is going to happen. To form the future tense, use the helping verb *will* or *shall* with the main verb.

Circle the verb in each sentence. Then write its tense on the line.

1. We (saved) our allowance for a month. past **(1)**
2. The package (will arrive) on time. future **(1)**
3. William (ordered) new track shoes. past **(1)**
4. We (will earn) money for our vacation. future **(1)**
5. Pat (saves) for the future. present **(1)**

Now rewrite each sentence using the verb tense shown.

1. **Future** We will save our allowance for a month. **(1)**
2. **Present** The package arrives on time. **(1)**
3. **Present** William orders new track shoes. **(1)**
4. **Past** We earned money for our vacation. **(1)**
5. **Future** Pat will save for the future. **(1)**

Assessment Tip: Total **10** Points

Copyright © Houghton Mifflin Company. All rights reserved.

Name _____

When Did That Happen?

Choosing the Correct Verb Tense Switch tenses when you write only to tell about different times.

Dorinda wrote the following paragraph. Rewrite her paragraph using correct verb tenses. The first sentence will not change.

> Every summer I visit my aunt and uncle. They lived in a mountain valley. I will like to walk there in my bare feet and waded in the creek behind their house. Last summer, I help my aunt and uncle with their vegetable garden. It is hard work, but we all will enjoy the vegetables. Vegetables fresh from a garden will taste so much better than vegetables from a store! Now I wanted to grow vegetables at home. When spring arrives, my parents helped me plant tomatoes and green beans. Then we enjoy eating vegetables from our garden.

Every summer I visit my aunt and uncle. They **live** in a mountain valley. I **like** to walk there in my bare feet and **wade** in the creek behind their house. Last summer, I **helped** my aunt and uncle with their vegetable garden. It **was** hard work, but we all **enjoyed** the vegetables. Vegetables fresh from a garden **taste** so much better than vegetables from a store! Now I **want** to grow vegetables at home. When spring arrives, my parents **will help** me plant tomatoes and green beans. Then we **will enjoy** eating vegetables from our garden. **(10 points)**

_____

_____

Copyright © Houghton Mifflin Company. All rights reserved.

Assessment Tip: Total **10** Points

Name _____

Writing a Problem-Solution Composition

Writing about a character's problems in a **problem-solution composition** can help you better understand characters and events in a story. In *Where the Red Fern Grows*, for example, Billy Colman faces a problem. How Billy solves his problem reveals the kind of person he is.

Brainstorm problems that Billy solves in this story as well as problems that characters solve in other stories you have read. Write three of these problems and solutions on the graphic organizer below. Answers will vary. (**2 points** for each answer.)

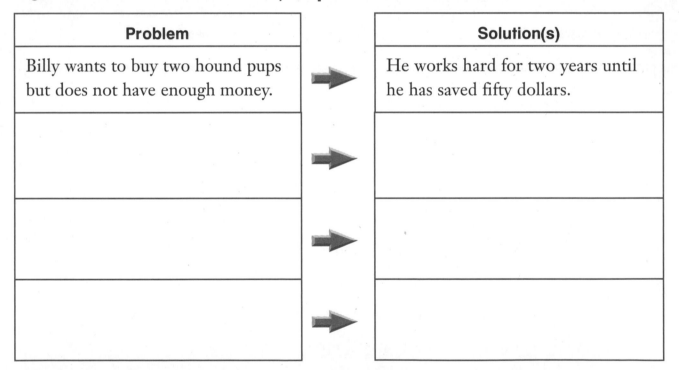

Problem	Solution(s)
Billy wants to buy two hound pups but does not have enough money.	He works hard for two years until he has saved fifty dollars.

Now pick one problem and its solution. On a separate sheet of paper, write your problem-solution composition. Begin with an introductory sentence that tells who or what you are writing about. Then state the problem in the first paragraph. In the second paragraph, describe how Billy or another character solves the problem. Include details that lead to the solution. Finally, end with a strong concluding sentence. (3 points)

Assessment Tip: Total **15** Points

Copyright © Houghton Mifflin Company. All rights reserved.

Name _____

Organization

Good writers organize their ideas by sequence of events, by causes and effects, or by main ideas and details.

Help to unscramble this composition. Write students' ideas in a logical order in the organization outline below.

> In the winter, he traps opossums and sells their hides to fur buyers. Through hard work and determination, Billy finally realizes his dream. Billy desperately wants to buy two hound pups. Billy Colman is growing up during the Great Depression. Also, he catches crawfish and minnows and sells them to fishermen. To earn what he needs, Billy decides to work hard and save the money. However, each dog costs twenty-five dollars. During the summer, he picks berries and sells them. After two years, Billy has saved fifty dollars. Neither Billy nor his parents have fifty dollars to spend.

Paragraph 1: Introductory sentence

Billy Colman, is growing up during the Great Depression.

Problem

Billy desperately wants to buy two hound pups. However, each dog

costs twenty-five dollars. Neither Billy nor his parents have fifty dollars to spend.

Paragraph 2: Solution

To earn what he needs, Billy decides to work hard and save the money. During

the summer, he picks berries and sells them. Also, he catches crawfish and

minnows and sells them to fishermen. In the winter, he traps opossums and sells

their hides to fur buyers. After two years, Billy has saved fifty dollars.

Concluding sentence

Through hard work, and determination, Billy finally realizes his dream.

Copyright © Houghton Mifflin Company. All rights reserved.

Assessment Tip: Total **20** Points

Name _____

Revising Your Description

Reread your description. Put a checkmark in the box for each sentence that describes your paper. Use this page to help you revise.

Loud and Clear!

☐ My description is focused on single topic.

☐ Sensory words and vivid details create a clear picture.

☐ The details are told in a clear order. The beginning introduces the topic, and the ending sums it up.

☐ My writing shows my feelings about the topic.

☐ Sentences flow smoothly. There are almost no mistakes.

Sounding Stronger

☐ The description is not always focused on a single topic.

☐ More sensory words and vivid details are needed.

☐ The order could be easier to follow. The beginning and ending may be weak.

☐ Readers can't always tell how I feel about the topic.

☐ Many sentences are choppy. There are a few mistakes.

Turn Up the Volume

☐ There is no focus. It isn't clear what my topic is.

☐ There are no sensory words and almost no details.

☐ The order is unclear. There is no beginning and ending.

☐ My writing sounds flat. I show no feelings about my topic.

☐ Most sentences are choppy. There are lots of mistakes.

Copyright © Houghton Mifflin Company. All rights reserved.

Sentence Combining

Combine each pair of sentences to make them flow more easily. Use the joining word in parentheses. Add commas where needed. Answers may vary. Possible responses are given.

1. Tom was born in Minnesota. (AND) Tom grew up there.

   Tom was born in Minnesota and grew up there. **(1)**

2. Toby was also born in Minnesota. (BUT) He grew up in Chicago.

   Toby was also born in Minnesota, but he grew up in Chicago. **(1)**

3. Tom and Toby were twins. (AND) They had been separated at birth.

   Tom and Toby were twins, and they had been separated at birth. **(1)**

4. The twins had different last names. (BUT) They shared many traits.

   The twins had different last names, but they shared many traits. **(1)**

5. Tom owned a beagle named Willie. (OR) Toby owned a beagle named Willie.

   Tom or Toby owned a beagle named Willie. **(1)**

6. The other owned a cat named Billy. (OR) The other owned a cat name Millie.

   The other owned a cat named Billy or Millie. **(1)**

7. Both twins loved baseball. (AND) Both twins hated fishing.

   Both twins loved baseball and hated fishing. **(1)**

8. Both twins owned the same kind of truck.(BUT) Tom's was blue and Toby's was red.

   Both twins owned the same kind of truck, but Tom's was blue and Toby's

   was red. **(1)**

9. They both liked the same movie. (OR) They both hated the same movie.

   They both liked the same movie, or they both hated the same movie. **(1)**

10. Once the twins were together, they were happy. (AND)
    Once the twins were together, they would never part.

    Once the twins were together, they were happy and would never part. **(1)**

Copyright © Houghton Mifflin Company. All rights reserved.

Name _____

Words Often Confused

Do cows graze in a pastor or a pasture? Is a glass ring a bauble or a bubble? It is easy to confuse words that have similar spellings and pronunciations even though the meanings are different. The Spelling Words in each pair on the list are often confused. Pay careful attention to their pronunciations, spellings, and meanings.

Spelling Words

1. bland
2. blend
3. below
4. bellow
5. pastor
6. pasture
7. moral
8. mortal
9. bauble
10. bubble
11. bisect
12. dissect
13. assent
14. ascent

Write the missing letters in the Spelling Words below.
Order of answers for 1–2, 9–10, and 13–14 may vary.

1. bl __a__ nd **(1 point)**

2. bl __e__ nd **(1)**

3. be __l__ __o__ __w__ **(1)**

4. be __l__ __l__ ow **(1)**

5. past __o__ __r__ **(1)**

6. pas __t__ __u__ __r__ __e__ **(1)**

7. mor __a__ __l__ **(1)**

8. mor __t__ __a__ __l__ **(1)**

9. b __a__ __u__ __b__ le **(1)**

10. b __u__ __b__ __b__ le **(1)**

11. b __i__ __s__ ect **(1)**

12. d __i__ __s__ __s__ ect **(1)**

13. a __s__ __s__ ent **(1)**

14. a __s__ __c__ ent **(1)**

Study List On a separate piece of paper, write each Spelling Word pair. Check your spelling against the words on the list. Order of word pairs may vary. **(2)**

Assessment Tip: Total 16 Points

Copyright © Houghton Mifflin Company. All rights reserved.

Spelling Spree

Contrast Clues **The second part of each clue contrasts with the first part. Write a Spelling Word to fit each clue.**

1. not a descent, but an _____
2. not spicy, but _____
3. not real jewelry, but a _____
4. not a whisper, but a _____
5. not living forever, but _____
6. not a forest, but a _____
7. not to cut into unequal pieces, but to _____

1. ascent **(1)**
2. bland **(1)**
3. bauble **(1)**
4. bellow **(1)**
5. mortal **(1)**
6. pasture **(1)**
7. bisect **(1)**

Spelling Words

1. bland
2. blend
3. below
4. bellow
5. pastor
6. pasture
7. moral
8. mortal
9. bauble
10. bubble
11. bisect
12. dissect
13. assent
14. ascent

Word Switch **For each item below, replace the underlined definition or synonym with a Spelling Word.**

8. Next week in my sister's biology class, they're going to cut apart in order to study frogs.
9. We were halfway up the mountain when we heard a cry for help from a lower position.
10. If you combine completely these red and yellow paints, you should get the right shade of orange.
11. Did your mom give her approval to our plan to go hiking?
12. The minister greeted the new couple the first time they walked into the church.
13. Each of Aesop's fables has a lesson.
14. There was a soap ball of air surrounded by a thin film of liquid on the surface of the dishwater.

8. dissect **(1)**
9. below **(1)**
10. blend **(1)**
11. assent **(1)**

12. pastor **(1)**
13. moral **(1)**
14. bubble **(1)**

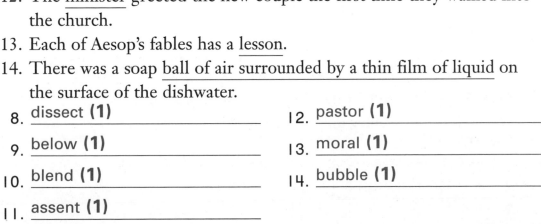

Copyright © Houghton Mifflin Company. All rights reserved.

Theme 3: **Growing Up**   213
Assessment Tip: Total **14** Points

Name _____

Proofreading and Writing

Proofreading Circle the five misspelled Spelling Words in this movie description. Then write each word correctly.

Spelling Words

1. bland
2. blend
3. below
4. bellow
5. pastor
6. pasture
7. moral
8. mortal
9. bauble
10. bubble
11. bisect
12. dissect
13. assent
14. ascent

Growing Up ★★★✔ is a welcome change from the typical, (blend) children's movie. The director manages to (bland) four stories into one film. Together, they give a picture of the often difficult (assent) from childhood to the teenage years. Each story has its own (morral) but teaches it quietly instead of trying to bellow it from the rooftops. Movie times are listed (balow.)

1. bland **(1 point)** _____

2. blend **(1)** _____

3. ascent **(1)** _____

4. moral **(1)** _____

5. below **(1)** _____

✏️➤ **Two for One** Pick four word pairs from the Spelling Word list. Then, for each pair, write a sentence using both words.
Responses will vary. (5)

Copyright © Houghton Mifflin Company. All rights reserved.

Name _____

City Similars

Read the word in each box from *Last Summer with Maizon*.
Then write a word from the list that is related to it in
meaning. Use a dictionary if necessary.

Vocabulary

earlier
lifeless
porch
imagining
help
platform
communicate

express
__communicate__ (1)

desolate
__lifeless__ (1)

daydreaming
__imagining__ (1)

previous
__earlier__ (1)

stoop
__porch__ (1)

relieve
__help__ (1)

Copyright © Houghton Mifflin Company. All rights reserved.

Inferences Chart

	Evidence from the Story	Own Experiences	Inference
How does Margaret feel about Maizon moving away? (page 279)	Maizon hasn't left yet, but Margaret has already written two letters to her. Margaret bites her cuticles. **(1 point)**	Example: I know people who chew their fingernails when they are worried about something. **(1)**	Margaret is very worried about losing her best friend. **(1)**
How does Margaret feel about her friendship with Maizon once Maizon has left? (pages 280–281)	Margaret says that they are "old friends" now. She says that Maizon kept her from doing some things. She thinks that sitting on the stoop was more fun when Maizon was still around. **(1)**	Answers will vary. **(1)**	Margaret is unsure how she feels about her friendship with Maizon. Some parts of the change seem bad, others seem good. **(1)**
How does Margaret feel about being in Ms. Peazle's class? (page 283)	She knows her essay isn't as good as she could make it. She wants very badly to stay in the class. She decides not to complain about the homework. **(1)**	Answers will vary. **(1)**	Margaret is worried that she won't make it in Ms. Peazle's class and wants to show that she belongs. **(1)**
How do you think Margaret's classmates feel about her poem? (page 286)	They stare at her blankly and remain silent when she is done reading. **(1)**	Answers will vary. **(1)**	Margaret's classmates are so moved by her poem that they don't know how to respond. **(1)**

Assessment Tip: Total **12** Points

Copyright © Houghton Mifflin Company. All rights reserved.

Name _____

Story Frames

Think about what happened in *Last Summer with Maizon*. Write what happened in each part of the story by completing the story frames.

I. On the M train:

Best Friends or Old Friends?

Margaret and Maizon say good-bye. Margaret wonders

whether she and Maizon are still best friends, or whether

they are old friends now. **(2 points)**

_____

---

2. First Day in 6–1:

The Essay

Margaret can't concentrate on the essay assignment.

Ms. Peazle asks her to write it over because she thinks

Margaret can do a better job. **(2)**

_____

---

3. Next Day in 6–1:

The Poem

Margaret reads her poem to the class. No one says

anything. Later, she gets a note from Mrs. Peazle, saying

she liked it. **(2)**

_____

---

4. On the Front Stoop:

What's Changed? What Hasn't?

Margaret still misses Maizon and her dad, but with the

support of her neighbors and Mrs. Peazle she is starting

to feel better about her loss and her ability to succeed in

6–1. **(2)**

Copyright © Houghton Mifflin Company. All rights reserved.

Assessment Tip: Total **8** Points

Name _____

Reading Between the Lines

Read the passage. Then complete the activity on page 219.

The Audition

Serena ran into the girls' dressing room and locked the door behind her. "It's not fair! It's just not fair!" she cried, breaking into uncontrollable sobs. Just one week before, she had been on top of the world. She had been picked for the leading role in the spring musical. Mr. O'Toole, the choir director, had had the choir choose the parts by show of hands, after hearing the auditions for each part. "I won the part fair and square!" Serena wailed. "How dare Rebecca show up this week and ask to audition for my part! How could Mr. O'Toole have let her to do it? He's never done anything like that before! Rebecca should have been here last week if she wanted the part!"

The audition had been short, with only Serena and Rebecca performing. At first Serena hadn't been concerned. She'd won the part once, and she had figured that everyone would love her singing again. Mr. O'Toole had had everyone close their eyes again and raise their hands to vote. "The winner is Rebecca," Mr. O'Toole had announced. At that moment, the color had drained out of Serena's face as the choir applauded for Rebecca. Ashen-faced, she had bolted for the dressing room.

Copyright © Houghton Mifflin Company. All rights reserved.

Name _____

Reading Between the Lines

continued

Answer the following questions about the passage on page 218.

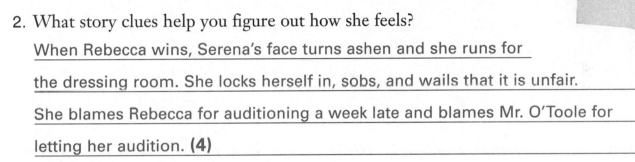

1. How does Serena feel when the choir votes for Rebecca?
   She feels surprised, upset, and cheated. She had expected
   everyone to vote for her again. She feels that she won the part
   fairly, and that it has been unfairly taken from her. **(4 points)**

2. What story clues help you figure out how she feels?
   When Rebecca wins, Serena's face turns ashen and she runs for
   the dressing room. She locks herself in, sobs, and wails that it is unfair.
   She blames Rebecca for auditioning a week late and blames Mr. O'Toole for
   letting her audition. **(4)**

3. Why do you think Mr. O'Toole allows Rebecca to audition for the role
   even though the choir already picked Serena? (To answer, think about
   what is probably important to Mr. O'Toole as the choir director.)
   He probably wants the best singer to star in the musical. **(4)**

   _____

   _____

4. How do you think Serena feels toward Rebecca at this moment in the story?
   She is angry at Rebecca for daring to audition late and for winning her part.
   She might also be jealous of her for winning more votes. **(4)**

5. What do you know from real life that can help you figure out how
   Serena feels toward Rebecca?
   Answers may vary. **(4)**

   _____

   _____

Copyright © Houghton Mifflin Company. All rights reserved.

Theme 3: **Growing Up**   219
Assessment Tip: Total **20** Points

Name _____

Words, Inc.

For each word in column 1, write the base word in column 2 and the ending in column 3. Check a dictionary if you are unsure about the spelling of a base word.

	Base word	Ending
1. whispered	whisper **(1 point)**	-ed **(1)**
2. stumbled	stumble **(1)**	-ed **(1)**
3. exaggerated	exaggerate **(1)**	-ed **(1)**
4. sweating	sweat **(1)**	-ing **(1)**
5. smiling	smile **(1)**	-ing **(1)**

Write the word from the chart that best completes each sentence.

6. When Margaret was unexpectedly asked to read her poem, she began sweating **(1)** _____.

7. Her classmates whispered **(1)** _____ among themselves.

8. They exaggerated **(1)** _____ their reactions as she got ready to read.

9. Margaret stumbled **(1)** _____ over her feet on her way back to her desk.

10. When Margaret looked up, her teacher was smiling **(1)** _____.

Assessment Tip: Total 15 Points

Copyright © Houghton Mifflin Company. All rights reserved.

Name _____

Words with *-ed* or *-ing*

Remember that when a one-syllable word ends with one vowel and one consonant, the final consonant is usually doubled before *-ed* or *-ing* is added. When a two-syllable word ends with a stressed syllable, double the final consonant before adding *-ed* or *-ing*.

map**ped**   fit**ting**   pilot**ing**   begin**ning**

Write each Spelling Word under the heading that tells how the word is changed when *-ed* or *-ing* is added.
Order of answers for each category may vary.

Copyright © Houghton Mifflin Company. All rights reserved.

8270 ○ **8270**

Final Consonant Doubled

mapped **(1 point)**   preferred **(1 point)**

permitting **(1)**   slipped **(1)**

beginning **(1)**   fitting **(1)**

forgetting **(1)**   knitting **(1)**

No Change

piloting **(1)**   listening **(1)**

bothered **(1)**   pardoned **(1)**

limited **(1)**   shoveled **(1)**

reasoning **(1)**   favored **(1)**

equaled **(1)**   answered **(1)**

wondering **(1)**   modeling **(1)**

Spelling Words

1. mapped
2. piloting
3. permitting
4. beginning
5. bothered
6. limited
7. forgetting
8. reasoning
9. preferred
10. equaled
11. wondering
12. slipped
13. listening
14. fitting
15. pardoned
16. shoveled
17. favored
18. knitting
19. answered
20. modeling

Assessment Tip: Total **20** Points

Name _____

Spelling Spree

Puzzle Play Write a Spelling Word to fit each clue.

(1 point each)

Spelling Words

1. posing for a photographer (m) o d e l i n g
2. forgiven p (a) r d o n e d
3. allowing p e (r) m i t t i n g
4. flying a plane p i l o t i n (g)
5. replied (a) n s w e r e d
6. liked better p (r) e f e r r e d
7. was the same as e q u a l (e) d
8. making a sweater k n i (t) t i n g

Now write the circled letters in order. They will spell the name of a character from *Last Summer with Maizon*.

M a r g a r e t

Meaning Match Each item below contains a meaning for a base word followed by an ending. Add the base word to the underlined ending to write a Spelling Word.

Example: collect + ing = gathering

9. be suitable for   + ing = fitting **(1)**
10. be for or partial to + ed = favored **(1)**
11. the ability to think + ing = reasoning **(1)**
12. disturb or annoy   + ed = bothered **(1)**
13. fail to remember   + ing = forgetting **(1)**
14. start   + ing = beginning **(1)**
15. plan in detail   + ed = mapped **(1)**

Spelling Words

1. mapped
2. piloting
3. permitting
4. beginning
5. bothered
6. limited
7. forgetting
8. reasoning
9. preferred
10. equaled
11. wondering
12. slipped
13. listening
14. fitting
15. pardoned
16. shoveled
17. favored
18. knitting
19. answered
20. modeling

Assessment Tip: Total **15** Points

Copyright © Houghton Mifflin Company. All rights reserved.

Name _____

Proofreading and Writing

Proofreading Circle the five misspelled Spelling Words in this letter. Then write each word correctly.

Copyright © Houghton Mifflin Company. All rights reserved.

C

Dear Leslie,

How's it going? I've been (lisening) to the tape you sent with your last letter. It's great! I really like the song you sang at the beginning. I'm sorry it's taken me so long to write. My mom (sliped) on our sidewalk last week. She was (shovelling) snow. Since then, I've been doing a lot of things around the house. I guess my time is pretty (limeted) right now. Actually, I should get going. Mom must be (wondring) why the laundry hasn't been done. I 'll write again soon!

Your friend,

Carmen

Spelling Words

1. mapped
2. piloting
3. permitting
4. beginning
5. bothered
6. limited
7. forgetting
8. reasoning
9. preferred
10. equaled
11. wondering
12. slipped
13. listening
14. fitting
15. pardoned
16. shoveled
17. favored
18. knitting
19. answered
20. modeling

1. listening **(1 point)**
2. slipped **(1)**
3. shoveling **(1)**
4. limited **(1)**
5. wondering **(1)**

Write a Poem Margaret wrote a poem to express her feelings about her father's death. Has there been an event in your life that caused you to feel great joy or sadness?

On a separate sheet of paper, write a poem about that event and the feelings you experienced then. Use Spelling Words from the list. Responses will vary. **(5)**

Finding Word Forms

Read each entry word, its inflected forms, and its definition. Write the form of the word that best completes each sentence.

choose (chōoz) *v.* **chose, chosen, choosing, chooses.** To decide.

close (klōs) *adj.* **closer, closest.** Near in space or time.

exchange (ĭks **chānj′**) *v.* **exchanged, exchanging, exchanges.** To give and receive mutually; interchange.

smart (smärt) *adj.* **smarter, smartest.** Intelligent, clever, or bright.

worry (wûr′ ē) *v.* **worried, worrying, worries.** To feel uneasy or concerned about something.

1. Maizon was the <u>smartest **(2 points)**</u> student at P.S. 102.

2. Margaret couldn't stop <u>worrying **(2)**</u> about whether Maizon would write to her.

3. Ms. Dell and Hattie <u>exhanged **(2)**</u> cautious looks as they talked about Maizon.

4. Hattie felt that poetry <u>chooses **(2)**</u> where it wants to live.

5. Margaret moved <u>closer **(2)**</u> to the women as they talked on the stoop.

Assessment Tip: Total **10** Points

Copyright © Houghton Mifflin Company. All rights reserved.

Name _____

Verb Trouble

Principal Parts of Regular and Irregular Verbs The **principal parts**, or basic forms, of a verb are the present form of the verb, the present participle, the past, and the past participle. All verb tenses are formed with these basic parts.

When the past and the past participle of a verb are formed by adding *-d* or *-ed*, the verb is **regular**. When the past and the past participle of a verb are formed in some other way, the verb is **irregular**.

	Present	Present Participle	Past	Past Participle
Regular	walk	(is) walking	walked	(has) walked
Irregular	ride	(is) riding	rode	(has) ridden

Margaret is having trouble with some verbs in a poem. The troublesome verbs are listed below. Complete the verb chart by writing the missing principal parts. Use a dictionary if needed. The first one is done for you.

Present	Present Participle	Past	Past Participle
sing	**(is) singing**	sang	**(has) sung**
write	(is) writing **(1)**	wrote **(1)**	(has) written **(1)**
search	(is) searching **(1)**	searched **(1)**	(has) searched **(1)**
feel	(is) feeling **(1)**	felt **(1)**	(has) felt **(1)**
become	(is) becoming **(1)**	became **(1)**	(has) become **(1)**
shout	(is) shouting **(1)**	shouted **(1)**	(has) shouted **(1)**

Copyright © Houghton Mifflin Company. All rights reserved.

Assessment Tip: Total **15** Points

Name _____

Score with Perfect Tenses

► There are three **perfect tenses:** **present perfect,** **past perfect,** and **future perfect.** Form the present perfect tense with *have* or *has* and a past participle.

► Form the past perfect tense with *had* and a past participle.

► Form the future perfect tense with *will have* and a past participle.

Complete the chart below with the verb in the proper tense. The first one has been done for you.

Verb	Present Perfect	Past Perfect	Future Perfect
work	**have worked**	**had worked**	**will have worked**
move	have moved	had moved	will have moved
play	have played	had played	will have played
write	have written	had written	will have written
feel	have felt	had felt	will have felt
take	have taken	had taken	will have taken

Write the correct form of the verb in parentheses ( ) in each sentence below. Use the verb forms from the chart. (2 points each)

1. Maria _____had moved_____ away before school started. (move)
   <small>past perfect</small>

2. At the beginning of the year, my teacher _____had worked_____ with me after school. (work)
   <small>past perfect</small>

3. We _____have played_____ together all day. (play)
   <small>present perfect</small>

4. I _____have felt_____ this way before. (feel)
   <small>present perfect</small>

5. In two weeks, she _____will have written_____ her report. (write)
   <small>future perfect</small>

Assessment Tip: Total 10 Points

Copyright © Houghton Mifflin Company. All rights reserved.

Name _____

Letter Perfect Tenses

Choosing the Correct Verb Form To correctly form a perfect tense, use the **past participle** form of the verb with *have*, *has*, and *had*.

Proofread the following letter that Margaret might have written to a friend who moved away. Insert the proper verb forms where needed.

taken

Example: I had took the long route.

Hi!

heard **(1 point)**
    It has been a long time since I have heared from you. Since you left,

asked **(1)**
John K. has ask me about you six times! Sarita says, "Hi." Even Ms.

said **(1)**   written **(1)**
Whitney has says she wonders how you are. J.D. has wrote you a letter, but

he has not mailed it yet.

gone **(1)**
    In the past month, I have went to the movies twice. Yesterday, I saw a

seen **(1)**
TV movie called My Friend Flicka. I had seed it before but I still liked it.

taken **(1)**
    Tomorrow I will have taked my fifth math quiz. We have one each week.

    I plan to rake leaves and shovel snow to make money this year. By

saved **(1)**
summertime, I will have save enough to visit you. Remember last summer

went **(1)**   run **(1)**
when we goed to the beach? I had ran errands for months to earn that

money.

Your friend,

Margaret

Copyright © Houghton Mifflin Company. All rights reserved.

Assessment Tip: Total **10** Points

Name _____

Responding to a Prompt

In *Last Summer with Maizon*, Ms. Peazle gives her sixth-grade class a writing prompt. She asks them to write an essay about their summer vacations. A **writing prompt** is a direction that asks for a written response of one or more paragraphs.

Read the following prompts and choose one you would like to respond to.

Prompt 1
Describe a time when you had to adjust to a change.

Prompt 2
Write about a person who is important to you. Describe the person and tell why he or she is important.

Prompt 3
Describe what you look for in a friend.

Use the chart below to help you plan your response. First, list key words in the prompt such as *compare, explain, describe,* or *discuss*. Next, jot down main ideas and details you might include. Finally, number your main ideas, beginning from most to least important. (15 points)

Key Words	Main Ideas	Details

Write your response on a separate sheet of paper. Start by restating the prompt. Then write your main ideas and supporting details in order of importance from most to least important. Finally, check your response to make sure it answers the prompt. Responses will vary. **(5)**

Assessment Tip: Total 20 Points

Copyright © Houghton Mifflin Company. All rights reserved.

Name _____

Correcting Sentence Fragments and Run-on Sentences

Good writers check to make sure that their sentences are complete.
**Rewrite the body of the letter on the lines below. Correct run-on
sentences and sentence fragments so that the reader can understand
them.**

1234 Winding Drive Lane
Greenfield, Connecticut 06606
September 15
Dear Bethany,
     How are you? Boarding school is okay I miss our old class.
Teachers are pretty strict and they give tons of homework and
they teach hard subjects. My tiny room at the end of the hall.
Is already crammed with books and papers. Yesterday I met
some other scholarship students. In my class. Unfortunately,
none of them can jump rope.
     I can't wait to come home on vacation Boston seems so far
away. I miss you! Write soon.

        Your friend,
        Allison

Responses may vary slightly. Suggested responses below. **(5 points)**

   How are you? Boarding school is okay, but I miss our old class. Teachers

are pretty strict, give tons of homework, and teach hard subjects. My tiny

room at the end of the hall is already crammed with books and papers.

Yesterday I met some other scholarship students in my class.

Unfortunately, none of them can jump rope.

   I can't wait to come home on vacation. Boston seems so far away. I

miss you! Write soon.

Copyright © Houghton Mifflin Company. All rights reserved.

Assessment Tip: Total **5** Points

Name _____

What a Racquet!

Answer each of the following questions by writing a vocabulary word.

Vocabulary

encourage
notice
conversation
awkward
managed
bragged
attention
briskly

1. Which word tells what a show-off tries to attract?
   attention **(1 point)**

2. Which word means "claimed to be great"?
   bragged **(1)**

3. Which word tells what friends do when they want you to do well? encourage **(1)**

4. Which word describes how you might feel if you accidentally walked into the wrong classroom?
   awkward **(1)**

5. Which word means the same as *swiftly* and *rapidly*?
   briskly **(1)**

6. Which word could replace *was able* in the sentence "Willa finally was able to return a serve"?
   managed **(1)**

7. Which word means "become aware of"?
   notice **(1)**

8. Which word means "to have a discussion"?
   conversation **(1)**

Write two new questions of your own that use at least one vocabulary word each.

9. Accept reasonable answers **(1)**

10. Accept reasonable answers **(1)**

Copyright © Houghton Mifflin Company. All rights reserved.

Name _____

Story Map

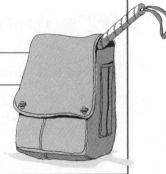

Setting

sometime during the school year at a

middle school and its surrounding

neighborhood in Fresno, California

(1 point)

Characters

José, Estela **(1)**

_____

_____

Plot

Story problem: José wants to get Estela's attention, but after three weeks of

trying he hasn't had any success. **(1)**

Events:

1: José tries impressing Estela by doing well on his history quiz and showing

off his scraped chin from a bike accident. Neither effort succeeds. **(1)**

2: José notices that Estela plays racquetball and challenges her to a game,

even though he's never played. She accepts after José brags he is good. **(1)**

3: José visits his Uncle Freddie to borrow his racket and get advice about

playing. **(1)**

4: Estela and José play, and she beats him twenty-one to nothing. **(1)**

_____

Resolution: José returns the racquet to his uncle. The game has left him with

a bruise on his back and a broken heart. **(1)**

_____

_____

Copyright © Houghton Mifflin Company. All rights reserved.

Name _____

Give Advice

What would you tell a friend who was thinking of lying to impress someone? Write your advice using José's experience as an example.

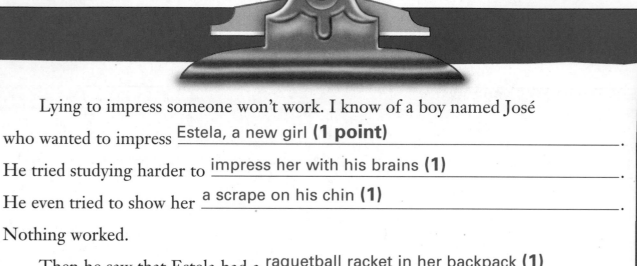

Lying to impress someone won't work. I know of a boy named José who wanted to impress Estela, a new girl **(1 point)** .

He tried studying harder to impress her with his brains **(1)** .

He even tried to show her a scrape on his chin **(1)** .

Nothing worked.

Then he saw that Estela had a raquetball racket in her backpack **(1)** .

That gave him the idea to challenge her to a game **(1)** .

Telling her that he could play racquetball was a lie, though, because he'd never played before **(1)** !

As soon as she said yes, José knew he was in trouble **(1)** .

He went to his uncle Freddy's house to borrow his racquet **(1)** .

Uncle Freddy was sure José would get beaten **(1)** .

When José met Estela at the courts, he saw right away that she was an excellent player **(1)** . Estela beat him 21 to nothing **(1)** . Instead of impressing her, José just felt humiliated **(1)** .

So don't lie! Just be yourself.

Assessment Tip: Total **12** Points

Copyright © Houghton Mifflin Company. All rights reserved.

Name _____

Story Building Blocks

Read the story. Then complete the story map on page 234.

The Spelling Bee

Marty had been nervous all morning. The Lincoln Middle
School Spelling Bee was about to begin, and he was the
representative from Ms. Higgins's sixth-grade class. Ms. Higgins
had asked Marty to compete earlier in the week. He'd said yes
because he was a good speller and he thought it might be fun.
However, now that he was up on the stage, he wondered what he
could have been thinking. "What if I make a mistake and
everyone laughs at me?" he worried.

The spelling bee began. Marty's first word was *nervous*.
"What a perfect word for me," he thought. He spelled the word
correctly, and his classmates applauded and cheered. Marty
smiled gratefully. "This isn't so bad after all," he decided.

After three rounds, only Marty and an eighth-grade girl
were left. Marty's next word was *enthusiastically*. "Wow. Long
word!" he thought. He started spelling the word, and then
stopped. He was trying to picture the word in his mind, but he
couldn't remember the last letter he had spoken! Marty made a
guess and continued at the *u*. When he finished, the judge said,
"I'm sorry, Marty. The word has only one *u*." The spelling bee
was over. Marty had lost.

As he was packing up his books, Marty saw Ms. Higgins.
He was about to apologize when she said, "Marty, what a great
job! You did better than all the seventh graders and most
of the eighth graders!" Marty smiled. He hadn't thought about
it that way. He hadn't lost. He'd finished near the top!

Copyright © Houghton Mifflin Company. All rights reserved.

Name _____

Story Building Blocks continued

Complete the story map with details from "The Spelling Bee."

Story Map

Setting	
When:	the day of the spelling bee **(1 point)**
Where:	Lincoln Middle School **(1)**

Characters	
Who:	Marty, a sixth grader;
	Ms. Higgins, his teacher;
	an eighth-grade girl **(2)**

Plot

Problem: Marty is afraid he will make a mistake and be laughed at. **(2)**

Events:

1. Marty worries and wonders why he agreed to be in the spelling bee. **(2)**

2. Marty spells his first word correctly, and his classmates cheer. **(2)**

3. After three rounds, only Marty and an eighth-grade girl are left. **(2)**

4. Marty pauses while spelling enthusiastically and makes a mistake. **(2)**

5. While Marty is packing up his books, he sees Ms. Higgins, who praises him. **(2)**

Resolution: Marty is proud of himself even though he didn't win. **(2)**

Copyright © Houghton Mifflin Company. All rights reserved.

Assessment Tip: Total **18** Points

Name _____

Suffix Chart

Read each sentence. For each underlined word, write the base and the suffix of the word in the chart. Then use sentence clues and what you know about the meaning of each suffix to write the meaning of each word. An example is provided.

1. José's class learned how the Egyptians would <u>mummify</u> their dead.
2. Estela's racket was <u>blackened</u> by her frequent playing.
3. She <u>flattened</u> her milk carton as she finished her lunch.
4. He tried to keep his face from <u>reddening</u> with shame.
5. José didn't want to <u>dramatize</u> his feelings, even though Estela could <u>terrify</u> him on the court.

Base word	Suffix	Meaning
mummy	-ify	make into a mummy
black **(1 point)**	-en **(1)**	made black **(1)**
flat **(1)**	-en **(1)**	made flat **(1)**
red **(1)**	-en **(1)**	becoming red **(1)**
drama **(1)**	-ize **(1)**	make dramatic **(1)**
terror **(1)**	-ify **(1)**	fill with terror; make afraid **(1)**

Copyright © Houghton Mifflin Company. All rights reserved.

Name _____

Endings and Suffixes

Remember that if a word ends with *e*, the *e* is usually dropped when a suffix or an ending beginning with a vowel is added. The *e* is usually not dropped when a suffix beginning with a consonant is added.

divide + ed = divid**ed**   grace + ful = grace**ful**

► In the starred words *mileage* and *manageable*, the final *e* of the base word is kept when a suffix beginning with a vowel is added.

Write each Spelling Word under the heading that tells what happens to its base word when a suffix or ending is added.
Order of answers for each category may vary.

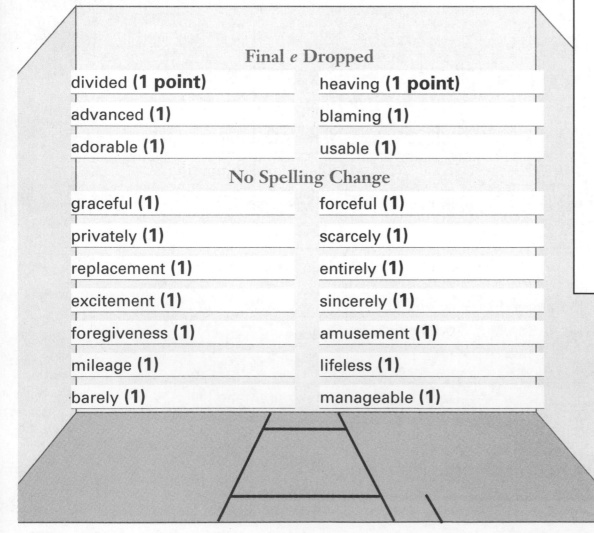

Final *e* Dropped

divided **(1 point)**	heaving **(1 point)**
advanced **(1)**	blaming **(1)**
adorable **(1)**	usable **(1)**

No Spelling Change

graceful **(1)**	forceful **(1)**
privately **(1)**	scarcely **(1)**
replacement **(1)**	entirely **(1)**
excitement **(1)**	sincerely **(1)**
foregiveness **(1)**	amusement **(1)**
mileage **(1)**	lifeless **(1)**
barely **(1)**	manageable **(1)**

Spelling Words

1. graceful
2. divided
3. advanced
4. privately
5. replacement
6. excitement
7. adorable
8. heaving
9. forgiveness
10. mileage*
11. barely
12. forceful
13. scarcely
14. blaming
15. entirely
16. usable
17. sincerely
18. amusement
19. lifeless
20. manageable*

Assessment Tip: Total **20** Points

Copyright © Houghton Mifflin Company. All rights reserved.

Name _____

Spelling Spree

Adding Suffixes or Endings Write the Spelling Word that has each base word below. The spelling of a base word may change.

1. use — usable **(1 point)**

2. forgive — forgiveness **(1)**

3. grace — graceful **(1)**

4. adore — adorable **(1)**

5. sincere — sincerely **(1)**

6. heave — heaving **(1)**

7. mile — mileage **(1)**

8. life — lifeless **(1)**

9. replace — replacement **(1)**

10. scarce — scarcely **(1)**

Spolling Words

1. graceful
2. divided
3. advanced
4. privately
5. replacement
6. excitement
7. adorable
8. heaving
9. forgiveness
10. mileage*
11. barely
12. forceful
13. scarcely
14. blaming
15. entirely
16. usable
17. sincerely
18. amusement
19. lifeless
20. manageable*

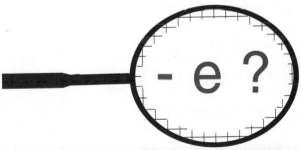

Contrast Clues The second part of each clue contrasts with the first part. Write a Spelling Word to fit each clue.

11. not united, but — divided **(1)**

12. not partly, but — entirely **(1)**

13. not basic, but — advanced **(1)**

14. not publicly, but — privately **(1)**

15. not impossible, but — manageable **(1)**

Copyright © Houghton Mifflin Company. All rights reserved.

Name _____

Proofreading and Writing

Proofreading Circle the five misspelled Spelling Words in this script for a scene from a movie. Then write each word correctly.

Setting: *A basketball court, with a boy and girl playing.*

LUCY: *(She makes a* (forcefull) *move to the basket and scores. Her face lights up with* (exitement).*)* Yes!
DANIEL: *(His chest is heaving.)* That was a lucky lay-up. You (barly) got past me. If it wasn't for these old, worn-out shoes . . .
LUCY: *(She looks at Daniel with* (amusment).*)* Quit (blamming) your shoes. It's my ball. The score's ten to ten. Next point wins.
DANIEL: Hold on! Let me catch my breath. . . . Okay, let's go.
LUCY: *(She gets the ball and shoots a graceful jump shot, which goes in.)* That's game, little brother!

Spelling Words

1. graceful
2. divided
3. advanced
4. privately
5. replacement
6. excitement
7. adorable
8. heaving
9. forgiveness
10. mileage*
11. barely
12. forceful
13. scarcely
14. blaming
15. entirely
16. usable
17. sincerely
18. amusement
19. lifeless
20. manageable*

1. forceful **(1 point)**
2. excitement **(1)**
3. barely **(1)**
4. amusement **(1)**
5. blaming **(1)**

✏ **Write a Challenging Invitation** Are you especially good at a sport or game? Is there someone whom you'd like to challenge to be your competitor?

On a separate sheet of paper, write an invitation challenging a friend to compete against you in your chosen sport or game. Use Spelling Words from the list. Responses will vary. **(5)**

Copyright © Houghton Mifflin Company. All rights reserved.

Name _____

Using Parts of Speech

Read the dictionary entries. For each word, write two sentences, using the word as a different part of speech in each sentence.

► **palm** (päm) *n.* The inside surface of the hand. –*tr.v.* **palmed, palming, palms.** To conceal an object in the palm of the hand.

► **quiz** (kwĭz) *tr.v.* **quizzed, quizzing, quizzes.** To test the knowledge of by asking questions. –*n.*, *pl.* **quizzes.** A short oral or written examination.

► **strain** (strān) *v.* **strained, straining, strains.** –*tr.* To exert or tax to the utmost. *n.* An injury resulting from excessive effort or twisting.

► **whip** (wĭp) *v.* **whipped, whipping, whips.** *Informal.* To defeat; outdo. –*n.* A flexible rod or thong attached to a handle, used for driving animals.

1. The girl's palms were sweating when she finished her speech. **(1)**

   The practical joker palmed a buzzer and surprised us all when we

   shook hands. **(1)**

2. The science teacher will quiz us this afternoon on chapter 10. **(1)**

   I did well on the quiz she gave us last week. **(1)**

3. Reading in the sunshine always strains my eyes. **(1)**

   The doctor checked Ramon's muscle strain in his leg. **(1)**

4. My grandmother can whip me at marbles any day. **(1)**

   Grandpa used to drive cattle with a whip. (1)

Copyright © Houghton Mifflin Company. All rights reserved.

Name _____

The Irregular Verb Challenge

Irregular verbs have the past or past participle formed, not by adding -*ed* or -*d*, but in some other way. You must memorize the forms of irregular verbs. Here are five irregular verbs to study.

Present	Past	Past Participle
become	became	become
feel	felt	felt
go	went	gone
see	saw	seen
take	took	taken

Now cover the chart above, and complete the exercise below. Fill in the blank in each sentence with either the past or the past participle form of the verb in parentheses. Remember that there must be a helping verb in order to use the past participle form.

1. Bob had __become **(1)**_____ a skilled tennis player. (become)

2. He __took **(1)**_____ his racket to the court. (take)

3. He __felt **(1)**_____ confident. (feel)

4. Bob's friends had __seen **(1)**_____ him play many times. (see)

5. Last week they __went **(1)**_____ to a big tournament with him. (go)

240   Theme 3: **Growing Up**
Assessment Tip: Total **5** Points

Copyright © Houghton Mifflin Company. All rights reserved.

Name _____

In Agreement

The verb in a sentence must agree in number with its subject. In the present tense, if the subject is singular, add *-s* or *-es* to the verb. Do not add *-s* or *-es* if the subject is *I* or *you* or if the subject is plural.

Kyle has started a conversation with Rosa, the new girl in his class. To find out what they are saying, choose from among these verbs to fill in the blanks. Make each verb agree with its subject.

smell	come	see
live	go	eat
taste	agree	
bake	take	

Kyle: This tomato soup _tastes **(1 point)**_ salty.

Rosa: You _come **(1)**_ from Ohio, don't you?

Kyle: Yes. My cousin still _lives **(1)**_ in Ohio.

Rosa: My cousin does too! He _goes **(1)**_ to college there.

Kyle: I _see **(1)**_ my cousin during the holidays.

Rosa: Our cafeteria chef _bakes **(1)**_ cookies every Friday.

Kyle: They _smell **(1)**_ terrific!

Rosa: Chris and Kelly always _eat **(1)**_ six cookies each.

Kyle: Our homework _takes **(1)**_ a long time to do.

Rosa: I _agree **(1)**_ with you!

Copyright © Houghton Mifflin Company. All rights reserved.

Name _____

Writing Challenge

Verbs That Agree The people below are facing challenges.
Complete each sentence by writing an appropriate verb to
describe each scene. Be sure that subjects and verbs agree.

Answers will vary, but subjects
and predicates should agree in
number.

1. Mark and Laura **(2)** _____ .

2. A girl with three rings **(2)** _____ .

3. Mary **(2)** _____ .

4. Latasha and Bill **(2)** _____ .

5. Roberto **(2)** _____ .

Assessment Tip: Total **10** Points

Copyright © Houghton Mifflin Company. All rights reserved.

Name _____

Writing a Character Sketch

A **character sketch** is a written profile that tells how either a real person or a character like Estela or José looks, acts, thinks, and feels.

Think about a real person or a story character from a selection you have read whom you would like to write about. Then use the web below to help you brainstorm details about this character's physical appearance and personality traits. (10 points for chart)

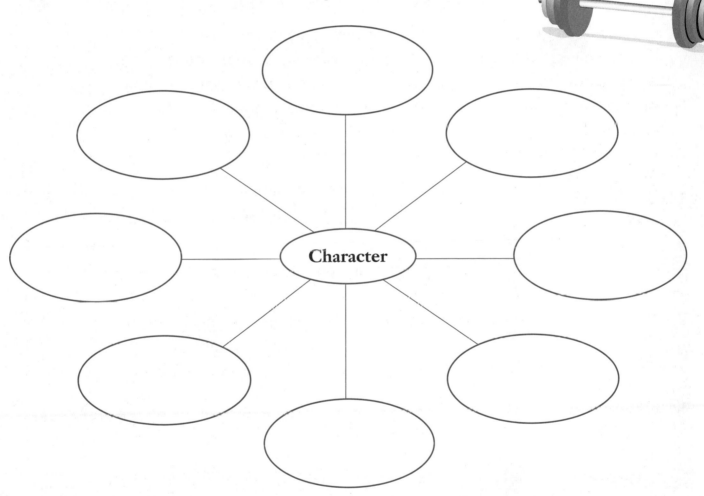

Character

On a separate sheet of paper, write your character sketch. Begin with an anecdote or quote about the character. Then write a sentence that summarizes the character's most significant traits. Next, give two or three details from the web that support your summary. Conclude by restating the traits that are most significant. (5 points)

Copyright © Houghton Mifflin Company. All rights reserved.

Name _____

Using Exact Nouns and Verbs

Which noun, *sport* or *racquetball*, is more exact? Which verb, *held* or *gripped*, is more exact? A good writer avoids using vague nouns and verbs. Exact nouns and verbs like *racquetball* and *gripped* will make your writing clearer and help readers get a more vivid mental picture of the people, places, and events you describe.

Imagine José gives Uncle Freddie a play-by-play account of his racquetball game with Estela. Read the following portion of his account. Circle vague nouns and pronouns and inexact verbs. Then replace them with more exact verbs and nouns from the list below. Write the exact verbs and nouns above the words you circled.
(1 point each)

Exact Verbs and Nouns
whizzed
smashed
winner
court
scored
racquetball
racket
sprinted
left ear
swatted

                                    smashed racquetball
Estela (hit) the (thing) hard against the front wall.
     scored   winner
She (got) her first point. Then she served another (one.)
                          whizzed   left ear sprinted
Point 2. Her third serve (flew) by my (head) I (ran) top
                                         court
speed right off the paved (playing area!) Point 3. Now I
                                          swatted
really had to concentrate. This time I (swung) at her
                 racket
serve, but my (equipment) slipped from my fingers. Four

to zip.

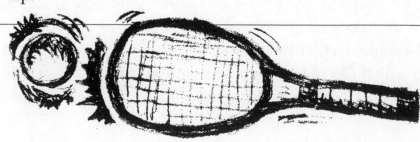

Assessment Tip: Total **10** Points

Copyright © Houghton Mifflin Company. All rights reserved.

Name _____

Turtle Patrol Puzzle

Words are missing in the sentences. Fill each blank with a vocabulary word. Then follow the directions to help you find the letters that need to be unscrambled to answer the question below.

Vocabulary

subtle
resettling
volunteers
interfering
commute
hover
permitted

1. If you go back and forth between two places, you

   _____.

   Directions: Circle the fifth letter.

2. If you are moving to a new place, you are

   _____.

   Directions: Circle the first and seventh letters.

3. If something is not very obvious, it is

   _____.

   Directions: Circle the first and second letters.

4. If you remain in one place in the sky, you

   _____.

   Directions: Circle the third and fourth letters.

5. If something is allowed, it is _____.
   Directions: Circle the fifth and eighth letters.

6. If you and your friends offer to do something, you are

   _____.

   Directions: Circle the third and ninth letters.

7. If you are too curious about other people's business, you are

   _____.

   Directions: Circle the seventh letter.

8. What do turtle patrols try to do during big storms?
   h ◯ ◯ p ___ t ◯ ◯ t ◯ ◯ ◯
   s ◯ ◯ v ◯ ◯ ◯

Copyright © Houghton Mifflin Company. All rights reserved.

Name _____

Problem-Solution Chart

Problem	Solution
If tall buildings hide the horizon's light, baby turtles head toward the city lights instead of the sea, and many die.	Turtle volunteers guide the baby turtles to the sea. **(2 points)**
Nadia is jealous when she learns that Dad wants to be listed on Margaret's permit. She feels left out.	Nadia decides that, from now on, she will not go on any more turtle walks. **(2)**
Dad knows that Nadia is upset and jealous of the time he spends with Margaret and the turtles.	Dad invites Nadia to go to Walt Disney World and bring a friend. **(2)**
A storm hits the Florida Coast, and the turtles are in danger.	Nadia decides to stay behind and help the turtles instead of going to Disney World. **(2)**
Dad and Nadia realize that, like the turtles, they too need help settling into their new lives.	They agree that there will be times when they need a lift from each other. **(2)**

Copyright © Houghton Mifflin Company. All rights reserved.

Assessment Tip: Total **10** Points

Name _____

How Does Nadia Feel?

The following questions ask about how Nadia feels about her new family situation in *The View from Saturday*. Answer each one.

Why does it upset Nadia to learn that Margaret set up her mother's job interview?

She feels that she has been spied on by Ethan because he did not tell her that he knew her. She is angry with Margaret for helping her mother start a new life apart from her father. **(2 points)**

Why does Nadia's father decide to take her to Disney World?

He realizes Nadia feels hurt and neglected, and wants to show her that he cares about her. **(2)**

How does Nadia feel about her grandfather's remarriage and her new family at first?

She is very unhappy about the new situation. She is resentful of the time her father spends with Margaret and Ethan. **(2)**

Why does Nadia decide not to go to Disney World?

She decides it's more important to stay and help rescue the hatchlings during the storm than to spend time just having fun. **(2)**

What connection does Nadia discover between her life and the lives of the sea turtles?

She realizes that, like the hatchlings, she and her father have been stranded in a difficult situation by the "storm" in their private lives. She also realizes that she, like the turtles, will learn to commute between her two new homes, with her father's help. **(2)**

Copyright © Houghton Mifflin Company. All rights reserved.

Name _____

What Would You Do?

Read the story. Then complete page 249.

The Tag-Along

Ben whooped with joy as he rode down the hill on his mountain bike. He heard Ann shout with glee as she started down the same trail. When he glanced over his shoulder, however, Ben noticed that someone else was following them. It was Joyce. Ben felt annoyed.

Joyce had arrived in their class a few months ago. She was new to town and didn't know anyone. That became a problem for Ben when Joyce decided she wanted to become Ann's friend. For the past few weeks, no matter where Ben and Ann went, Joyce always seemed to show up a few minutes later.

Last week, Joyce came across Ben and Ann as they read comic books in Ben's tree house. She watched them for a while, but Ben did not invite her to join them. Yesterday, when Ann and Ben went swimming at the local pool, Joyce showed up and put her towel down right next to theirs.

Ben wanted to resolve the situation one way or another. He stopped his bike and waited for Joyce to catch up. He decided he was going to tell Joyce to stop following Ann around.

Copyright © Houghton Mifflin Company. All rights reserved.

Name _____

What Would You Do? continued

Complete the chart and answer the questions based on
"The Tag-Along." Sample answers shown.

Character	Problem	Solution
Joyce	She is new in town and doesn't know anyone. **(2 points)**	She decides she wants Ann to be her friend and starts following her around. **(2)**
Ben	He is annoyed by Joyce interfering in his friendship with Ann. **(2)**	He decides he will tell Joyce to stop following Ann. **(2)**

1. Is Joyce's way of dealing with her problem a good one?
   Why or why not?

   No. Following other people around when you have not been

   invited is not a good way to make friends. **(4)**

   _____

2. How else can Joyce handle her problem?

   She can tell Ann that she likes her and would like to be her friend.

   She can also invite Ann to do something with her. **(4)**

   _____

3. Do you think Ben handles his problem in the best way possible?
   Explain your answer.

   No. He should ask Ann what she wants to do about Joyce before

   he acts. He could also invite Joyce to join them rather than being

   annoyed with her for tagging along. **(4)**

Copyright © Houghton Mifflin Company. All rights reserved.

Name _____

Prefix Puzzle

Each of the words in the eggs begins with the prefix *in-, im-,* or *con-*.
Find the word that matches each clue and write it in the letter spaces.

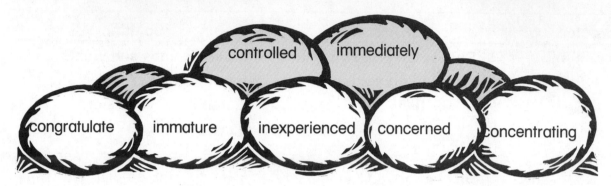

1. worried; anxious; troubled

      c   o   n   **c**   e   r   n   e   d   **(2)**

2. held in check; restrained

      c   o   n   t   r   **o**   l   l   e   d   **(2)**

3. not fully grown or developed

      i   m   **m**   a   t   u   r   e   **(2)**

4. taking place at once; happening without delay

      i   **m**   m   e   d   i   a   t   e   l   y   **(2)**

5. to express joy or good wishes to someone for an achievement

      c   o   n   g   r   a   t   **u**   l   a   t   e   **(2)**

6. thinking very hard; focusing attention on something

      c   o   n   c   e   n   **t**   r   a   t   i   n   g   **(2)**

7. not having knowledge or experience

      i   n   e   x   p   **e**   r   i   e   n   c   e   d   **(2)**

**Read the tinted letters down. Write the word, which means "to travel
regularly between one place and another." (2)**

commute _____

Assessment Tip: Total **16** Points

Copyright © Houghton Mifflin Company. All rights reserved.

Name _____

Prefixes: *in-* and *con-*

A **prefix** is a word part added to the beginning of a base word or a word root to add meaning. A **word root** is a word part that has meaning but cannot stand alone.

The prefix *in-* is spelled *im* before a base word or a word root beginning with *m* or *p*. The prefix *con-* is often spelled *com* before the consonant *m* or *p*.

Copyright © Houghton Mifflin Company. All rights reserved.

Prefix + Base Word

incomplete, **im**polite

contest

Prefix + Word Root

involve, **im**mense

control, **com**ment, **com**pete

To spell words with these prefixes, find the prefix, the base word or word root, and any ending. Spell the word by parts.

Write each Spelling Word under the spelling of its prefix.
Order of answers for each category may vary.

Spelling Words

1. computer
2. impolite
3. control
4. include
5. immigrant
6. compete
7. consumer
8. involve
9. immediate
10. comment
11. infection
12. concert
13. import
14. conversation
15. community
16. incomplete
17. immense
18. contest
19. inactive
20. complicate

in-

include **(1 point)**

involve **(1)**

incfection **(1)**

incomplete **(1)**

inactive **(1)**

con-

control **(1)**

consumer **(1)**

concert **(1)**

conversation **(1)**

contest **(1)**

impolite **(1)** *im-*

immigrant **(1)**

immediate **(1)**

import **(1)**

immense **(1)**

computer **(1)** *com-*

compete **(1)**

comment **(1)**

community **(1)**

complicate **(1)**

Theme 3: **Growing Up** 251

Assessment Tip: Total **20** Points

Name _____

Spelling Spree

Alphabetizing Write the Spelling Word that fits alphabetically between the two words in each group.

Spelling Words

1. computer
2. impolite
3. control
4. include
5. immigrant
6. compete
7. consumer
8. involve
9. immediate
10. comment
11. infection
12. concert
13. import
14. conversation
15. community
16. incomplete
17. immense
18. contest
19. inactive
20. complicate

1. indoors, ___infection **(1 point)**___, inform

2. contract, ___control **(1)**___, convene

3. compromise, ___computer **(1)**___, comrade

4. income, ___incomplete **(1)**___, increase

5. compass, ___compete **(1)**___, complain

6. inability, ___inactive **(1)**___, incentive

7. consonant, ___consumer **(1)**___, contain

8. concern, ___concert **(1)**___, conduct

Base Word/Word Root Match Write the Spelling Word that has the same base word or word root as each word below.

9. detest ___contest **(1)**___

10. export ___import **(1)**___

11. exclude ___include **(1)**___

12. duplicate ___complicate **(1)**___

13. emigrant ___immigrant **(1)**___

14. politeness ___impolite **(1)**___

15. immunity ___community **(1)**___

Assessment Tip: Total **15** Points

Copyright © Houghton Mifflin Company. All rights reserved.

Name _____

Proofreading and Writing

Proofreading Circle the five misspelled Spelling Words in these instructions. Then write each word correctly.

Spelling Words

Instructions for Permitted Volunteers

1. Watch the hatching quietly. Keep (conversasion) to a minimum.

2. Don't (involv) yourself in the hatching process. Let the turtles do it!

3. The turtles' (inmediate) goal is to reach the water. Don't get in their way.

4. You will seem (immence) to the hatchlings. Don't stand too close to them.

5. Take notes about the results of the hatching. Include figures for all the eggs as well as for any dead or half-pipped turtles. Add a (coment) about anything unusual.

1. computer
2. impolite
3. control
4. include
5. immigrant
6. compete
7. consumer
8. involve
9. immediate
10. comment
11. infection
12. concert
13. import
14. conversation
15. community
16. incomplete
17. immense
18. contest
19. inactive
20. complicate

1. conversation **(1 point)**   4. immense **(1)**

2. involve **(1)**   5. comment **(1)**

3. immediate **(1)**

✏️➤ **Write a Personal Narrative** Have you ever taken part in a project or program as a volunteer? What was the experience like?

On a separate piece of paper, write a personal narrative about a time when you served as a volunteer. Use Spelling Words from the list. Responses will vary. **(5)**

Copyright © Houghton Mifflin Company. All rights reserved.

Name _____

Connotation Correction

You are writing a screenplay for the selection, and the director would like to see some changes. Rewrite each sentence replacing the underlined word with a word from the box that has a negative connotation. Then rewrite it again using a word with a positive connotation. If you don't know the meanings of the words, use a dictionary to find them.

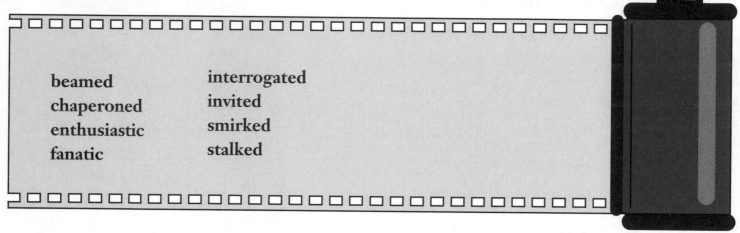

beamed
chaperoned
enthusiastic
fanatic

interrogated
invited
smirked
stalked

1. People who volunteer to help turtles can be <u>excited</u> about their work.
   People who volunteer to help turtles can be fanatic about their work. **(1 point)**

   People who volunteer to help turtles can be enthusiastic about their work. **(1)**

2. Nadia <u>asked</u> Ethan about the comments he had heard.
   Nadia interrogated Ethan about the comments he had heard. **(1)**

   Nadia invited Ethan to tell about the comments he had heard. **(1)**

3. The volunteers <u>followed</u> the turtles as they moved from the beach to the sea.
   The volunteers stalked the turtles as they moved from the beach to the sea. **(1)**

   The volunteers chaperoned the turtles as they moved from the beach to the sea. **(1)**

4. Ethan <u>smiled</u> during the performance of *Phantom of the Opera*.
   Ethan smirked during the performance of *Phantom of the Opera*. **(1)**

   Ethan beamed during the performance of *Phantom of the Opera*. **(1)**

Assessment Tip: Total **8** Points

Copyright © Houghton Mifflin Company. All rights reserved.

Name _____

Up in the Sky

sit, set; lie, lay; rise, raise Some verb pairs can be confusing. Below are the definitions of three such pairs of words.

> **sit**—to rest in an upright position
> **set**—to put or place an object
>
> **lie**—to rest or recline
> **lay**—to put or place an object
>
> **rise**—to get up or go up
> **raise**—to move something up

Complete the sentences below by filling in the blanks with the correct verb in parentheses ( ) .

1. (sits/sets) A robin __sits **(1 point)**__ on its nest.

2. (lie/lay) I __lie **(1)**__ on my back to watch geese fly overhead.

3. (rises/raises) Mario __rises **(1)**__ from his chair when the flock flies over.

4. (sits/sets) That bird watcher __sets/set **(1)**__ down his binoculars.

5. (rise/raise) I __rise **(1)**__ at dawn when I go bird watching.

6. (lie/lay) I will __lay **(1)**__ my backpack on the grass.

7. (sit/set) We __set **(1)**__ out food for the migrating birds.

8. (lics/lays) She __lies **(1)**__ under the tree listening to the chirping birds.

9. (sit/set) I __set **(1)**__ the fallen baby bird back in its nest.

10. (rise/raise) I __raise **(1)**__ my binoculars to my eyes.

Copyright © Houghton Mifflin Company. All rights reserved.

Assessment Tip: Total **10** Points

Name _____

Dog Days

lend, borrow; let, leave; teach, learn Here are the definitions of three more easily confused word pairs:

lend—to give

borrow—to take

let—to permit

leave—to go away

teach—to give instruction

learn—to receive instruction

Complete the sentences below by filling in the blanks with the correct verb in parentheses ( ).

1. Sadie <u>borrows **(1 point)**</u> from Mr. Karol a book on dog training. (lends/borrows)

2. She <u>learns **(1)**</u> from the book how to train puppies. (teaches/learns)

3. Sadie and her puppy, Kipper, <u>leave **(1)**</u> for dog obedience school. (let/leave)

4. The instructor <u>teaches **(1)**</u> Sadie how to handle her dog. (teaches/learns)

5. Sadie <u>lets **(1)**</u> me take Kipper to obedience school one day. (lets/leaves)

6. The instructor <u>lends **(1)**</u> me a better leash. (lends/borrows)

7. Kipper <u>learns **(1)**</u> to sit on command. (teaches/learns)

8. We <u>leave **(1)**</u> for home. (let/leave)

9. My parents <u>let **(1)**</u> me have a puppy. (let/leave)

10. I <u>learn **(1)**</u> to be responsible for her well-being. (teach/learn)

Assessment Tip: Total **10** Points

Copyright © Houghton Mifflin Company. All rights reserved.

Name _____

Autumn in New England

Choosing the Correct Verb Proofread the following passage written by a girl on her way to New England in the fall. Correct each incorrect verb form.

lent
Example: The libarian borrowed me a book.
^

let **(1)**
Please leave me explain something. I like setting on Florida *sitting* **(1)**
^ ^

beaches, but when it is autumn, I'd rather head to New England.

teach **(1)** *raise* **(1)**
Teachers learn me better and I rise my hand more often when it is cool
^ ^

outside. I look forward to seeing the trees turn red and gold. I set in *sit* **(1)**
^

newly raked leaves and watch the sky. Sometimes my mother leaves me *lets* **(1)**
^

make hot chocolate with marshmallows, and I wonder who learns *teaches* **(1)**
^

squirrels to gather nuts. When I come home, I sit my books on my desk *set* **(1)**
^

and lie my good school clothes over a chair. By February I will want to *lay* **(1)**
^

lend a little warmth from Florida, and by June I will be ready to fly south *borrow* **(1)**
^

again, but in autumn, I am a New England girl.

Copyright © Houghton Mifflin Company. All rights reserved.

Name _____

Writing a Speech

In *The View from Saturday*, Nadia gives an informal speech to persuade her father to let her help Grandpa with the sea turtles. Now you will write your own speech. Choose a topic listed below or come up with an idea of your own.

► Write a speech in which the mayor of the Florida town where Nadia lives thanks the turtle volunteers for their efforts.

► Write a speech to persuade local residents to clean up a beach or park.

► Write a speech to inform a group of children about what the turtle patrol's job is and why it is important.

Use the chart below to help you get started. First, identify the purpose of your speech—to entertain, to persuade, to inform, or to thank—and the audience to whom you will speak. Then jot down facts about the situation and reasons why you feel a certain way about it. Before you begin to write, number your ideas, in the order you in which you will present them. (15 points for chart)

Purpose	Audience	Facts and Reasons

Write your speech on a separate sheet of paper. At the beginning, mention whom you are addressing and the purpose of your speech. Then present your facts and reasons in a logical order. Finally, end with a conclusion that sums up or restates the purpose. (5)

Assessment Tip: Total **20** Points

Copyright © Houghton Mifflin Company. All rights reserved.

Name _____

Audience

Speech writers not only keep in mind their purpose for writing but also the **audience** they are addressing. Their audience affects what they say and how they say it. When you write a speech, you need to use language and examples that will best reach your audience.

Read each of the following excerpts from different speeches. What audience do you think the speech writer most likely had in mind when writing the speech? Choose a possible audience from the list and write it on the lines.

1. The Plum Beach condominium will offer lucky owners wonderful views from each unit, including a close look at this area's marine life.

   real-estate developers **(2 points)**

2. Although small turtles used to be commonly available, stores no longer sell them. If you want to observe sea life at home and up close, you might consider buying tropical fish.

   pet owners **(2)**

3. Thank you so much for a job well done! You greatly contributed to this year's successful turtle patrol. Most importantly, you have helped Florida's sea turtles.

   turtle patrol volunteers **(2)**

4. Sea turtles face extinction. Some are hunted for their meat, and turtle eggs are sold as a delicacy. Tragically, beach-front development has also destroyed the traditional breeding grounds of some species.

   environmental club members **(2)**

Audiences

family members

voters

environmental club members

real-estate developers

turtle patrol volunteers

pet owners

residents of Florida

biologists

young children

fishing industry representatives

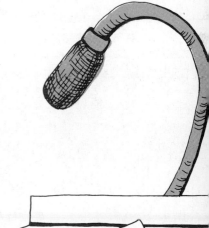

Copyright © Houghton Mifflin Company. All rights reserved.

Name _____

Artwork Words

Write each word from the box next to its meaning.

Vocabulary

apprentice
nib
consolation
timidly
highlights

in a nervous, careful way   timidly **(2 points)**

brightly drawn parts   highlights **(2)**

an assistant learning a trade   apprentice **(2)**

an ink pen's point   nib **(2)**

something that comforts   consolation **(2)**

Now use three words from the box in a short paragraph describing a scene at an art studio.

Answers will vary, but should include at least three Vocabulary words. **(6 points)**

_____

_____

_____

_____

Copyright © Houghton Mifflin Company. All rights reserved.

Story Problems

Use the chart below to list problems the main characters of *The Ink-Keeper's Apprentice* and *Jerry Pickney* face and the solutions they devise to solve these problems. Look back at the stories if necessary.

Sample answers are provided. Accept reasonable responses.

	Problems	**Solutions**
The Ink-Keeper's Apprentice: Kiyoi	1. how to paint with control 2. how to find the sharp part of the brush	1. When Kiyoi overcomes his nervousness, he paints with more control. 2. Kiyoi learns that the amount of ink on the brush has a lot to do with finding its sharp part.
Jerry Pickney	1. how to become an artist 2. how to find out what kind of drawing he liked best	1. Pickney draws, takes help from artists he meets, and goes to art school. 2. Pickney does all kinds of different drawing until he finds the kind that he likes best.

Copyright © Houghton Mifflin Company. All rights reserved.

Assessment Tip: Total **12** Points

Name _____

Story Predictions

Use the chart below to make inferences about the main characters of *The Ink-Keeper's Apprentice* and *Last Summer with Maizon*. Look back at the stories if necessary.

Sample answers are provided. Accept reasonable responses.

	The Ink-Keeper's Apprentice: Kiyoi	*Last Summer with Maizon:* Margaret
Story Detail	He asks to be Noro Shinpei's apprentice even though they don't know each other. **(2 points)**	She reveals her feelings in a poem. **(2)**
What I Know	It takes determination to ask for things from people you don't know. **(2)**	It can be hard to express feelings in writing. **(2)**
Inference	Kiyoi is determined to be an artist. **(2)**	Margaret is a talented writer. **(2)**

Copyright © Houghton Mifflin Company. All rights reserved.

Assessment Tip: Total **12** Points

Name _____

Inspirational Words

**Choose the word from the Vocabulary box that best fits each
definition below.**

Vocabulary

influence
testimony
springboard
commitment
climate

I. springboard **(1 point)** _____

something that helps
launch ideas or activities

2. climate **(1)** _____

an overall mood and spirit

4. commitment **(1)** _____

dedication to a cause

3. influence **(1)** _____

something that affects a
person's life

5. testimony **(1)** _____

a statement about what
really happened

Assessment Tip: Total **5** Points

Copyright © Houghton Mifflin Company. All rights reserved.

Name _____

Test Practice

Use the three steps you've learned to write a personal response to both these questions about *Jerry Pinkney*. Make a chart on a separate piece of paper. Then write your response on the lines below. Use the checklist to revise your response.

1. What advice would you give someone who wants to become an artist? Use information from *Jerry Pinkney* and your own ideas.

   Use the Personal Response Checklist to score each student's response.

   _____

   _____

   _____

   _____

   _____

   _____

   _____

   _____

   _____

   _____

   _____

Copyright © Houghton Mifflin Company. All rights reserved.

Personal Response Checklist

✔ Did I restate the question at the beginning? **(2 points)**

✔ Can I add more details from what I read to support my answer? **(5)**

✔ Can I add more of my thoughts or experiences to support my answer? **(5)**

✔ Do I need to delete details that do not help answer the question? **(2)**

✔ Where can I add more exact words? **(2)**

✔ Did I use clear handwriting? Did I make any mistakes? **(4)**

Continue on page 266.

Name _____

Test Practice continued

2. **Connecting/Comparing** Do you think it's important for adults to
encourage children to develop their talents? Explain why you think
as you do. Use your own experience, as well as details from both
Last Summer with Maizon and *Jerry Pinkney*.

Use the Personal Response Checklist to score each student's response.

_____

_____

_____

_____

_____

_____

_____

_____

_____

_____

_____

Personal Response Checklist

✔ Did I restate the question at the beginning? **(2 points)**

✔ Can I add more details from what I read to support my answer? **(5)**

✔ Can I add more of my thoughts or experiences to support my answer? **(5)**

✔ Do I need to delete details that do not help answer the question? **(2)**

✔ Where can I add more exact words? **(2)**

✔ Did I use clear handwriting? Did I make any mistakes? **(4)**

**Read your answers to Questions 1 and 2 aloud to a partner.
Then discuss the checklist. Make any changes that will improve
your answers.**

Assessment Tip: Total **40** Points

Copyright © Houghton Mifflin Company. All rights reserved.

Name _____

Inferring a Character's Feelings

Read the story. Then answer the questions.
Wording of answers will vary.

The Wrestler

Clem paced back and forth behind the row of folding chairs where some of his teammates were sitting. Kelvin, the team's 95-pound wrestler, was in the middle of the wrestling mat on the other side. His match had just begun. Soon it would be Clem's turn.

Clem tried to relax, but he was finding it hard to breath. "Why did I join the wrestling team?" thought Clem. "Why do I always follow in my older brother's footsteps?" Clem shook his head. He wanted to remain focused.

Then, out of the corner of his eye, he saw Kelvin on his back, fighting not to get pinned. "Come on, Kelvin," thought Clem. "Get off your back." Kelvin somehow managed to squirm free and went on the attack. "Go, Kelvin, go!" shouted Clem. Seconds later, Kelvin had pinned his opponent.

Now it was Clem's turn. He took a deep breath, clenched his teeth, and ran to the center of the mat.

1. How does Clem feel about his upcoming wrestling match?
   Clem is very nervous and filled with doubt. **(2 points)**

2. What story clues help you figure out his feelings? He paces back and forth, has trouble breathing; he wonders why he decided to join the wrestling team in the first place. **(2)**

3. Why do you think Clem joined the wrestling team?
   He wanted to be like his older brother. **(2)**

4. What do you know from your own experience that helps you understand Clem?
   Answers will vary. **(2)**

Copyright © Houghton Mifflin Company. All rights reserved.

Assessment Tip: Total **8** Points

Name _____

Making the Right Choice

Read the story. Then answer the questions.
Sample answers shown.

The Party Choice

Maya looked at the two birthday party invitations on the table. The one from Grace, her best friend, had arrived on Tuesday. Jessica's came just today. Both parties were scheduled for the same day at the same time.

Jessica was the new girl in class. She lived in the house on the hill with the swimming pool. Maya really wanted to go to that party to get a chance to swim in the pool and get to know Jessica better.

Maya looked at both invitations once more. She decided she would go to Jessica's party. "If I just pretend I didn't get Grace's invitation, I won't have to tell her I'm not coming," she thought.

1. What is Maya's problem?   She has received invitations to two
   birthday parties that are taking place on the same day. **(2 points)**

2. How does she decide to solve her problem?
   She decides to accept Jessica's invitation, while ignoring Grace's invitation. **(2)**

3. Do you think Maya's solution is a good one? Why or why not? Sample answer:
   No. Ignoring an invitation from a friend is not a good way to treat that person.
   Also, avoiding a situation will not make it go away. **(2)**

4. How else do you think Maya can handle her problem?
   She can tell Grace about the problem and ask for
   her help in finding a solution. She can accept
   both invitations but say that she can only attend
   each party for part of the time. **(2)**

268   Theme 3: **Growing Up**
Assessment Tip: Total 8 Points

Copyright © Houghton Mifflin Company. All rights reserved.

Name _____

Meaning Matching

**Read the base words in the box. Then read the
sentences. Write the word from each sentence
that contains one of the base words and the
suffix *-en*, *-ify*, or *-ize*. Then write the meaning
of the word.**

> | | | |
> |---|---|---|
> | glad | just | sign |
> | harmony | sad | sympathy |

1. The singer's voices harmonize beautifully.

   harmonize: work in harmony **(2 points)**

2. The sounds of their voices gladden the audience.

   gladden: become glad or happy **(2)**

3. I sympathize with the young boy who cannot see the stage.

   sympathize: feel sympathy for **(2)**

4. When the lights come on, it will signify the end of the show.

   signify: make a sign **(2)**

5. The end of the show will sadden me.

   sadden: become sad **(2)**

6. Spending time at a concert is easy for me to justify.

   justify: to show to be right or valid **(2)**

Copyright © Houghton Mifflin Company. All rights reserved.

Name _____

Inflection Connection

Read each entry word and its definition. Pay attention to inflected endings such as *-s, -es, -ed, -ing, -er,* and *-est.* Then use inflected forms of each word to complete the sentences below.

> **cham•pi•on (chăm′** pē ən) *n, pl.* **cham•pi•ons.** Someone or something acknowledged as the best of all; have defeated others in competition.
>
> **com•pete (kəm pēt′)** *v.* **com•pet•ed, com•pet•ing, com•petes.** To strive against another or others to win something; to take part in a contest.
>
> **de•liv•er (dĭ lĭv′ ər)** *v.* **de•liv•ered, de•liv•er•ing, de•liv•ers.** 1. To set free. 2. To hand over. 3. To give or utter.
>
> **edg•y (ĕj′ ē)** *adj.* **edg•i•er, edg•i•est.** On edge; tense; nervous.
>
> **he•ro (hîr′ ō)** *n, pl.* **he•roes.** A person noted for courage or special achievements.
>
> **hud•dle (hŭd′ l)** *v.* **hud•deled, hud•dling, hud•dles.** To crowd together.
>
> **hard (härd)** *adj.* **hard•er, hard•est.** 1. Resistant to pressure. 2. Toughened. 3. Requiring great effort; difficult.
>
> **vic•to•ry (vĭk′ tə rē)** *n, pl.* **vic•tor•ies.** The act or fact of winning in a contest or struggle.

1. The students <u>huddled **(1 point)**</u> together to decide who would be responsible for <u>delivering **(1)**</u> the first answer.

2. If the team can win a series of <u>victories **(1)**</u>, the members will be looked up to as <u>heroes **(1)**</u>.

3. Nadia seemed the <u>edgiest **(1)**</u> of all, knowing that it was the team's last chance to become the <u>champions **(1)**</u>.

4. The teams were <u>competing **(1)**</u> fiercely.

5. Each event seemed <u>harder **(1)**</u> to win than the one before.

Assessment Tip: Total **8** Points

Copyright © Houghton Mifflin Company. All rights reserved.

Name _____

Spelling Review

1–30. **Write each Spelling Word.** Order of answers may vary.

1. conversation **(1 point)**
2. supply **(1)**
3. minus **(1)**
4. impolite **(1)**
5. graceful **(1)**
6. author **(1)**
7. beginning **(1)**
8. forgiveness **(1)**
9. immediate **(1)**
10. forgetting **(1)**
11. slipped **(1)**
12. method **(1)**
13. answered **(1)**
14. relief **(1)**
15. consumer **(1)**
16. heaving **(1)**
17. amusement **(1)**
18. include **(1)**
19. advanced **(1)**
20. listening **(1)**
21. adorable **(1)**
22. scarcely **(1)**
23. excitement **(1)**
24. control **(1)**
25. balance **(1)**
26. complicate **(1)**
27. preferred **(1)**
28. involve **(1)**
29. community **(1)**
30. lawyer **(1)**

Spelling Words

1. conversation
2. supply
3. minus
4. impolite
5. graceful
6. author
7. beginning
8. forgiveness
9. immediate
10. forgetting
11. slipped
12. method
13. answered
14. relief
15. consumer
16. heaving
17. amusement
18. include
19. advanced
20. listening
21. adorable
22. scarcely
23. excitement
24. control
25. balance
26. complicate
27. preferred
28. involve
29. community
30. lawyer

Copyright © Houghton Mifflin Company. All rights reserved.

Assessment Tip: Total **30** Points

Name _____

Spelling Spree

Contrast Clues The second part of each clue contrasts with the first part. Write a Spelling Word to fit each clue.

Copyright © Houghton Mifflin Company. All rights reserved.

Spelling Words

1. relief
2. author
3. forgetting
4. consumer
5. slipped
6. conversation
7. minus
8. immediate
9. advanced
10. complicate
11. scarcely
12. heaving
13. answered
14. balance
15. excitement

1. not remembering, but <u>forgetting **(1 point)**</u>

2. not boredom, but <u>excitement **(1)**</u>

3. not plus, but <u>minus **(1)**</u>

4. not simplify, but <u>complicate **(1)**</u>

5. not asked, but <u>answered **(1)**</u>

6. not distress, but <u>relief **(1)**</u>

7. not retreated, but <u>advanced **(1)**</u>

Code Breaker Parts of some Spelling Words have been written in code. Use the code below to figure out each word. Then write the words correctly.

@ = con	¤ = or	$ = ed	# = ing	* = ate
% = ance	+ = im	Ø = er	& = ation	¶ = ly

8. + medi * <u>immediate **(1)**</u>

9. slipp $ <u>slipped **(1)**</u>

10. bal % <u>balance **(1)**</u>

11. @ sum Ø <u>consumer **(1)**</u>

12. heav # <u>heaving **(1)**</u>

13. scarce ¶ <u>scarcely **(1)**</u>

14. @ vers & <u>conversation **(1)**</u>

15. auth ¤ <u>author **(1)**</u>

272   Theme 3: **Growing Up**
Assessment Tip: Total **15** Points

Name _____

Proofreading and Writing

Proofreading Circle the five misspelled Spelling Words in these rules. Then write each word correctly.

Rules for Growing Up

You can learn a lot by (lissening) to what older people say. Never be (impalite) to anyone. Keep your temper under (controal.) This might (invollve) biting your tongue once in a while, but it's worth doing. If you hurt someone's feelings, ask for (forgivness.)

1. listening **(1 point)**
2. impolite **(1)**
3. control **(1)**
4. involve **(1)**
5. forgiveness **(1)**

Copyright © Houghton Mifflin Company. All rights reserved.

Spelling Words

1. method
2. listening
3. lawyer
4. include
5. amusement
6. adorable
7. graceful
8. forgiveness
9. supply
10. control
11. impolite
12. preferred
13. beginning
14. community
15. involve

Write the Spelling Words that best complete this discussion.

Question: All of you must be 6. beginning **(1)** to think about your futures. What kinds of jobs do you 7. include **(1)** in your thinking?

Amy: I'd like to be a comedian! I love to see the 8. amusement **(1)** on people's faces when I tell jokes.

Jaime: I'm 9. graceful **(1)**, so I might be a dancer. Later, if I 10. preferred **(1)** to, I could teach dance.

Laura: As a vet, I'd have a steady 11. supply **(1)** of 12. adorable **(1)** animals in my life!

Dion: I would like to be a 13. lawyer **(1)**, like my mom. She helps people in the 14. community **(1)** fight for their rights.

Bart: I'll invent a fast 15. method **(1)** for growing up!

✏ **Write a Song** On a separate sheet of paper, write a song about growing up. Use Spelling Review Words. **Responses will vary. (5)**

Assessment Tip: Total **20** Points

Name _____

Working with Verb Tenses

**Underline the verb in each sentence. Then write the tense of the
verb, *past*, *present*, or *future*, on the line.**

1. Millie will learn from the elderly artist.

   future **(1 point)** _____

2. She sketched an elephant on her third day.

   past **(1)** _____

3. The artist picked her as his new apprentice.

   past **(1)** _____

4. The apprentices finish the cartoon panels for the master.

   present **(1)** _____

5. Millie will color the clothes in these cartoon panels.

   future **(1)** _____

**Working in the order in which the sentences above appear, rewrite
each sentence above using the indicated verb tense.**

6. **Past**   Millie learned from the elderly artist. **(1)**

7. **Future**   She will sketch an elephant on her third day. **(1)**

8. **Present** The artist picks her as his new apprentice. **(1)**

9. **Past**   The apprentices finished the cartoon panels for the master. **(1)**

10. **Present** Millie colors the clothes in these cartoon panels. **(1)**

Assessment Tip: Total 10 Points

Copyright © Houghton Mifflin Company. All rights reserved.

Writing Perfect Tense Verbs

Complete the chart below. Write the correct form of the
verb in each column. The first one has been done for you.

Verb notice	Present Perfect have noticed	Past Perfect had noticed	Future Perfect will have noticed
1. use	have used	had used	will have used
2. attend	**(1 point)** have attended	had attended **(1)**	**(1)** will have attended
3. take	have taken **(1)**	had taken **(1)**	will have taken **(1)**
4. give	have given **(1)**	had given **(1)**	will have given **(1)**
5. become	have become **(1)**	had become **(1)**	**(1)** will have become

Write on the line below the correct form of the verb in
parentheses after each sentence.

6. An artist ___ had noticed **(2 points)** ___ the boy's talent last summer. (notice)
   past perfect

7. The boy ___ has used **(2)** ___ oil paints and watercolo
   present perfect

8. By Friday the boy ___ will have attended **(2)** ___ art school for
   future perfect
   three months. (attend)

9. He ___ has become **(2)** ___ an excellent artist. (become)
   present perfect

10. His aunt ___ had given **(2)** ___ him lessons before he started
    past perfect
    art school. (give)

Copyright © Houghton Mifflin Company. All rights reserved.

Theme 3: **Growing Up**   275
Assessment Tip: Total 22 Points

Student Handbook

Copyright © Houghton Mifflin Company. All rights reserved.

Contents

Copyright © Houghton Mifflin Company. All rights reserved.

How to Study a Word

1. LOOK at the word.
- ► What does the word mean?
- ► What letters are in the word?
- ► Name and touch each letter.

2. SAY the word.
- ► Listen for the consonant sounds.
- ► Listen for the vowel sounds.

3. THINK about the word.
- ► How is each sound spelled?
- ► Close your eyes and picture the word.
- ► What familiar spelling patterns do you see?
- ► Did you see any prefixes, suffixes, or other word parts?

4. WRITE the word.
- ► Think about the sounds and the letters.
- ► Form the letters correctly.

5. CHECK the spelling.
- ► Did you spell the word the same way it is spelled in your word list?
- ► If you did not spell the word correctly, write the word again.

Copyright © Houghton Mifflin Company. All rights reserved.

affectionate
again
all right
a lot
always
another
anyone
anything
anyway
applicable

beautiful
because
before
believe
brought
bureau

cannot
can't
captain
catastrophe
caught
clothes
coming
cousin

didn't
different
don't

eighth
embarrass
enough
essential
everybody
everything
everywhere

family
fatigue
favorite
field
finally
forfeit
friend

getting
going
guess
guy

happened
happily
haven't
heard
height
here

illustrator
indictment
instead
interpret
irreplaceable
its
it's

knew
know

might
millimeter
morning

o'clock
once

pennant
people
perceive
perspiration
pneumonia
pretty
probably

questionnaire

really
received
reversible
right

Saturday
school
someone
sometimes
stopped
stretch
sufficient
suppose
suppress
swimming

that's
their
there
there's
they're
thought
through
to
tonight
too
two

usually

weird
we're

whole
would
wouldn't
write
writing

your
you're

Words Often Confused

affect
effect

alley
ally

ascent
assent

bauble
bubble

bellow
below

bisect
dissect

bazaar
bizarre

bland
blend

confidant
confident

decent
descent

desert
dessert

eclipse
ellipse

hurdle
hurtle

illegible
ineligible

eminent
imminent

moral
mortal

pastor
pasture

sleek
slick

Copyright © Houghton Mifflin Company. All rights reserved.

Passage to Freedom

Long Vowels

/ā/	→	g**aze**, tr**ait**
/ē/	→	th**eme**, pr**ea**ch, sl**ee**ve
/ī/	→	str**ive**
/ō/	→	qu**ote**, r**oam**
/yōō/	→	m**ute**

Spelling Words

1. theme
2. quote
3. gaze
4. pace
5. preach
6. strive
7. trait
8. mute
9. sleeve
10. roam
11. strain
12. fade
13. league
14. soak
15. grease
16. throne
17. fume
18. file
19. toast
20. brake

Challenge Words

1. microphone
2. emphasize
3. refugee
4. pertain
5. coax

My Study List
Add your own spelling words on the back. ➡

Courage
Reading-Writing Workshop

Look for familiar spelling patterns in these words to help you remember their spellings.

Spelling Words

1. your
2. you're
3. their
4. there
5. they're
6. its
7. it's
8. wouldn't
9. we're
10. to
11. too
12. that's
13. knew
14. know

Challenge Words

1. pennant
2. bureau
3. interpret
4. forfeit
5. perspiration

My Study List
Add your own spelling words on the back. ➡

Hatchet

Short Vowels

/ă/	→	cr**a**ft
/ĕ/	→	d**e**pth
/ĭ/	→	f**i**lm
/ŏ/	→	b**o**mb
/ŭ/	→	pl**u**nge

Spelling Words

1. depth
2. craft
3. plunge
4. wreck
5. sunk
6. film
7. wince
8. bomb
9. switch
10. length
11. prompt
12. pitch
13. else
14. cliff
15. pledge
16. scrub
17. brass
18. grill
19. stung
20. bulk

Challenge Words

1. habitat
2. cobweb
3. tepid
4. magnetic
5. deft

My Study List
Add your own spelling words on the back. ➡

Copyright © Houghton Mifflin Company. All rights reserved.

Name _____

 My Study List

1. _____
2. _____
3. _____
4. _____
5. _____
6. _____
7. _____
8. _____
9. _____
10. _____

Review Words

1. swift
2. tense
3. bunch
4. grasp
5. ditch

How to Study a Word

Look at the word.
Say the word.
Think about the word.
Write the word.
Check the spelling.

Name _____

My Study List

1. _____
2. _____
3. _____
4. _____
5. _____
6. _____
7. _____
8. _____
9. _____
10. _____

How to Study a Word

Look at the word.
Say the word.
Think about the word.
Write the word.
Check the spelling.

Name _____

My Study List

1. _____
2. _____
3. _____
4. _____
5. _____
6. _____
7. _____
8. _____
9. _____
10. _____

Review Words

1. greet
2. boast
3. brain
4. code
5. squeak

How to Study a Word

Look at the word.
Say the word.
Think about the word.
Write the word.
Check the spelling.

Copyright © Houghton Mifflin Company. All rights reserved.

Courage
Spelling Review

Spelling Words

1. wince	16. craft
2. league	17. throne
3. strive	18. rhythm
4. routine	19. vault
5. prompt	20. avoid
6. strain	21. depth
7. meant	22. roam
8. foul	23. reply
9. hoist	24. stout
10. naughty	25. squawk
11. bulk	26. gaze
12. theme	27. sleeve
13. mute	28. ravine
14. sponge	29. sought
15. bloom	30. annoy

See the back for Challenge Words.

The True Confessions of Charlotte Doyle

The /ou/, /ō͞o/, /ô/, and /oi/ Sounds

/ou/ ➡ st**ou**t
/ō͞o/ ➡ bl**oo**m
/ô/ ➡ v**au**lt, squ**aw**k, s**ou**ght, n**augh**ty
/oi/ ➡ av**oi**d, ann**oy**

Spelling Words

1. bloom	11. mound
2. stout	12. groove
3. droop	13. foul
4. crouch	14. hoist
5. annoy	15. gloom
6. vault	16. trout
7. squawk	17. noun
8. avoid	18. roost
9. sought	19. clause
10. naughty	20. appoint

Challenge Words

1. bountiful
2. adjoin
3. nauseous
4. turquoise
5. heirloom

Climb or Die

More Vowel Spellings

/ē/ ➡ rout**ine**
/ĕ/ ➡ sw**ea**t
/ī/ ➡ c**y**cle
/ĭ/ ➡ rh**y**thm
/ŭ/ ➡ sh**ove**
(o consonant e)

Spelling Words

1. cycle	11. sponge
2. sweat	12. apply
3. rhythm	13. threat
4. rely	14. myth
5. pleasant	15. deny
6. routine	16. leather
7. cleanse	17. rhyme
8. shove	18. thread
9. reply	19. meadow
10. meant	20. ravine

Challenge Words

1. endeavor
2. oxygen
3. nylon
4. realm
5. trampoline

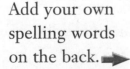

My Study List
Add your own spelling words on the back. ➡

My Study List
Add your own spelling words on the back. ➡

My Study List
Add your own spelling words on the back. ➡

Copyright © Houghton Mifflin Company. All rights reserved.

Name _____

 My Study List

1. _____
2. _____
3. _____
4. _____
5. _____
6. _____
7. _____
8. _____
9. _____
10. _____

Review Words

1. breath
2. measure
3. typical
4. deaf
5. crystal

How to Study a Word

Look at the word.
Say the word.
Think about the word.
Write the word.
Check the spelling.

Name _____

 My Study List

1. _____
2. _____
3. _____
4. _____
5. _____
6. _____
7. _____
8. _____
9. _____
10. _____

Review Words

1. scoop
2. moist
3. haul
4. loose
5. hawk

How to Study a Word

Look at the word.
Say the word.
Think about the word.
Write the word.
Check the spelling.

Name _____

My Study List

1. _____
2. _____
3. _____
4. _____
5. _____
6. _____
7. _____
8. _____
9. _____
10. _____

Challenge Words

1. cobweb
2. tepid
3. refugee
4. coax
5. nylon
6. endeavor
7. oxygen
8. nauseous
9. bountiful
10. heirloom

How to Study a Word

Look at the word.
Say the word.
Think about the word.
Write the word.
Check the spelling.

Copyright © Houghton Mifflin Company. All rights reserved.

The Girl Who Married the Moon

Homophones
Homophones are words that sound alike but have different spellings and meanings.

Spelling Words

1. fir	11. manor
2. fur	12. manner
3. scent	13. who's
4. sent	14. whose
5. scene	15. tacks
6. seen	16. tax
7. vain	17. hangar
8. vein	18. hanger
9. principal	19. died
10. principle	20. dyed

Challenge Words

1. phase
2. faze
3. burrow
4. burro
5. borough

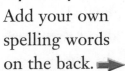

My Study List
Add your own spelling words on the back. ➡

What Really Happened?
Reading-Writing Workshop

Look for familiar spelling patterns in these words to help you remember their spellings.

Spelling Words

1. tonight	9. clothes
2. everywhere	10. height
3. everybody	11. always
4. another	12. right
5. because	13. might
6. whole	14. really
7. people	15. everything
8. cousin	

Challenge Words

1. essential
2. questionnaire
3. affectionate
4. illustrator
5. embarrass

My Study List
Add your own spelling words on the back. ➡

Amelia Earhart: First Lady of Flight

Vowel + /r/ Sounds
/ûr/ ➡ sk**ir**t, **ur**ge, **ear**th
/ôr/ ➡ th**or**n, c**our**t
/är/ ➡ ch**ar**t
/îr/ ➡ f**ier**ce

Spelling Words

1. fierce	11. whirl
2. sword	12. mourn
3. court	13. rehearse
4. snarl	14. curb
5. thorn	15. earnest
6. earth	16. starch
7. skirt	17. purse
8. chart	18. birch
9. urge	19. pierce
10. yarn	20. scorn

Challenge Words

1. circumstances
2. turmoil
3. absurd
4. territory
5. sparse

My Study List
Add your own spelling words on the back. ➡

Copyright © Houghton Mifflin Company. All rights reserved.

Name _____

 My Study List

1. _____
2. _____
3. _____
4. _____
5. _____
6. _____
7. _____
8. _____
9. _____
10. _____

Review Words

1. pearl
2. stir
3. inform
4. pour
5. scar

How to Study a Word

Look at the word.
Say the word.
Think about the word.
Write the word.
Check the spelling.

Name _____

My Study List

1. _____
2. _____
3. _____
4. _____
5. _____
6. _____
7. _____
8. _____
9. _____
10. _____

How to Study a Word

Look at the word.
Say the word.
Think about the word.
Write the word.
Check the spelling.

Name _____

My Study List

1. _____
2. _____
3. _____
4. _____
5. _____
6. _____
7. _____
8. _____
9. _____
10. _____

Review Words

1. berry
2. bury
3. soar
4. sore

How to Study a Word

Look at the word.
Say the word.
Think about the word.
Write the word.
Check the spelling.

Copyright © Houghton Mifflin Company. All rights reserved.

Where the Red Fern Grows

VCV, VCCV, and VCCCV Patterns

VC|V:	**bal | ance**
V|CV:	**mi | nus**
VC|CV:	**law | yer**
V|CCV:	**au | thor**
VCC|V:	**meth | od**
VC|CCV:	**sup | ply**

Spelling Words

1. balance
2. lawyer
3. sheriff
4. author
5. minus
6. method
7. item
8. require
9. supply
10. whisper
11. spirit
12. tennis
13. adopt
14. instant
15. poison
16. deserve
17. rescue
18. journey
19. relief
20. laundry

Challenge Words

1. enhance
2. delete
3. precious
4. structure
5. decade

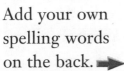

My Study List
Add your own spelling words on the back. ➡

What Really Happened?
Spelling Review

Spelling Words

1. chart
2. starch
3. hangar
4. manner
5. gallon
6. whirl
7. curb
8. vein
9. similar
10. rural
11. sword
12. purse
13. hanger
14. manor
15. direction
16. mourn
17. who's
18. scent
19. channel
20. passenger
21. pierce
22. thorn
23. vain
24. struggle
25. frighten
26. rehearse
27. whose
28. sent
29. familiar
30. calendar

See the back for Challenge Words.

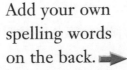

My Study List
Add your own spelling words on the back. ➡

Dinosaur Ghosts

Final /ər/, /ən/, and /əl/

/ər/ ➡	messeng**er**, direct**or**, simil**ar**
/ən/ ➡	weap**on**, fright**en**
/əl/ ➡	strugg**le**, chann**el**, ment**al**

Spelling Words

1. struggle
2. director
3. weapon
4. similar
5. mental
6. frighten
7. channel
8. messenger
9. familiar
10. acre
11. error
12. gallon
13. rural
14. calendar
15. elevator
16. stumble
17. youngster
18. kitchen
19. passenger
20. quarrel

Challenge Words

1. agricultural
2. colonel
3. predator
4. corridor
5. maneuver

My Study List
Add your own spelling words on the back. ➡

Copyright © Houghton Mifflin Company. All rights reserved.

Name _____

 My Study List

1. _____
2. _____
3. _____
4. _____
5. _____
6. _____
7. _____
8. _____
9. _____
10. _____

Review Words

1. matter
2. novel
3. mayor
4. consider
5. dozen

How to Study a Word

Look at the word.
Say the word.
Think about the word.
Write the word.
Check the spelling.

Name _____

 My Study List

1. _____
2. _____
3. _____
4. _____
5. _____
6. _____
7. _____
8. _____
9. _____
10. _____

Challenge Words

1. territory
2. absurd
3. turmoil
4. phase
5. burrow

6. predator
7. colonel
8. faze
9. burro
10. corridor

How to Study a Word

Look at the word.
Say the word.
Think about the word.
Write the word.
Check the spelling.

Name _____

My Study List

1. _____
2. _____
3. _____
4. _____
5. _____
6. _____
7. _____
8. _____
9. _____
10. _____

Review Words

1. protect
2. effort
3. actor
4. credit
5. merchant

How to Study a Word

Look at the word.
Say the word.
Think about the word.
Write the word.
Check the spelling.

Copyright © Houghton Mifflin Company. All rights reserved.

The Challenge

> **Endings and Suffixes**
> divide + ed = divid**ed**
> grace + ful = grace**ful**

Spelling Words

1. graceful
2. divided
3. advanced
4. privately
5. replacement
6. excitement
7. adorable
8. heaving
9. forgiveness
10. mileage
11. barely
12. forceful
13. scarcely
14. blaming
15. entirely
16. usable
17. sincerely
18. amusement
19. lifeless
20. manageable

Challenge Words

1. deflated
2. disciplined
3. consecutively
4. silhouetted
5. refinement

Last Summer with Maizon

> **Words with -ed or -ing**
> map**ped**   pilot**ing**
> fit**ting**   begin**ning**

Spelling Words

1. mapped
2. piloting
3. permitting
4. beginning
5. bothered
6. limited
7. forgetting
8. reasoning
9. preferred
10. equaled
11. wondering
12. slipped
13. listening
14. fitting
15. pardoned
16. shoveling
17. favored
18. knitting
19. answered
20. modeling

Challenge Words

1. propelling
2. equipped
3. transmitted
4. recurring
5. beckoned

Growing Up
Reading-Writing Workshop

Look for familiar spelling patterns in these words to help you remember their spellings.

Spelling Words

1. bland
2. blend
3. below
4. bellow
5. pastor
6. pasture
7. moral
8. mortal
9. bauble
10. bubble
11. bisect
12. dissect
13. assent
14. ascent

Challenge Words

1. imminent
2. eminent
3. illegible
4. ineligible

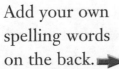

My Study List
Add your own spelling words on the back. ➡

My Study List
Add your own spelling words on the back. ➡

My Study List
Add your own spelling words on the back. ➡

Copyright © Houghton Mifflin Company. All rights reserved.

Name _____

 My Study List

1. _____
2. _____
3. _____
4. _____
5. _____
6. _____
7. _____
8. _____
9. _____
10. _____

How to Study a Word

Look at the word.
Say the word.
Think about the word.
Write the word.
Check the spelling.

Name _____

 My Study List

1. _____
2. _____
3. _____
4. _____
5. _____
6. _____
7. _____
8. _____
9. _____
10. _____

Review Words

1. ordered
2. planned
3. spotted
4. winning
5. gathering

How to Study a Word

Look at the word.
Say the word.
Think about the word.
Write the word.
Check the spelling.

Name _____

My Study List

1. _____
2. _____
3. _____
4. _____
5. _____
6. _____
7. _____
8. _____
9. _____
10. _____

Review Words

1. breathless
2. collapsed
3. valuable
4. retirement
5. government

How to Study a Word

Look at the word.
Say the word.
Think about the word.
Write the word.
Check the spelling.

Copyright © Houghton Mifflin Company. All rights reserved.

Growing Up
Spelling Review

Spelling Words

1. method
2. author
3. answered
4. forgiveness
5. complicate
6. supply
7. beginning
8. heaving
9. scarcely
10. include
11. rclicf
12. forgetting
13. amusement
14. excitement
15. consumer
16. balance
17. slipped
18. advanced
19. control
20. impolite
21. minus
22. listening
23. adorable
24. immediate
25. involve
26. lawyer
27. preferred
28. graceful
29. conversation
30. community

See the back for
Challenge Words.

The View from
Saturday

Prefixes: *in-* and *con-*
in + active = **in**active
in + volve = **in**volve
in + polite = **im**polite
in + mense = **im**mense
con + trol = **con**trol
con + test = **con**test
con + ment = **com**ment
con + pete = **com**pete

Spelling Words

1. computer
2. impolite
3. control
4. include
5. immigrant
6. compete
7. consumer
8. involve
9. immediate
10. comment
11. infection
12. concert
13. import
14. conversation
15. community
16. incomplete
17. immense
18. contest
19. inactive
20. complicate

Challenge Words

1. imply
2. consequence
3. comprehensive
4. inadequate
5. communicate

My Study List
Add your own
spelling words
on the back. ➡

My Study List
Add your own
spelling words
on the back. ➡

Copyright © Houghton Mifflin Company. All rights reserved.

Name _____

 My Study List

1. _____
2. _____
3. _____
4. _____
5. _____
6. _____
7. _____
8. _____
9. _____
10. _____

Review Words

1. concern
2. insist
3. compare
4. improve
5. convince

How to Study a Word

Look at the word.
Say the word.
Think about the word.
Write the word.
Check the spelling.

Name _____

 My Study List

1. _____
2. _____
3. _____
4. _____
5. _____
6. _____
7. _____
8. _____
9. _____
10. _____

Challenge Words

1. precious   6. consecutively
2. enhance   7. refinement
3. beckoned   8. communicate
4. propelling   9. imply
5. deflated   10. consequence

How to Study a Word

Look at the word.
Say the word.
Think about the word.
Write the word.
Check the spelling.

Copyright © Houghton Mifflin Company. All rights reserved.

Focus on Plays

Focus on Poetry

Compound Words
A compond word is a word made up of two or more smaller words.

Consonant Changes
A consonant that is silent in one word may be sounded in a word related in meaning.

Spelling Words

1. headache	11. handwriting
2. warehouse	12. nighttime
3. cupboard	13. self-respect
4. old-fashioned	14. shipwreck
5. teammate	15. penknife
6. rattlesnake	16. mother-in-law
7. blueberry	17. wristwatch
8. headquarters	18. handkerchief
9. space shuttle	19. bulletin board
10. baby-sit	20. software

Spelling Words

1. autumn	11. haste
2. autumnal	12. hasten
3. muscle	13. column
4. muscular	14. columnist
5. crumb	15. heir
6. crumble	16. inherit
7. sign	17. hymn
8. signal	18. hymnal
9. bomb	19. design
10. bombard	20. designate

Challenge Words

1. windshield
2. guinea pig
3. self-conscious
4. videocassette
5. elementary school

Challenge Words

1. doubt
2. dubious
3. condemn
4. condemnation

My Study List
Add your own spelling words on the back. ➡

My Study List
Add your own spelling words on the back. ➡

Copyright © Houghton Mifflin Company. All rights reserved.

Name _____

 My Study List

1. _____
2. _____
3. _____
4. _____
5. _____
6. _____
7. _____
8. _____
9. _____
10. _____

Review Words

1. soft
2. soften
3. limb
4. limber

How to Study a Word

Look at the word.
Say the word.
Think about the word.
Write the word.
Check the spelling.

Name _____

My Study List

1. _____
2. _____
3. _____
4. _____
5. _____
6. _____
7. _____
8. _____
9. _____
10. _____

Review Words

1. salesperson
2. whoever
3. seat belt
4. highway
5. make-believe

How to Study a Word

Look at the word.
Say the word.
Think about the word.
Write the word.
Check the spelling.

Copyright © Houghton Mifflin Company. All rights reserved.

Problem Words

Words	Rules	Examples
bad badly	*Bad* is an adjective. It can be used after linking verbs like *look* and *feel*. *Badly* is an adverb.	This was a <u>bad</u> day. I feel <u>bad</u>. I play <u>badly</u>.
borrow lend	*Borrow* means "to take." *Lend* means "to give."	You may <u>borrow</u> my pen. I will <u>lend</u> it to you for the day.
can may	*Can* means "to be able to do something." *May* means "to be allowed or permitted."	Nellie <u>can</u> read quickly. May I borrow your book?
good well	*Good* is an adjective. *Well* is usually an adverb. It is an adjective only when it refers to health.	The weather looks <u>good</u>. She sings <u>well</u>. Do you feel <u>well</u>?
in into	*In* means "located within." *Into* means "movement from the outside to the inside."	Your lunch is <u>in</u> that bag. He jumped <u>into</u> the pool.
its it's	*Its* is a possessive pronoun. *It's* is a contraction of *it is*.	The dog wagged <u>its</u> tail. <u>It's</u> cold today.
let leave	*Let* means "to permit or allow." *Leave* means "to go away from" or "to let remain in place."	Please <u>let</u> me go swimming. I will <u>leave</u> soon. <u>Leave</u> it on my desk.
lie lay	*Lie* means "to rest or recline." *Lay* means "to put or place something."	The dog <u>lies</u> in its bed. Please <u>lay</u> the books there.

Copyright © Houghton Mifflin Company. All rights reserved.

Problem Words continued

Words	Rules	Examples
sit	*Sit* means "to rest in one place."	Please <u>sit</u> in this chair.
set	*Set* means "to place or put."	<u>Set</u> the vase on the table.
teach	*Teach* means "to give instruction."	He <u>teaches</u> us how to dance.
learn	*Learn* means "to receive instruction."	I <u>learned</u> about history.
their there they're	*Their* is a possessive pronoun. *There* is an adverb. It may also begin a sentence. *They're* is a contraction of *they are*.	<u>Their</u> coats are on the bed. Is Carlos <u>there</u>? <u>There</u> is my book. <u>They're</u> going to the store.
two to too	*Two* is a number. *To* means "in the direction of." *Too* means "more than enough" and "also."	I bought <u>two</u> shirts. A squirrel ran <u>to</u> the tree. May we go <u>too</u>?
whose who's	*Whose* is a possessive pronoun. *Who's* is a contraction for *who is*.	<u>Whose</u> tickets are these? <u>Who's</u> that woman?
your you're	*Your* is a possessive pronoun. *You're* is a contraction for *you are*.	Are these <u>your</u> glasses? <u>You're</u> late again!

Copyright © Houghton Mifflin Company. All rights reserved.

Read each question below. Then check your paper. Correct any mistakes you find. After you have corrected them, put a check mark in the box next to the question.

☐ 1. Did I spell all words correctly?

☐ 2. Did I indent each paragraph?

☐ 3. Does each sentence state a complete thought?

☐ 4. Are there any run-on sentences or fragments?

☐ 5. Did I begin each sentence with a capital letter?

☐ 6. Did I capitalize all proper nouns?

☐ 7. Did I end each sentence with the correct end mark?

☐ 8. Did I use commas, apostrophes, and quotation marks correctly?

Are there other problem areas you should watch for? Make your own proofreading checklist.

☐ _____

☐ _____

☐ _____

☐ _____

☐ _____

☐ _____

☐ _____

Copyright © Houghton Mifflin Company. All rights reserved

Mark	Explanation	Examples
¶	Begin a new paragraph. Indent the paragraph.	¶The boat finally arrived. It was two hours late.
∧	Add letters, words, or sentences.	My best friend ate lunch with me today.
℘	Take out words, sentences, and punctuation marks. Correct spelling.	We looked at and admired, the moddel airplanes.
≡	Change a small letter to a capital letter.	New York city is exciting.
/	Change a capital letter to a small letter.	The Fireflies blinked in the dark.
ⱽ ⱽ	Add quotation marks.	Where do you want the piano? asked the movers.
∧	Add a comma.	Carlton my cat has a mind of his own.
⊙	Add a period.	Put a period at the end of the sentence.
∼	Reverse letters or words.	Raed carefully the instructions.
?	Add a question mark.	Should I put the mark here?
!	Add an exclamation mark.	Look out below!

Copyright © Houghton Mifflin Company. All rights reserved.

Copyright © Houghton Mifflin Company. All rights reserved.

Copyright © Houghton Mifflin Company. All rights reserved.

Copyright © Houghton Mifflin Company. All rights reserved.

CURRICULUM

Weeks-Townsend Memorial Library
Union College
Barbourville, KY 40906

Copyright © Houghton Mifflin Company. All rights reserved.

My Notes